AF588251

WEEKEND ART

# WATERCOLOUR

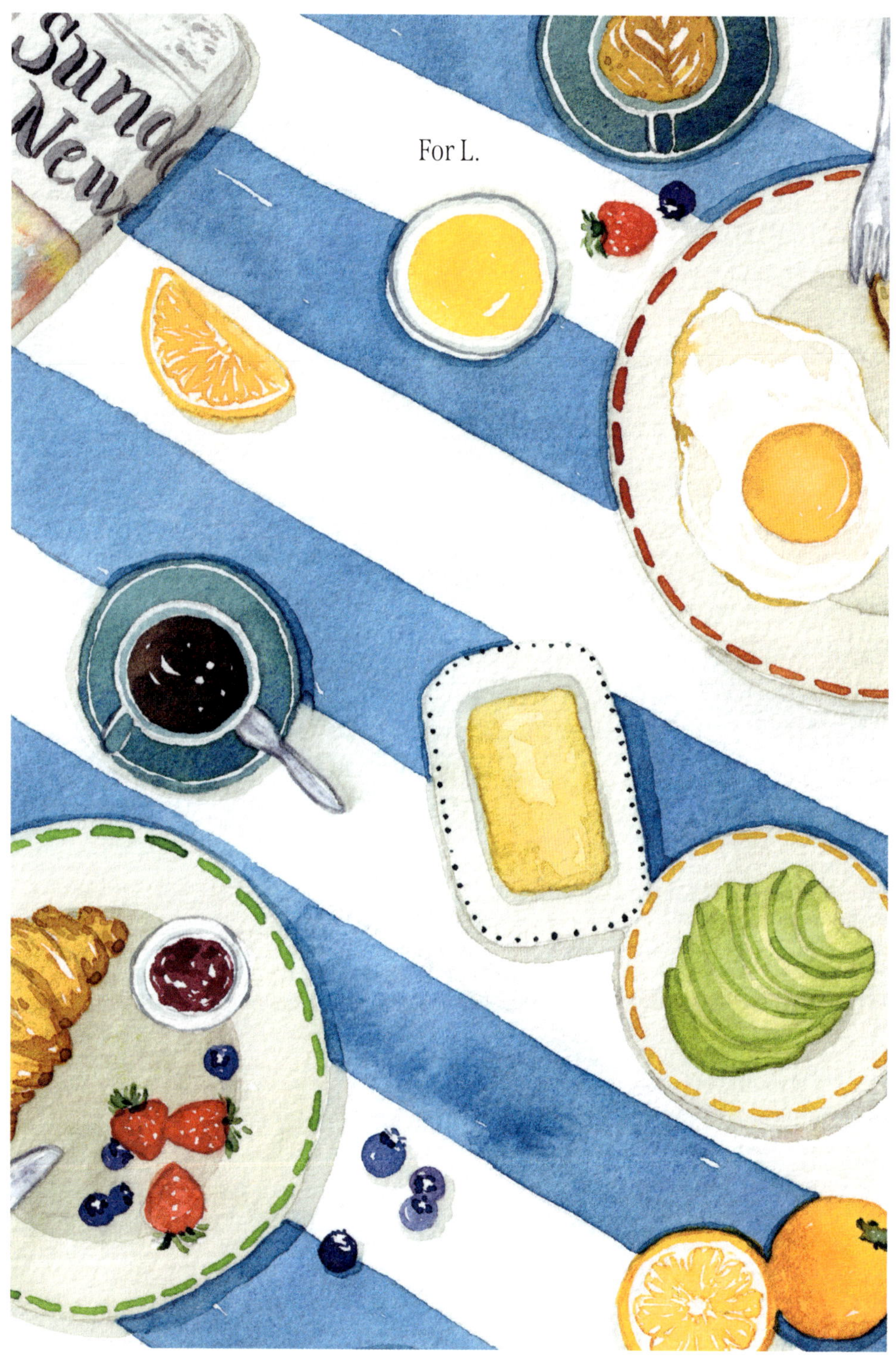

For L.

WEEKEND ART

# WATERCOLOUR

PAINT AT YOUR
OWN PACE

JOLA SOPEK

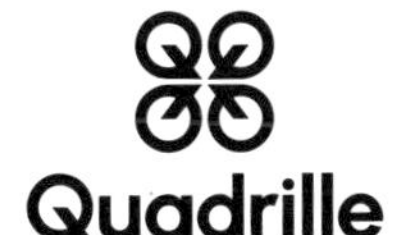

Quadrille

# CONTENTS


*6* Introduction
*9* Art Supplies
*16* Painting Techniques
*25* Colour Theory Expanded
*37* Warm-up Exercises

## 44 Up to 35 Minutes

*45* Duotone Abstract Pattern
*48* Beetroot
*51* Snowy Tree
*54* Pebbles
*56* Tropical Fruit
*60* Abstract Landscapes
*64* Blueberries
*68* Fish, Shells and Seaweed
*72* Cucumbers
*76* Flowers at Dusk


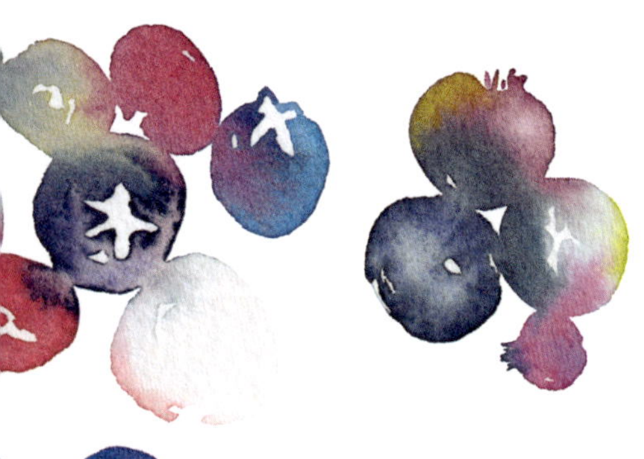

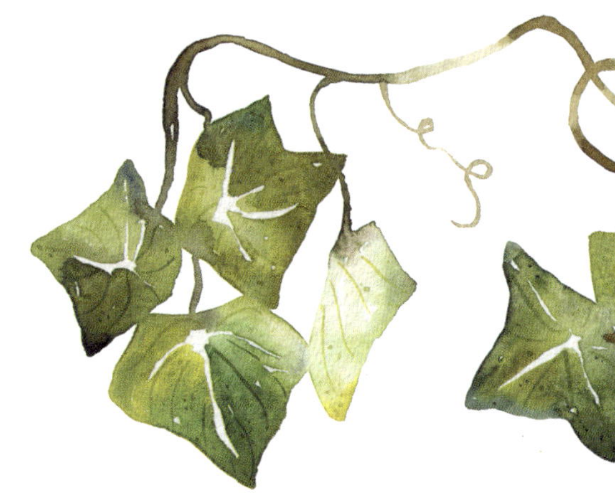

## 80 Up to One Hour


*81* Autumn Leaves
*84* Leaf Vine
*88* Moon
*92* Stork
*96* Apples and Pears
*100* Countryside Flowers
*104* Milky Way Sky
*109* Glass Flower Vase
*114* Artichokes
*118* Sea Waves
*123* Forest Mushrooms
*128* People


## 132 More Than an Hour


*133* Winter Landscape
*138* A Spring Walk
*144* Fig Lemon Vine
*150* Zebra
*154* View of an Abbey
*160* White Wisteria Flowers
*166* Italian Oranges
*172* Summer Breakfast

*178* Sketch Templates
*191* About the Author/
Acknowledgements

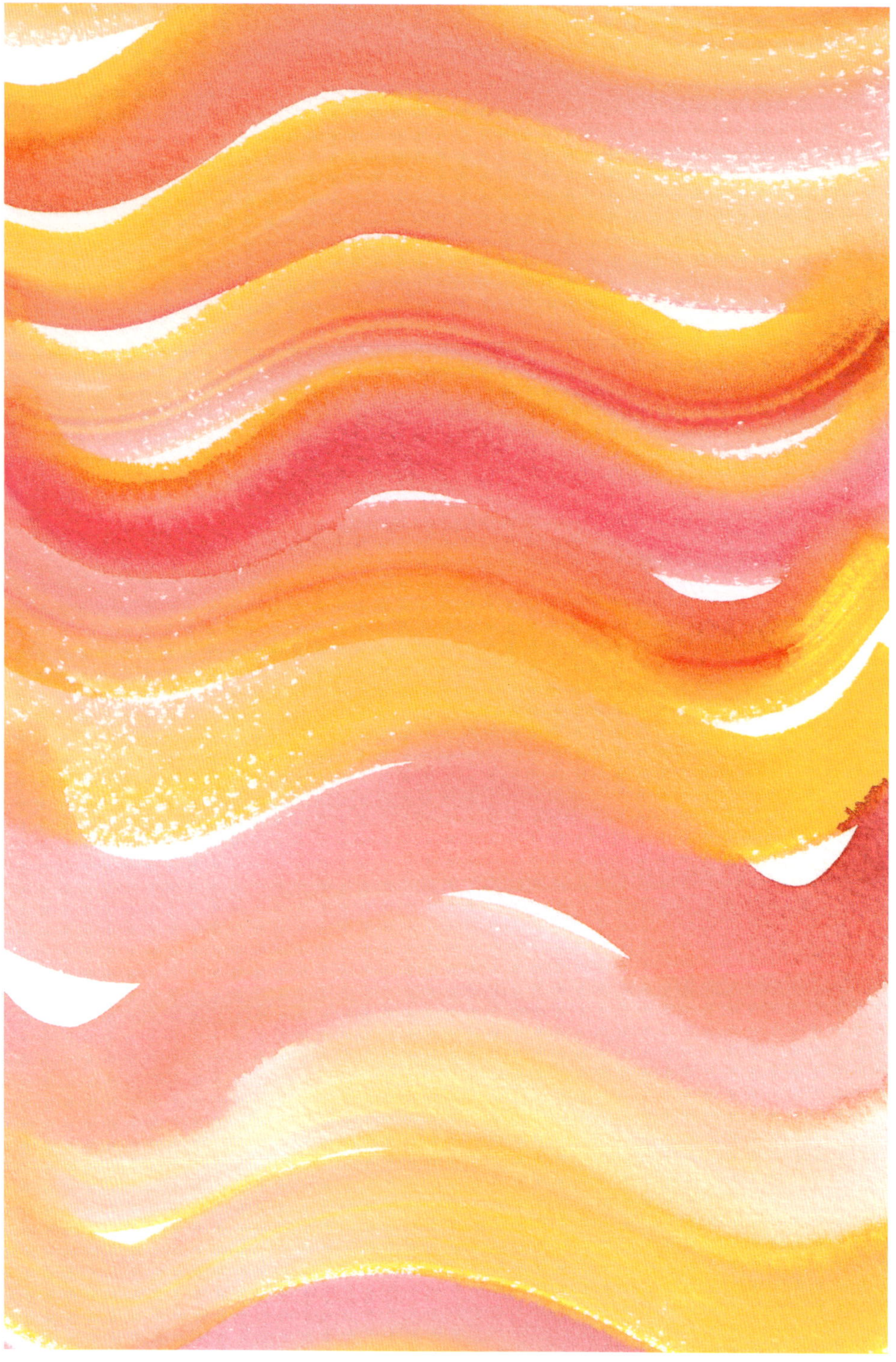

# Introduction

Hello! Thank you for picking up this book. I am so pleased you did. It tells me you are a curious individual who enjoys a challenge – mastering watercolour painting surely is one, but what an utterly wonderful and versatile medium it is. There is good reason why it is such a popular technique worldwide, regardless of it being tricky to learn – its ethereal, innate transparency and vibrancy of colours captivate and inspire like nothing else.

My name is Jola Sopek. I am a freelance illustrator and the author of *15 Minute Art: Watercolour* (2024). My fascination with the medium is immense and has been growing for a decade – yet I still find myself learning new aspects every time I sit down to paint.

The motivation behind writing my second book about watercolours is to give you an opportunity to dive deeper into the endless possibilities the medium has to offer. You will exercise muscle memory to become fearless with your brushstrokes. With step-by-step guidance, you will discover techniques to tackle a wide range of subjects from plants, landscapes and animals to people and food.

The discussion of colour theory on pages 25–36 will open your eyes to the near-infinite possibilities of informed colour mixing, which will greatly advance your approach to creating specific moods in illustrations.

The exercises in this book are divided into three timed sections: up to 35 minutes, up to one hour and over an hour. I wanted you to be able to sketch some illustrations relatively quickly when you have less time on your hands but still want a creative fix – but also to be able to spend longer to work on more complex paintings over a weekend, or whenever suits.

When sketching on watercolour paper, make sure to use a soft pencil and make the drawings lightly, applying hardly any pressure. Watercolour paints are transparent and pencil lines easily show underneath, which is not necessarily desirable. Try to make faint lines and use a kneadable eraser to soften the sketches further by gently dabbing on the surface of the paper. I recommend that you use high-quality dedicated watercolour papers to practise these exercises for best results.

Some of the exercises in this book come with sketch templates included on pages 178–190, which you are welcome to copy or use as inspiration. Not all the projects have a sketch, because I want to encourage you to practise freehand, loose painting – the rigidity of a sketch can sometimes block this flow.

It is now time for you to enjoy working with watercolours and unwind in a creative way!

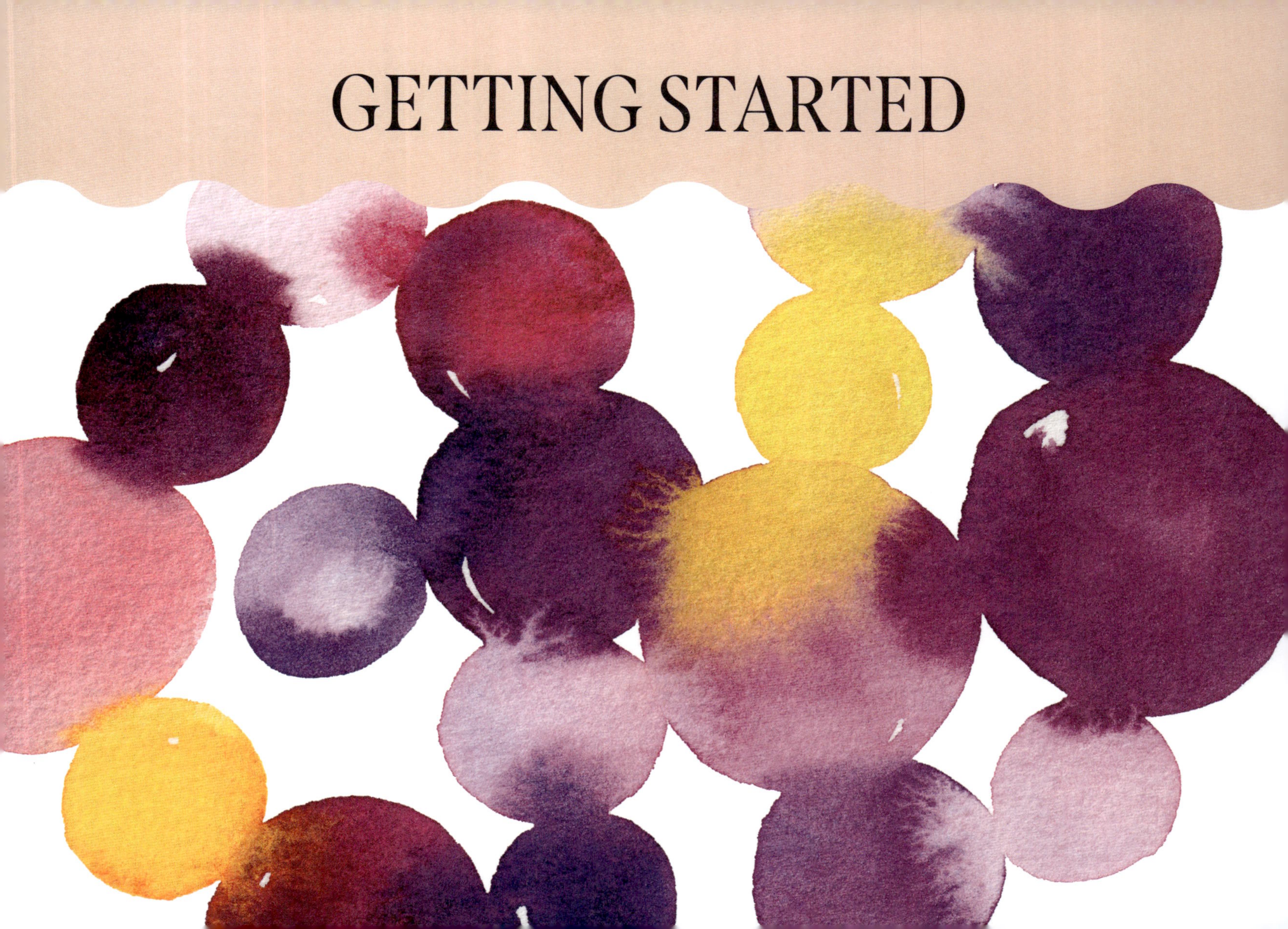

# GETTING STARTED

# Art Supplies

Choosing the right watercolour supplies can seem like a daunting task. I encourage you not to spend a ton of money on a multitude of tools. It is best to buy less, but better quality – and that rule goes for paints and brushes as well as papers.

Luckily for our pockets, the more expensive art supplies tend to be much better value and go a long way, so they probably save us money in the long run. In addition, better-quality materials give improved effects, which in turn increases satisfaction in painting and reduces unnecessary frustration when we don't get the results we are after.

Having said that, there are fantastic ranges of art materials that don't break the bank but still feel high-end. I will first outline the essential watercolour supplies you need to have in your inventory and then suggest some of my favourite, tested brands. Please bear in mind this list is not exhaustive, and access to certain makes of materials may be limited depending on your location.

# 1/Watercolour papers

Watercolour paper comes in a few formats – pads, sketchbooks and loose sheets. These come in various sizes, and the format you choose will depend on your preferences and needs.

Sketchbooks are great for keeping all your doodles and tests in one place, fantastic for developing visual concepts, and handy if you want to paint when travelling. Pads are useful for paintings you may want to hang on a wall, or to make into greeting cards; they are often glued on the edges, which means you can apply a lot of water to the paper, and it won't buckle or warp easily. Loose sheets tend to be large, which means you can practise painting big and with fewer restrictions.

Regardless of the format, I recommend you opt for 100% cotton papers with a minimum weight of 300gsm, as they absorb water and pigments beautifully, allowing you to really notice the extraordinary qualities of watercolour. Lower-quality papers are not quite able to deliver the visual results we all expect to achieve, and they cannot withstand repeated water applications.

There are three main paper types: cold-pressed, hot-pressed and rough. To demonstrate the difference, I tested the same six brushstrokes and techniques on all three surfaces (see opposite page).

## PAPER TYPES

**COLD-PRESSED** (CP) papers are the most popular and versatile of watercolour papers, because they hold pigments well due to their mildly bumpy texture. Most of the exercises in this book were prepared on cold-pressed papers. The term 'cold press' refers to the paper's uneven surface, achieved by pressing the pulp with cold felt rollers during manufacturing. The paper absorbs water and pigment easily, which lends itself to working wet-on-wet and gives the distinct watercolour look that most of us seek. The irregular surface allows for working in layers and is suitable for dry brush techniques.

My favourite cold-pressed papers: Stonehenge Aqua Coldpress by Legion Paper, Moulin du Roy by Canson and Saunders Waterford Cold Pressed by St Cuthberts Mill.

**HOT-PRESSED** (HP) papers are smooth and even in texture without any bumps. To a beginner, they may look like any other drawing paper as their surface isn't very distinctive. The term 'hot press' means the pulp has been pressed with hot metal rollers during the manufacturing process, leaving no texture underneath. This paper doesn't absorb water or pigment as well as CP sheets – without any texture to help the water sink into, wet paint tends to sit on the surface for longer. This means they are not the best choice for large washes and wet-on-wet techniques, and dry brush strokes will have a harder time showing up on their smooth surface.

However, HP papers are fantastic for detailed illustrations, botanical art and paintings that don't require a lot of water application. They also expose the vibrancy of pigments more than CP papers because light reflects off their smooth surface more intensely than off textured sheets.

Some recommended hot-pressed papers: hot-pressed pads by Arches, Professional Watercolour Hot-Pressed Blocks by Winsor & Newton and Stonehenge Aqua Hotpress by Legion Paper.

**ROUGH** papers, as the name suggests, have very bumpy and irregular textures with lots of

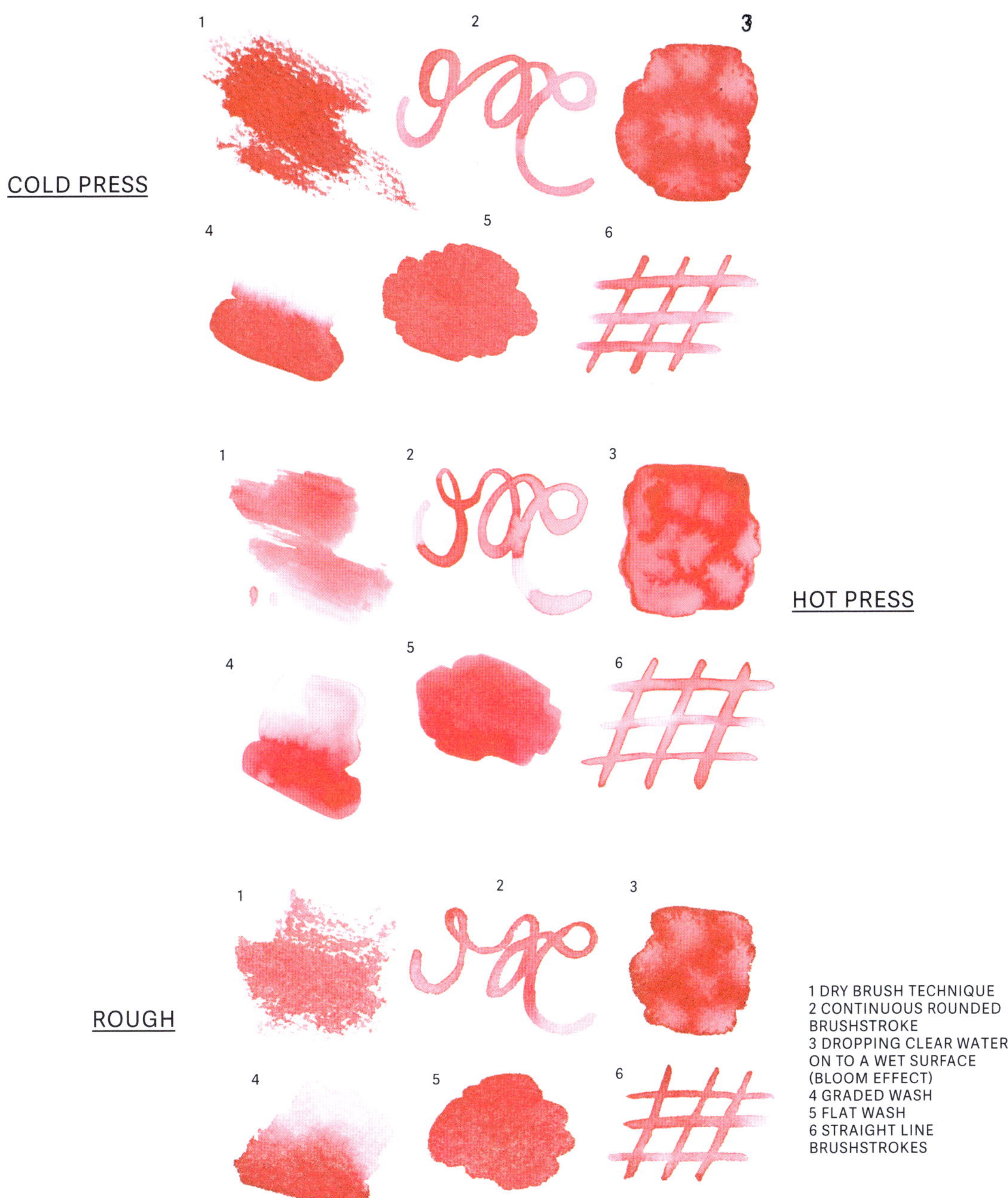


1 DRY BRUSH TECHNIQUE
2 CONTINUOUS ROUNDED BRUSHSTROKE
3 DROPPING CLEAR WATER ON TO A WET SURFACE (BLOOM EFFECT)
4 GRADED WASH
5 FLAT WASH
6 STRAIGHT LINE BRUSHSTROKES

indents. They are manufactured by pressing wet pulp with textured felt and leaving the sheets to dry until they mould into a coarse surface. Rough paper is very absorbent and hence good for large washes, but it is difficult to make even, smooth brushstrokes with it. It can sustain layers of paint applications and is therefore suitable for landscape painting, loose abstract works and dry brush techniques. Colours will appear less vibrant on it as the bumps will not let light reflect off the surface as easily as on CP or HP papers. Overall, it is the trickiest surface to work with of the three, but it is worth experimenting with all of them to see which one speaks to you the most, keeping in mind that different painting topics may require different surfaces.

I do not have specific recommendations for rough papers as I don't use them regularly, but I always go for 100% cotton for best results.

Different brushstrokes and techniques interact differently with different kinds of papers. The Painting Techniques section on pages 16–24 will give you an in-depth understanding of these techniques but, in general, the dry brush technique is mostly effective on a rough surface, and least effective on a hot-pressed one. The graded wash tends to be most effective on cold-pressed papers and least on hot-pressed. Continuous rounded and straight-line brushstrokes are the most seamless on a hot-pressed surface and least on rough.

From the get-go, the biggest difference can be seen in the dry brush technique and the graded wash, although the three papers feel distinctive when you interact with them. If you want to familiarise yourself with this well, try painting a few of the same illustrations on all three surfaces to really grasp each one's pros and cons. And keep in mind that in painting everything is relative – there is no right and wrong, only what you deem to look good!

## 2/*Watercolour brushes*

There is a very wide range of watercolour brushes available, and to be perfectly honest I have not tried even half the types available in art shops. You are of course welcome to try whichever you fancy!

I have always used **ROUND** (1) and **MOP BRUSHES** (3) in various sizes as they are most versatile for multiple techniques, and they make up most of the brushes I own. A good round brush will be able to hold a lot of water in its bristles, it should be flexible enough to allow for rounded, soft brushstrokes, but also come to a fine point. A mop brush tends to soak up even more water, making it ideal for loose, effortless strokes and expressive, large washes. I like to use medium to large-sized brushes as they are most versatile.

A **FLAT BRUSH** (2) is a fantastic addition to a watercolour inventory as it allows for laying down large washes quickly (especially useful in landscape painting). Its bristles can be cut flat or at an angle, which means the strokes have a less rounded shape and will therefore offer you further possibilities for evoking different moods with the brush marks.

Owning at least one small **DETAIL BRUSH** (4) is essential – these tiny but mighty tools are for adding final details and textures to your illustrations and let you paint small objects precisely (for example, animal eyes or citrus pips), as you will discover while working on exercises in this book.

I usually opt for synthetic brushes, which are fantastic in quality and more affordable than animal-hair ones. If your budget allows, feel free to try the latter too and see if you have a preference.

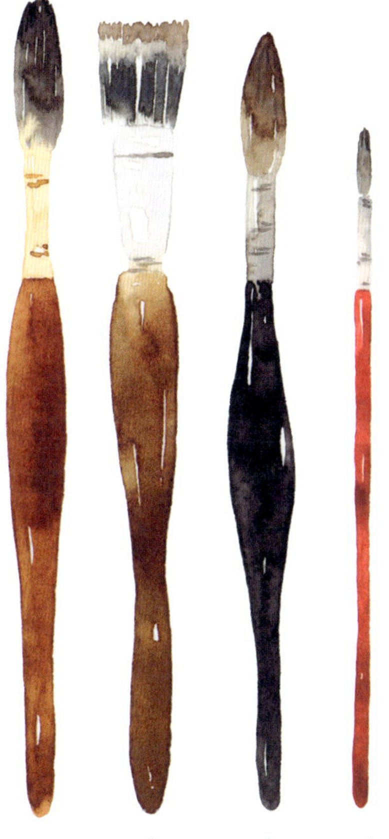


## 3/*Watercolour paints*

The two most common watercolour paint formulations are tubes and pans. Tubes are filled with wet paint, which you squeeze out onto a palette and can use immediately. Be careful to dilute the pigments to achieve transparency. Freshly squeezed tubed paint is easy to pick up with a brush, which also means we need to be careful not to use too thick a formulation.

Pans are dried pigments in tiny square plastic 'cakes', usually sold as a set, which makes them portable for travelling or painting *en plein air*. Pans need to be sprayed with water a few minutes before painting to ensure the pigments activate.

There are other exciting types of paints available in art shops, such as liquid watercolour (very wet and highly pigmented paint in small jars) and watercolour pencils, markers and pastels, whose application is different – you can draw with them on paper, then apply a layer of water to activate and enliven them.

Gouache paint is a type of opaque watercolour, which means it is less transparent. It is also a water-based paint; you use water to paint with it, much like with watercolour, but it has more pigment and less binder in it, giving flatter, denser washes.

In this book, every exercise has been painted using tubed watercolours, because they are my favourite to work with. I could write a separate book on the various types of paints, but to keep things as clear and straightforward as possible, I have focused solely on tubed watercolours – apart from one white gouache paint called 'bleed-proof white', which is fantastic for adding opaque detail.

A crucial distinction in paints is their quality. More expensive, professional grade watercolours are way more effective and saturated than student grade watercolours. Professional paints have a higher proportion of pigment in their formulation, which means your paintings will be more vibrant and lightfast (resistant to fading over time). To avoid disappointment, I recommend purchasing fewer colours, but of higher quality.

## THE ESSENTIAL COLOURS NEEDED FOR THIS BOOK

I structured *Weekend Art Watercolour* to guide you through the process of mixing most of the colours from just six pigments. I explain this process in depth on pages 25–26.

The entire content of this book has been prepared using primary colours (red, yellow, blue) in two temperatures: cool and warm. These six colours, in various combinations, offer you endless possibilities for colour mixing, as you will soon discover. This means you do not need to buy a huge set of watercolours – just six tubes will suffice!

In this book, my recommendation for paints is the Daniel Smith Extra-Fine Watercolour Essentials Set, which consists of two blues, two reds and two yellows.

I suggest getting two extra colours: a professional-grade Lamp Black from any brand, as well as a jar of opaque white gouache called 'bleed-proof white' by Dr. Ph. Martin's, for adding the odd highlight detail.

The six colours that make up the Daniel Smith's Essentials set are:

- WARM BLUE (WB) – FRENCH ULTRAMARINE
- COOL BLUE (CB) – PHTHALO BLUE (GREEN SHADE)
- WARM RED (WR) – PYRROL SCARLET
- COOL RED (CR) – QUINACRIDONE ROSE
- WARM YELLOW (WY) – NEW GAMBOGE
- COOL YELLOW (CY) – HANSA YELLOW LIGHT

If you cannot get this set of paints, here are

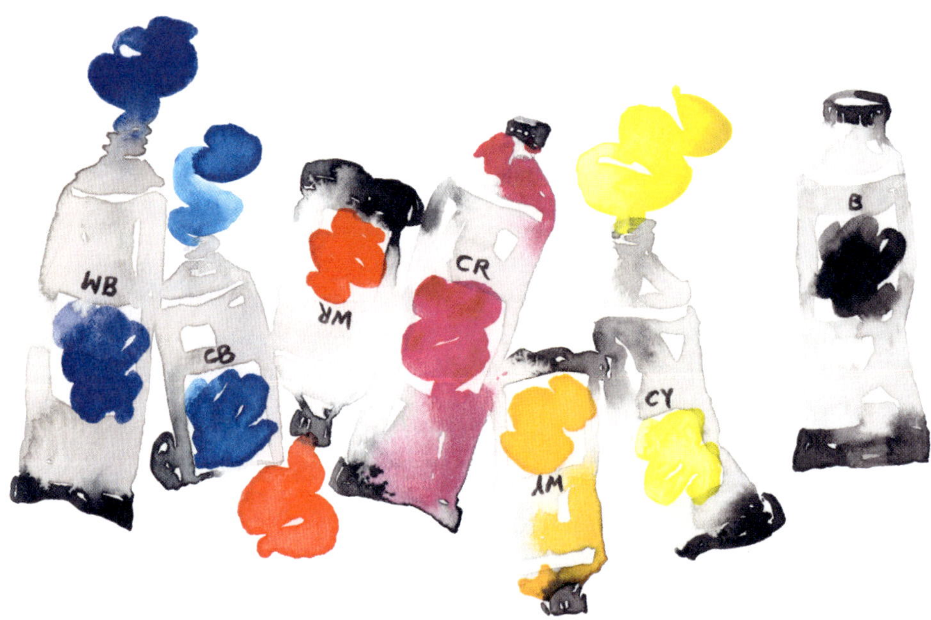

my recommendations for pigments that will work very well as substitutes for the warm and cool primaries listed. You will be able to find most of the colours named below from other art-supply brands.

- WARM BLUE (WB) – COBALT BLUE OR FRENCH ULTRAMARINE
- COOL BLUE (CB) – PHTHALO BLUE OR WINSOR BLUE
- WARM RED (WR) – CADMIUM RED OR PYRROL SCARLET
- COOL RED (CR) – PERMANENT ROSE OR QUINACRIDONE ROSE
- WARM YELLOW (WY) – INDIAN YELLOW OR NEW GAMBOGE
- COOL YELLOW (CY) – HANSA YELLOW MEDIUM OR LEMON YELLOW

## *4/Other essential supplies*

For diluting paint, laying down washes and cleaning brushes I recommend having at least three glass jars of water on your desk. We will be mixing a lot of colours, so having a few jars of clean water means you can spare one to be the 'dirty water jar' in which you dispose of excess pigments and still have spares for fresh water, which can be used for further painting. This is crucial to avoid creating muddy colours.

You will need at least two mixing dishes or palettes, so that you can squeeze paints onto one, and use the other for your colour preparation. I sometimes use three palettes so I can mix a lot of colours simultaneously, and it really helps to have this extra space!

Prepare some paper towels to remove excess water and pigment with, and to use for a colour lifting technique called 'blotting' (see page 21).

A soft pencil and a kneadable art eraser are a fantastic duo – watercolour papers have a delicate surface, so a sharp pencil and a regular eraser could damage it quickly.

Kneadable erasers are soft and mouldable and gently remove pencil lines without rubbing.

Regular table salt will be used in two exercises, and it is an unassuming but very special ingredient in watercolour painting.

I always have a few scraps of paper to hand to test colour mixes on. It is essential to be able to see a colour you prepared before you apply it to your painting.

A fine-line waterproof graphic pen in black can be used to add hard edges and detail.

Lastly, a hairdryer or other heat tool can be used to speed up the paint-drying process when painting in layers.

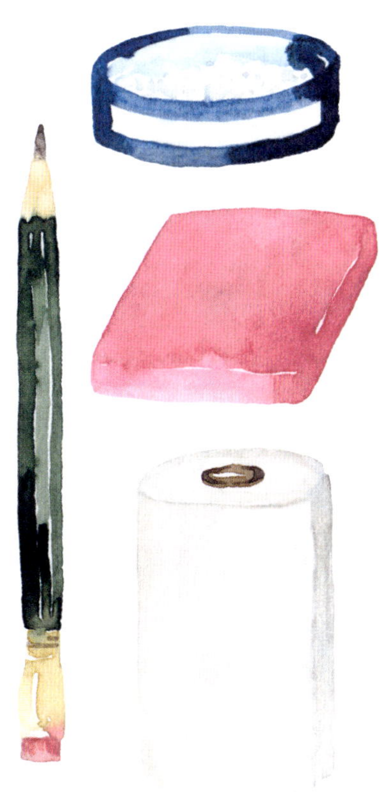

# Painting Techniques

I'm going to begin by showing you a range of fundamental watercolour techniques that you should be familiar with, and practise, before you tackle the projects in this book. Establishing a firm technical base is a key to success as it eliminates a lot of guesswork, of which there can be plenty in this fascinating medium!

Even if you are not a beginner watercolourist anymore, it is always beneficial to remind yourself of the basics and sharpen up your muscle memory. To this day, I practise basic techniques regularly just to keep in touch with what made me fall in love with this medium in the first place – the transparency, the complex simplicity, the ethereal quality of watercolours that is tricky to control fully – and therefore pushes us to let go of excess control.

# 1/ Flat wash or wet-on-dry

Load up your brush with a generous amount of water and pick up a colour of your choice. Mix a rich consistency, somewhere between the texture of butter and milk. Apply a flat wash of colour, trying to make the shape as seamless as possible. This is also called the wet-on-dry technique, which just means applying wet paint onto a dry surface.

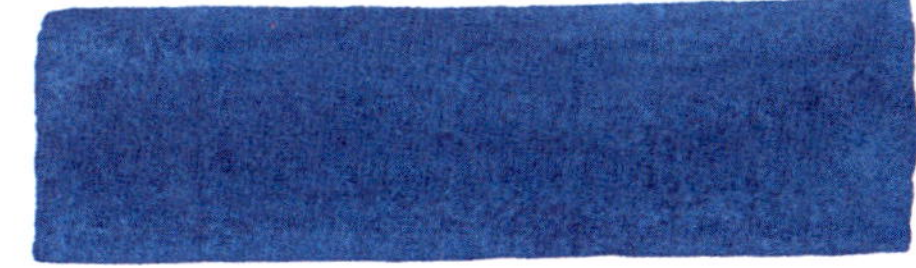

Now wash most of the blue off the brush in your 'dirty water jug', leaving just a tiny bit of pigment, and paint the same shape. This time there is very little colour, so the consistency of the mix will be much more watery.

To make the third shape, go back to the original colour and the initial consistency and apply it starting from the left, gradually adding more water and expending the shape as you move towards the right. You are creating a gradient, or a graded wash, and hence exploring this colour's transparency possibilities.

# 2/Wet-on-wet

Everyone's favourite technique is the famous way in which watercolours explode on wet paper – the wet-on-wet technique. In short, it means applying wet paint onto a moist surface, which allows the pigments to move and bloom.

The image to the right shows a wet-on-dry brushstroke at the top and similar brushstrokes dropped onto a wetted surface below. You can see the pigment merging slowly with the water: there are no hard edges, and the colour becomes less vibrant as it is diluted with water.

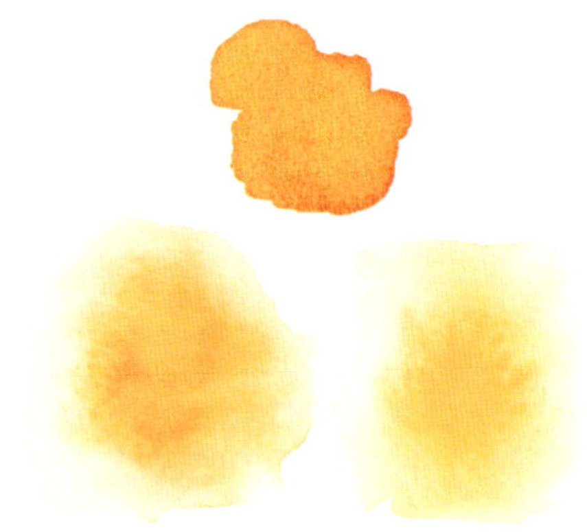

A very common problem with achieving desirable wet-on-wet effects is putting too much or too little water on the paper. The sweet spot of how much water to lay down initially is enough to produce a sheen or glaze, which still shows a little bit of the paper's texture when you hold it against a source of light. If you see puddles forming, there is too much water. If you notice the paper is drying quickly, that means there is not enough water on it. If you see a little grain of paper showing from underneath the layer of water, that is the right amount, and you can go ahead and drop in wet paint onto it! It takes some time to develop muscle memory for the correct water application.

Take a look at these examples. The first two rectangles have a different saturation, but they are both wet.

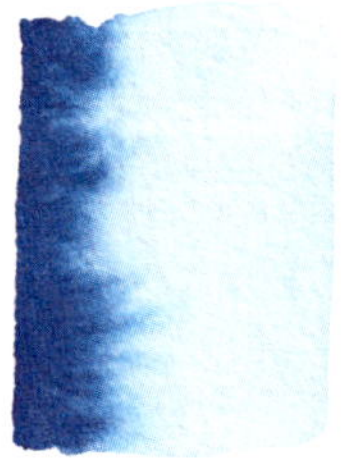

If you apply more paint to the side of the pale shape when it is still wet, you will see colour blending from that side.

To expand the exercise further, try merging the pale rectangle with the dark blue, and repeat that a few times. You will get merging shapes. Each time you undertake this exercise, the effects will vary a bit. It will never look exactly the same, because watercolour pigments travel in their own rhythm, which means we need to embrace not being in full control.

## 3/*Glazing*

One of the predominant ways to build contrast and colour depth in watercolour is to lay down layers. It's also a great way to discover the full potential of any one colour.

Starting with a pale mix with hardly any pigment, lay down a flat wash as you did in the first exercise. Using a hairdryer or other heat tool, dry it and add another flat wash of the same concentration on top, but make the shape slightly narrower so that you can still see a strip of the first wash underneath. The idea is that you are increasing the depth and saturation of your colour by gradually layering transparent, thin washes over coats of colour that have already dried. It is important that after each layer, you dry everything completely.

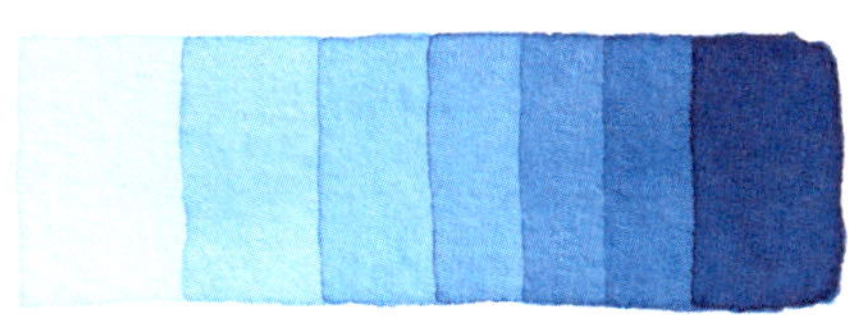

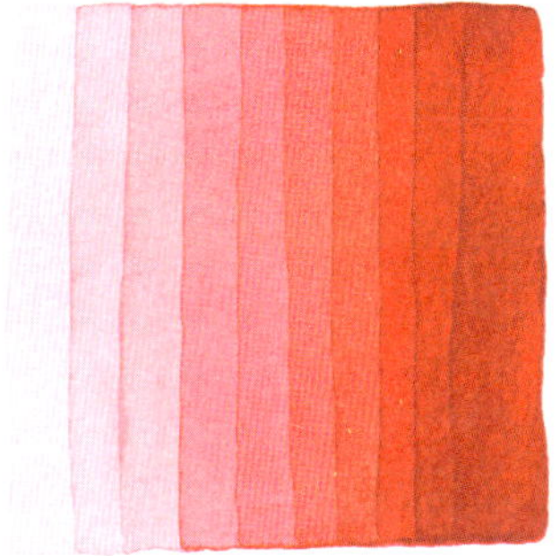

## 4/Dry brush

You can also paint with a dry brush that has hardly any water on it. This technique is great for adding texture and irregular structure to parts of your paintings.

Load up your brush with water and a colour of choice. Then gently remove excess water from the brush using paper towels, until the brush feels just damp to touch. Hold it at a 45-degree angle and sweep the paper with the semi-dry bristles for a rough, irregular effect.

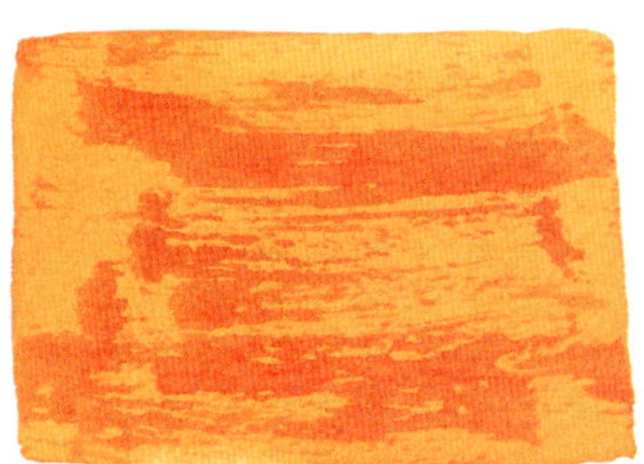

## 5/Dry-on-dry

Now that you have practised a dry brush technique, you can utilise it to add layers of texture on top of existing washes of colour. In the example below, I applied a flat yellow wash as in the first exercise, waited for it to dry and then went over it with some red using a dry brush as explored in the previous technique.

## 6/Feathering

Feathering is a way of softening an edge when a shape is still wet.

First, lay down a flat, even brushstroke. Then, quickly get rid of excess pigment from the brush in a jar of water. Now that your brush is damp, go over the edge of the brushstroke and drag out the hard edges to soften them.

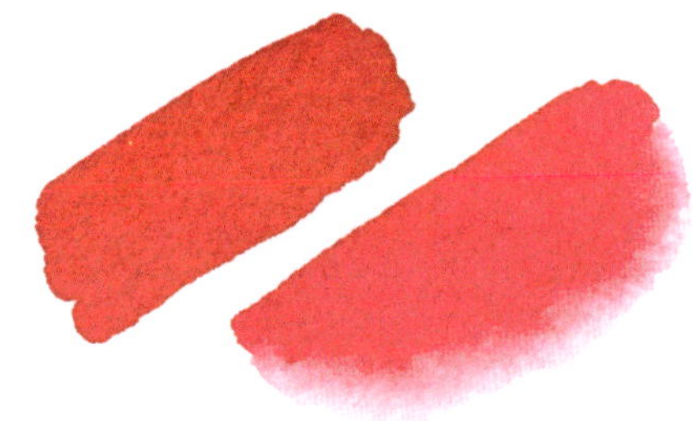

# 7/Lifting colour and blotting

Lifting is the method of removing some of the pigment from an existing layer of watercolour in order to pull out highlights and create contrast.

Look at the green squares below. Colour has been lifted in three different ways.

The first green wash (top left) was still wet when I cleaned off my brush and dried it completely with a paper towel. I then went over the moist shape with dry bristles and picked up excess colour.

The second wash (bottom left) had dried completely before I went over it with a damp brush to release highlights.

The third wash (right) was still damp when I dropped in a few drops of clean water, which pushed the existing pigment of the wash sideways, creating awesome blooming effects.

Finally, you can use a tissue or paper towel to pick up excess pigment from a damp wash – this is called blotting. While the watercolour paper is still wet, dab the kitchen paper around to elevate highlights. I enjoy painting clouds like this as it gives them an irregular, naturalistic feel.

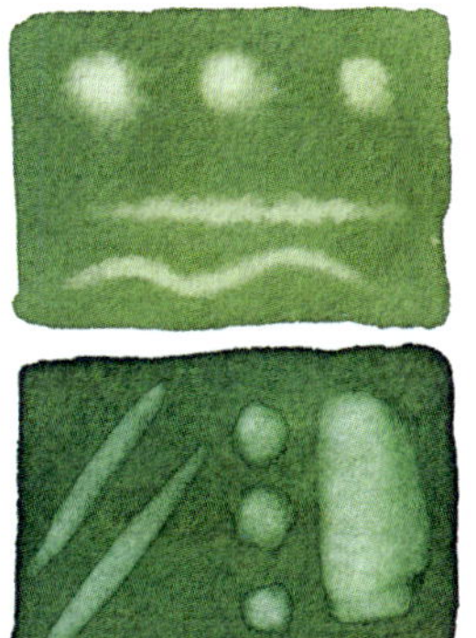

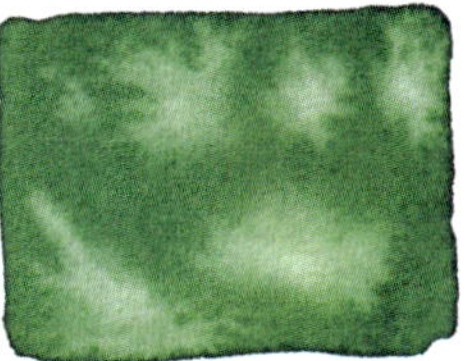

## 8/'Cauliflower' blooms

It seems to me that a lot of people are afraid of the unexpected bleeding, or blooming, effects in watercolour where a wet area meets an area that is drying quicker, resulting in 'cauliflower' edges. I personally love this look and strongly urge you to start seeing watercolour's unique beauty in it; it reminds me of the white tips of sea waves.

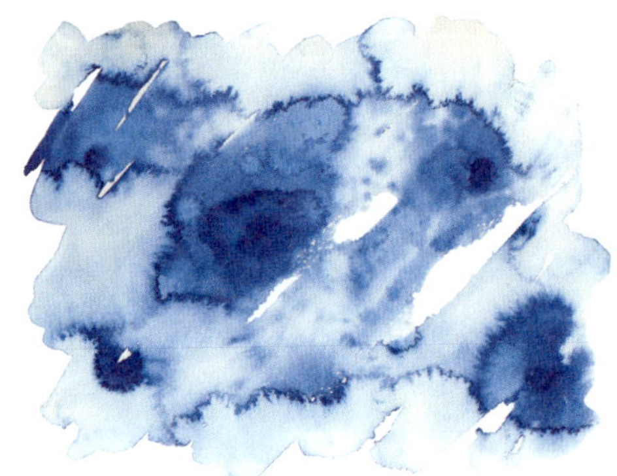

## 9/Granulation

Granulation is an effect in watercolour which creates uneven, grainy, clumpy textures. It is created by using granulating colours, which are paints made of heavy, coarse pigments. This means the pigment particles sink and settle into the paper texture, creating a mottled appearance. Granulation is enhanced when working on textured papers (cold-pressed and rough) and is most prominent in earthy tones (e.g. raw umber, raw sienna, oxide black), and very commonly in ultramarine blue, but can also be present in the popular cerulean blue, cobalt green and viridian colours.

Note that some brands of watercolour paints are more granulating than others.

While granulating paints separate on paper creating unexpected effects, there are paints which are smoother and allow for even washes – we call those 'staining colours'. They are made of finely-milled pigments, and some prominent examples are quinacridone magenta, Indian yellow, phthalo blue and sap green. Note that staining pigments seep deep into the paper and are therefore more difficult to lift off than granulating ones once they have dried.

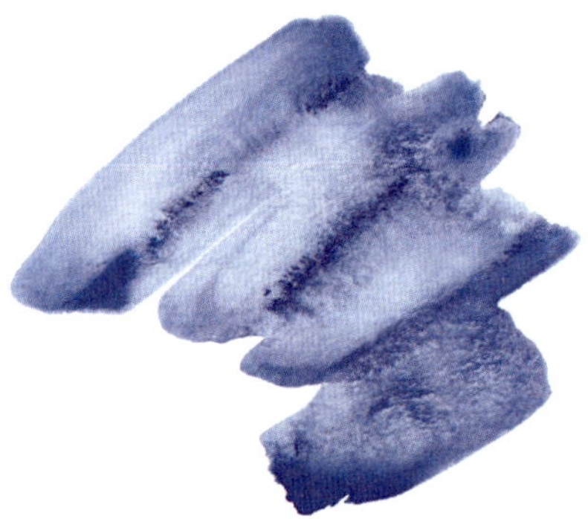

## 10/*Underpainting*

A fantastic way to darken a colour is to use its opposite on the colour wheel (a complementary colour), a colour theory technique I look at on page 31. Underpainting means applying a light wash of diluted paint to establish a base tone, which will alter the value of the colour we put on next.

In the lemon example to the right, I laid down a pale wash of purple (the colour opposite yellow on the colour wheel), waited for it to dry, and then painted a lemon shape like the one on the right on top of the purple underpainting. Notice how much more natural the bottom lemon looks with a shadow created this way.

## 11/*Leaving gaps vs. adding white paint*

I generally discourage using white watercolour paint, which sometimes comes in store-bought watercolour sets. White is a chalky, non-transparent pigment which turns colours pastel (see page 33 for more detail). White bleed-proof gouache can be used to add highlights and accentuate elements of an illustration, but make sure the initial layer has dried completely before it is applied.

However, hands down the best way to accentuate highlights and imitate light reflecting off surfaces is to avoid putting down colour in certain areas – in other words, leaving empty gaps between brushstrokes. I use that method a lot in this book.

The square on the left has had white bleed-proof white gouache applied on top to achieve the shapes. The one on the right did not need any white pigment, as I simply left gaps, in which you can see the paper beneath. Both effects can be useful, depending on context and desired effect.

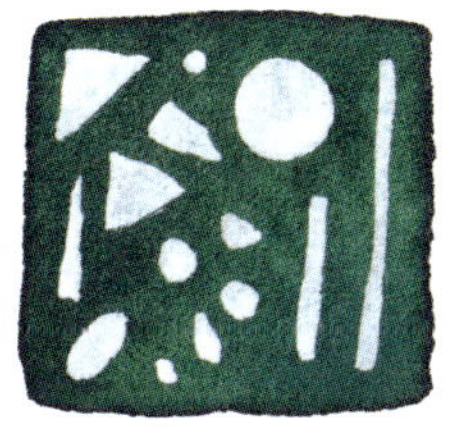

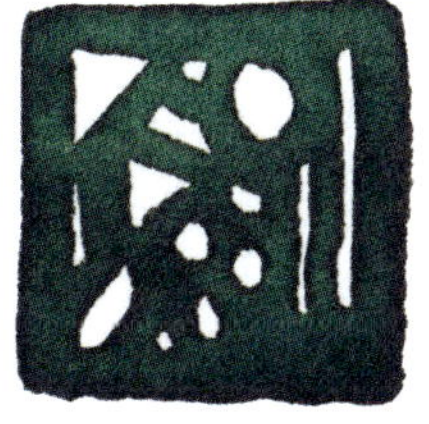

## 12/*Duotone brushstrokes*

A wonderful and dynamic technique is to lay down brushstrokes in two colours simultaneously. To do this, load your brush with lots of water, then pick up a generous amount of your base colour (lemon yellow works well) to cover the brush bristles nicely. Then, dunk just the very tip of the brush in a strong, saturated mix of another colour and watch the magic unfold as you move your brush on the surface of the paper.

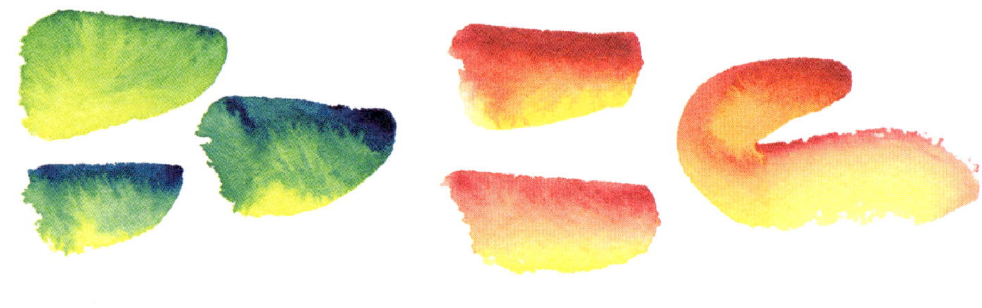

## 13/*Salt*

Humble table salt is a wonderful tool that can add mysterious, unexpected texture to your washes. Lay down a flat wash and before it dries, drop some grains of salt on top. Leave the paper to dry completely and naturally (do not use a hairdryer, as it could push the salt particles around). Then observe the awesome blooms the salt crystals created by pulling the pigment away from the paper surface. Below is a comparison of using salt on a flat wash on cold-pressed, hot-pressed and rough papers.

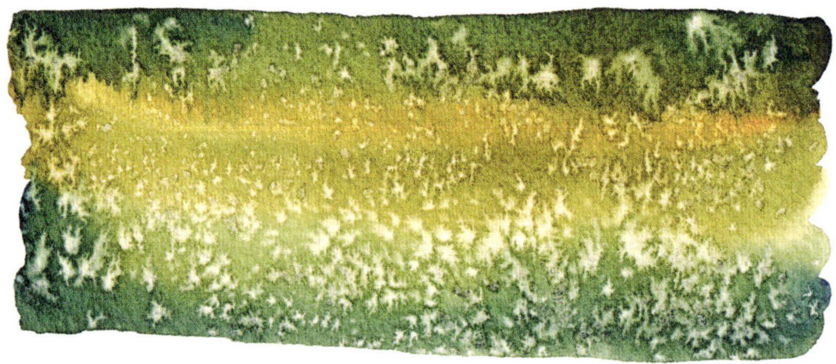

# Colour Theory Expanded

You do not need a huge selection of watercolour paints to start your journey.

Just as important as mastering basic watercolour techniques is grasping the concepts of essential colour theory for successful colour mixing. When I first understood that a plethora of colours can be mixed just from six colours – two reds, two blues and two yellows – I was astonished and excited!

I carried out the projects for this entire book using a minimal palette – all the colours I used for the exercises are hand-mixed from the six primaries, plus one additional tube of black paint in case I needed a really dark colour, and bleed-proof white opaque paint for the odd highlight. Working that way was incredible for my understanding of colour mixing, and I find myself painting with just the six paints every time I work now – this method gives you heaps of informed control.

Let me go into more detail to explain. You may be familiar with the concept of 'primary colours', which are blue, red and yellow. Secondary colours are green (blue + yellow), purple (blue + red) and orange (red + yellow). The problem in colour mixing arises when secondary colours don't meet our expectations – for example purple often turns out closer to brown, and is muted rather than vibrant. We get frustrated and feel that the best shortcut would be to buy a ready-made palette with more colour choices.

The reason for this confusion is that a comprehensive understanding of the colour wheel needs to incorporate the temperature of colours into the equation. Pigments are divided into colours that evoke a sense of warmth, and those with cool undertones. Depending on which temperature of primaries you use to mix a secondary, you will achieve a duller or a more vibrant colour. Look at the comparison of cool and warm primary colours on the following page to see the difference in temperature (see page 14 for more detail about the set of colours I used in this book).

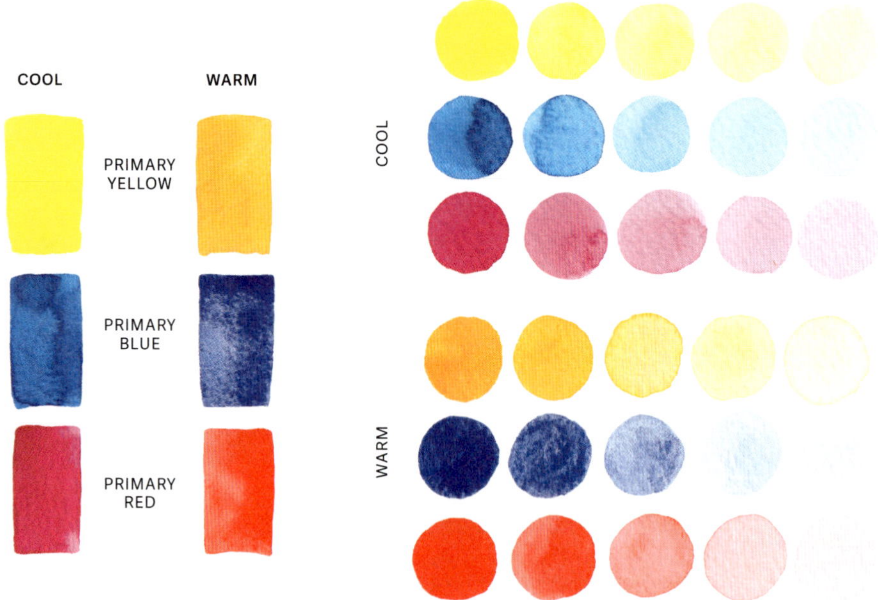


The cool yellow is very bright and almost neon-like, whereas the warm has a sunny feel to it. The cool blue has a little green tint to it, while the warm leans more towards a purple tone. The cool red is vibrant and saturated; the warm red feels more organic and natural.

To see the full scope of the six colours we are working with, it is beneficial to test each colour in its most saturated version, and then gradually add more water to each swatch to see their full potential.

To get an idea of the kinds of secondary and tertiary mixes you can achieve in both temperatures, look at the cool and warm colour wheel comparison opposite.

# Cool and warm colour wheels

Secondary colours are the mixes of primaries; tertiary colours are made of one primary and one neighbouring secondary colour.

The difference in tonal ranges is significant – the cool purple is vibrant, whereas the warm one is dull and closer to brown. The cool green is bright and vivid; the warm one is softer and more organic.

The temperature of primary colours affects the tonal range of your mixes. This gives you the ability to adjust the moods of colours, cutting out the guesswork. For example, warm greens will be more appropriate for realistic botanical paintings than cool ones because they are more naturalistic. If you are after a more vibrant artwork, you will opt for the cooler tones rather than the warm.

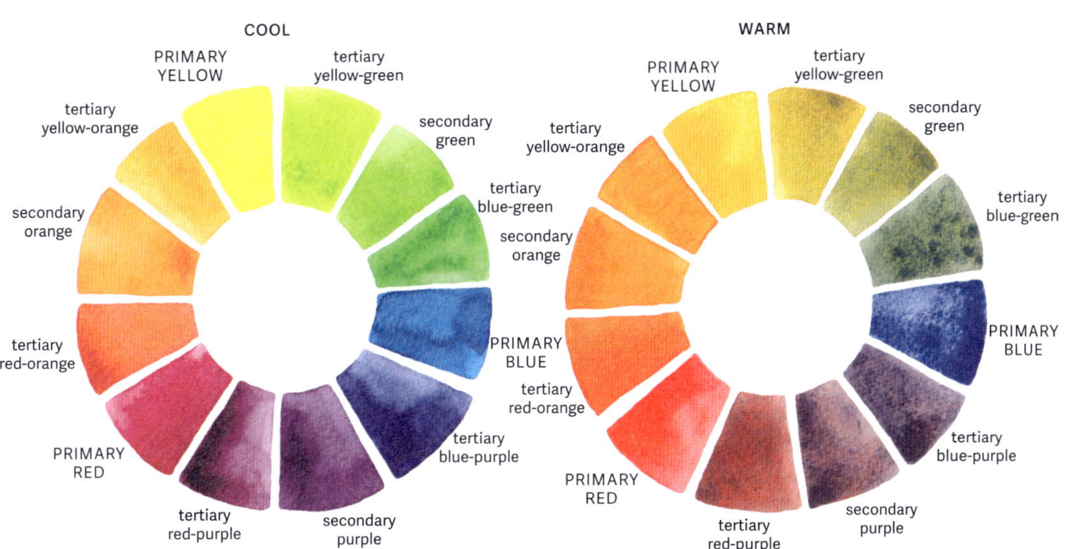


# Split-primary colour wheels

To ascertain which primary mixes will give you the brightest and most radiant secondaries, and in turn which will produce duller, muted ones, we can use split-primary colour wheels. Notice that the only thing that changes between the vibrant and muted colour wheels is the position of the cool and warm primaries. They have been swapped for the best colour outcome.

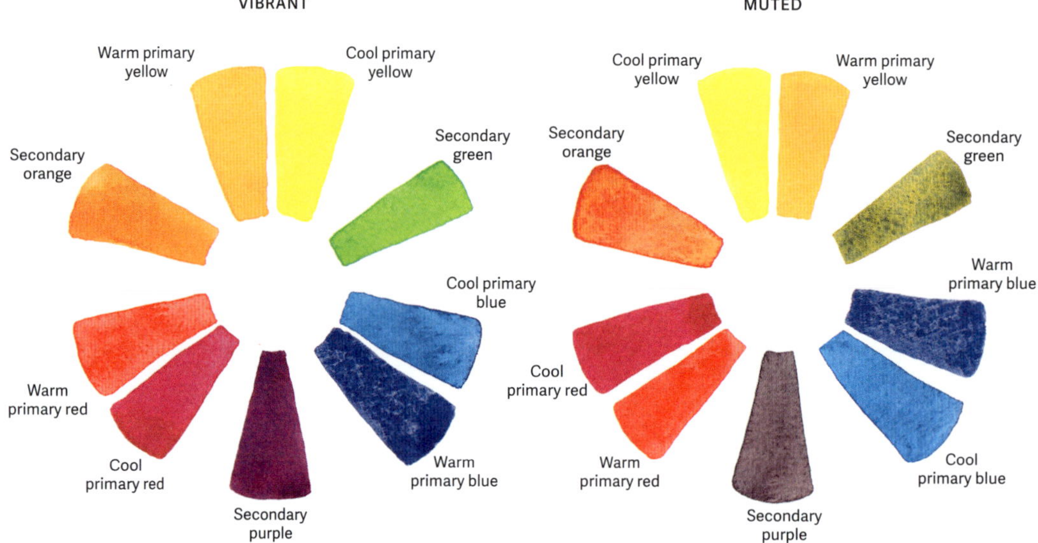


The richest purples are achieved by mixing a cool red with a warm blue. The most vibrant greens are made of cool yellow and cool blue. The brightest oranges are a mix of warm yellow and warm red.

On the flip side, the dullest purples are a combination of warm red and cool blue. The organic, nature-like greens are created with warm yellow and warm blue. More muted, calmer oranges are a mix of cool yellow and cool red.

Of course, you can also combine the cool and warm primaries of the same colour (warm and cool yellow, warm and cool red, warm and cool blue) to mix a primary colour that would land somewhere in the middle of the temperatures.

I tend to use such mixes of the primaries when I want to achieve a middle ground between a vibrant and a duller tone – the mixed yellow is a wonderful colour to use for painting flowers, for example.

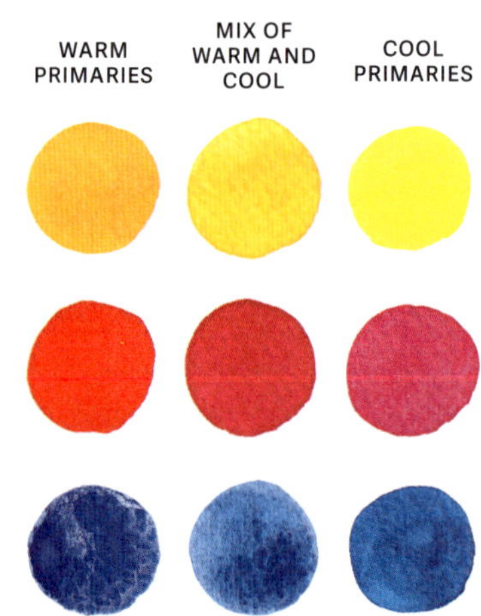

# *Colour charts*

I recommend creating a few colour charts so you can always refer to them and find the shade you need. Seeing all the possibilities of colour mixes on a sheet of paper is a wonderful reference guide to consult whenever you are unsure what tone you are after.

Start with a cool colours chart. The primary colours (I) are placed on the far left and far right, with their secondary mixes in the centre (II), and tertiary ones (III) in between the primary and the secondary on either side.

The second row in each combination of primaries is a more diluted version of every colour to give you an idea of each one's transparency potential.

Do the same with the warm colours.

**COOL secondary and tertiary mixes**

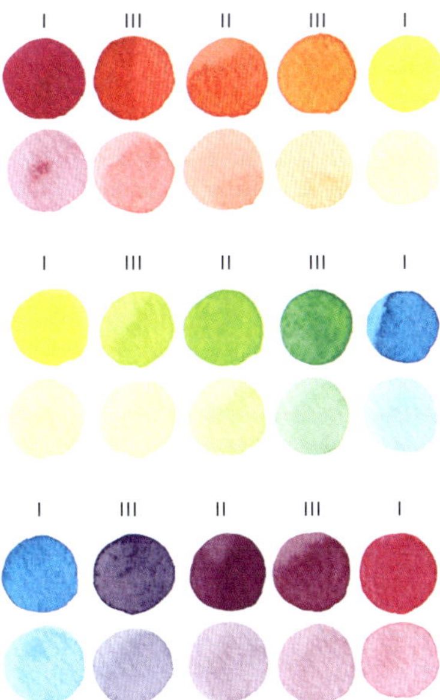


**WARM secondary and tertiary mixes**

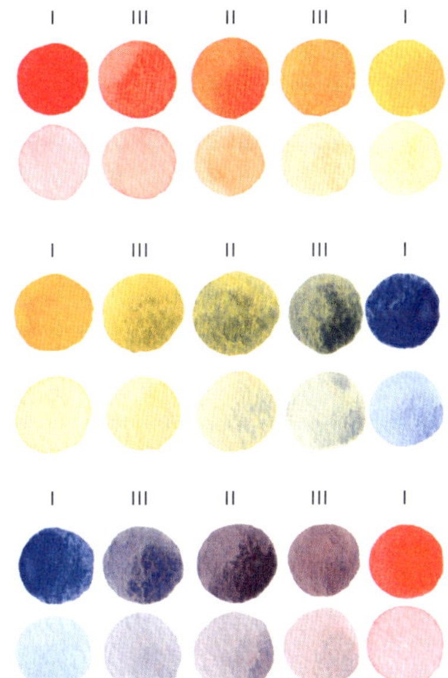

To complete the charts, now create one where you mix warm and cool primaries, to see the wide array of tones you can achieve with just six paints. Notice how many different greens, purples and oranges you can create by being aware of the temperature of your primary colour combinations – the possibilities grow exponentially.

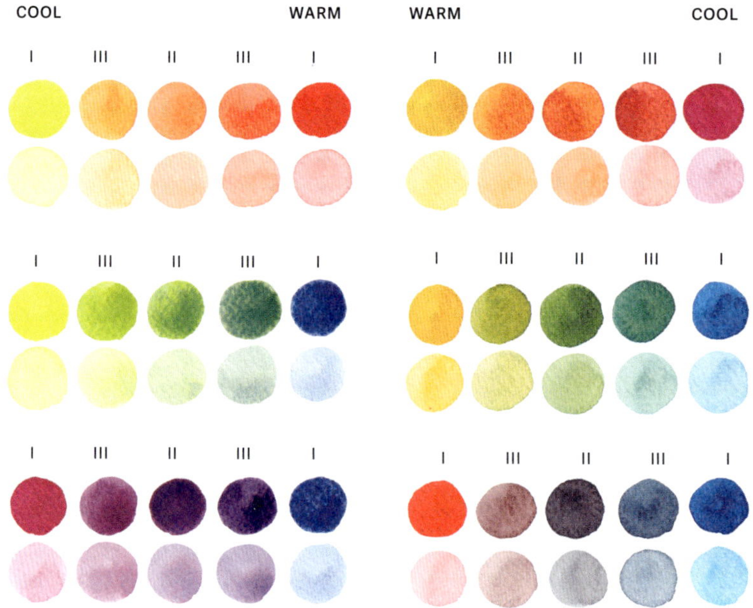


# *Muting colours*

You may be wondering how to tone down or darken your colours. Most of us would assume that adding black paint would be the way, but to achieve more natural darker shades we will use each colour's complement.

Complements are the colours opposite each other on the colour wheel – they are the most contrasting tones when coupled together, and when mixed they neutralise each other and create duller, darker colours.

The black and grey lines within the wheels above indicate each colour's complement opposite. To darken red, add a little secondary green; to make yellow a shade darker, introduce a tiny bit of purple; to dull down blue, mix in some orange. This can of course be flipped to darkening secondary colours too – for example to darken purple, add a tiny bit of yellow to it, and so on.

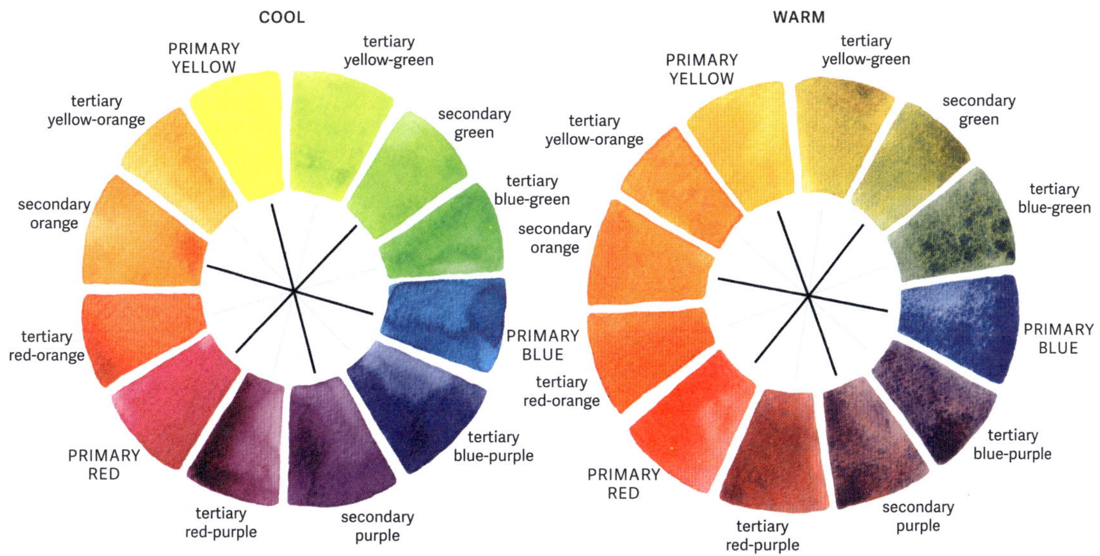


# *Darkening colours*

When darkening a colour with a complementary one, it is important to use a diluted version of the complement to merely tone down the original colour. In the charts below, 'I' indicates a primary colour, 'II' a secondary colour.

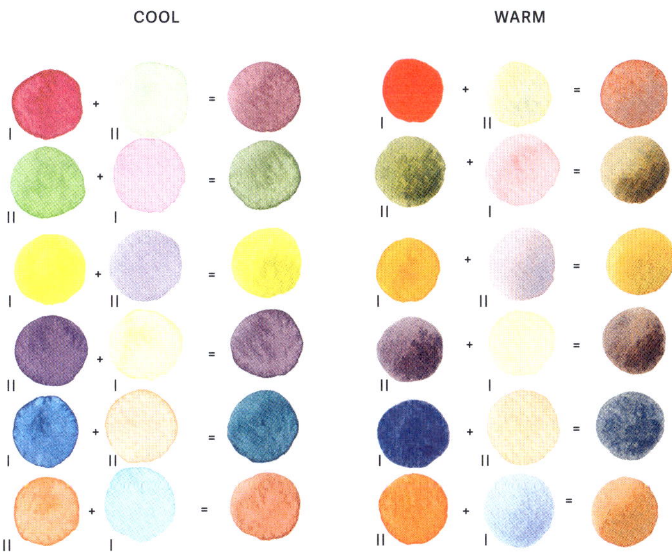

# *Neutralising colours*

The next step after darkening colours is neutralising them, meaning that you use the same amount of each complement to mix a neutral shade. This is extremely useful knowledge, because neutrals can elevate your paintings to a new level due to their nuanced nature.

Imagine you are painting a muted autumnal landscape that includes shades of brown, dark green, rust red and subdued orange. To build variety in such a scene, you can use complementary colour neutralisation and achieve a wide range of hues even within similar tones. Suddenly you can mix warm and cool browns, each with their own individual characters.

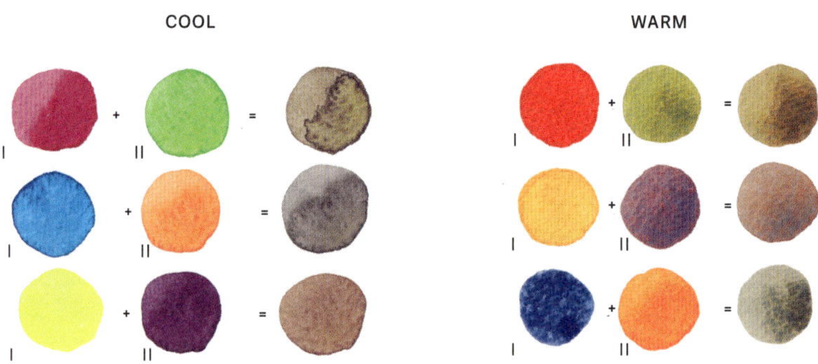


# *Mixing with black*

To show you the difference between darkening colours using their complements and darkening using a black pigment, I made a chart where I used Lamp Black to darken cool and warm primaries and secondaries. A colour mixed with black is called a shade.

The effect is different – by mixing in black paint we get colours that are flatter, with less nuanced vibrancy. Such tones also serve a purpose and can be useful in your paintings. The key is to be aware of both ways in which you can darken colours, and how much variety you can achieve by using both mixing methods mindfully.

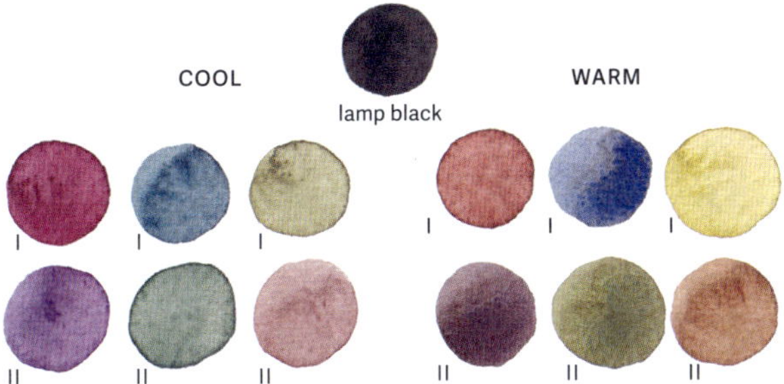


# *Mixing with white*

When we begin our journey with watercolours, a lot of us assume that adding white paint will lighten a mix. This may be true for other paint media, but not for watercolours: white is a chalky, opaque pigment that dulls the vibrancy of watercolours.

To brighten a colour, we simply add more water to the mix to make it more translucent. Mixing in white pigment does create wonderful pastel shades, but it simultaneously mutes the original saturation by flattening the depth of colour.

In this demo, I used Chinese White paint, which is often included in watercolour sets, but be careful with how and when you use it. When you do, you are making a conscious choice to mix flatter, pastel-like colours.

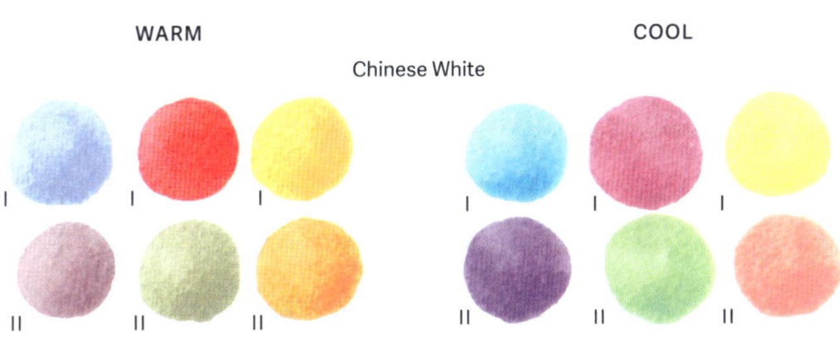

# *Mixing black with primary colours*

As mentioned in the Art Supplies section, I recommend using a ready-made Lamp Black watercolour paint, because having a deep, dense black paint available is very handy. However, I want you to know that you can mix your own black shades by using primary colours.

Black is formed when all primaries are combined. This requires a little time and practice, because yellow is a naturally lighter and paler colour than blue or red, which means you will need a bigger quantity of yellow than red or blue to achieve a neutral black.

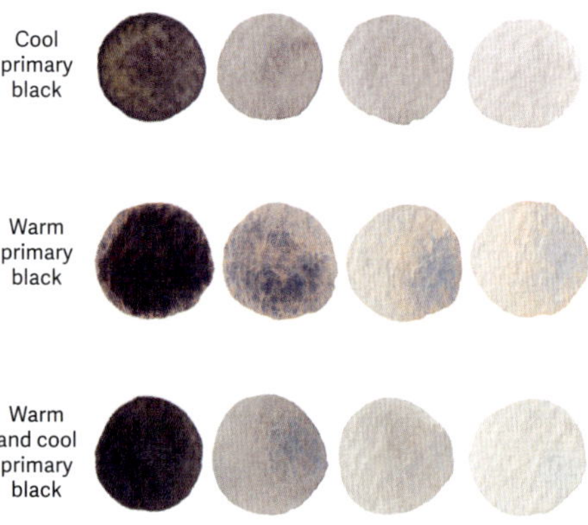


It is worth spending a little time mixing your own black tones to add another nuanced skill to your watercolour set. You can adjust the temperature of the black depending on whether you use cool or white primaries to put it together – and for a well-rounded black, use both temperatures; in other words mix all six colours together.

# Skin tones

It may come as a surprise that to mix human skin tones, we only need primary colours. While complexions vary from pale to dark, in painting we can use the same base colour mixes and adjust their darkness and saturation by varying the ratio of water to pigment. The more water you add, the paler your skin tones. The more pigment you use, the darker they will become.

The base of all skin tones will be a peach colour. The below example is a red (a combination of cool and warm primary reds), coupled with a yellow (a combination of cool and warm primary yellows). Those two colours combined give us a middle-range peach tone.

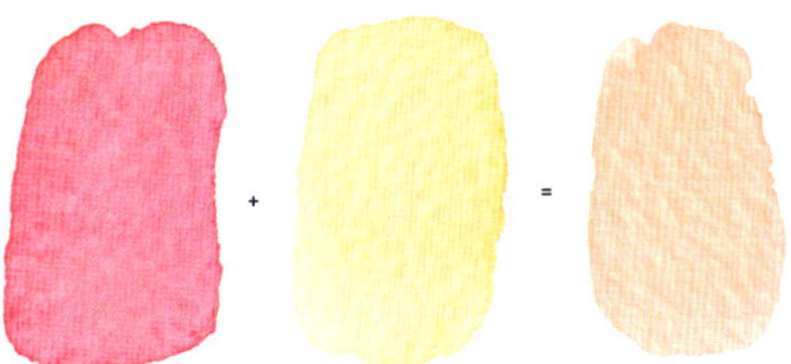


## 1 FAIR SKIN TONES

Use the peach tone with a little diluted blue (a mix of cool and warm blue primaries) to create fair skin tones like in the examples below.

The more peach in your mix, the warmer the tones will be. The more blue you add, the more neutral the tones.

## 2 MEDIUM SKIN TONES

To create skin tones a shade darker, you will use the same combination of colours but using a little more pigment and a little less water.

Notice that you can achieve a whole range of skin tones using the same colours, merely adjusting the amount of peach and blue tones you mix in and controlling the amount of water in each variation.

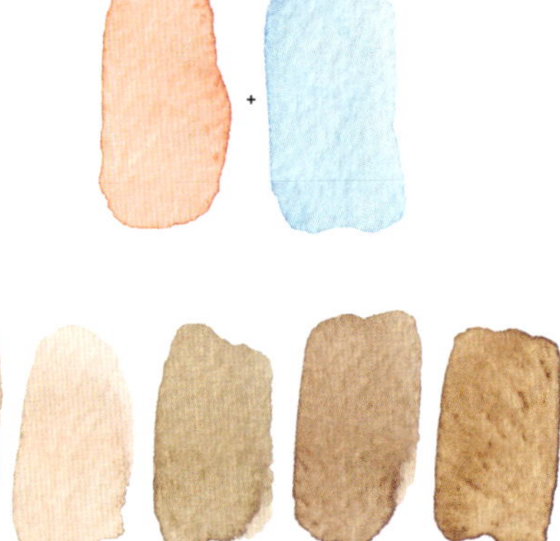

## 3 DARK SKIN TONES

The darkest skin tones will require a more saturated version of the peach and blue base combination. Simply use more pigment and less water to achieve this.

The more blue you use, the darker the tones, but remain careful to avoid diverting into green shades.

When it comes to skin-tone mixing overall, spend time practising the colour combinations to get used to the process. We are after natural-looking, muted variations of browns, beige and cream tones. Bear in mind that even miniscule additions of a certain pigment will affect the overall effect, so take some time to practise.

# Warm-up Exercises

Some people may say that sketching is a fun way to learn, relax and have fun with painting. They are right of course – but I take this statement further. I believe that playing around with art supplies, doodling, keeping a sketchbook and engaging your hands with a paintbrush as often as possible is essential for making progress, and paramount to developing a solid muscle memory for painting. The more you fool around and experiment with watercolours, the quicker your confidence and ingenuity will grow.

Each time you open this book and intend to work on an exercise prompt, I would really like you to do a couple of easy warm-ups beforehand. Much like warming up before a sports class, it is crucial to loosen up your wrists and set your mind onto a creative wavelength before you tackle a specific illustration subject.

Feel free to use the examples that follow as inspiration – they are all abstract, so that your brain can focus solely on colour mixing, brushstroke motions and unspecific but beautiful forms. I am positive that you will soon find your own favourite warm-up exercises, and the habit of loosening up before painting will become part of your artistic process. You could dedicate a sketchbook to become your collection of warm-ups, and see where that takes you!

# 1/*Simple stripe patterns*

Pick two primary colours and make flat, straight brushstrokes, varying the amount of water and pigment you use. Then, combine those brushstrokes to make a simple repeated pattern where the shapes blend into one another.

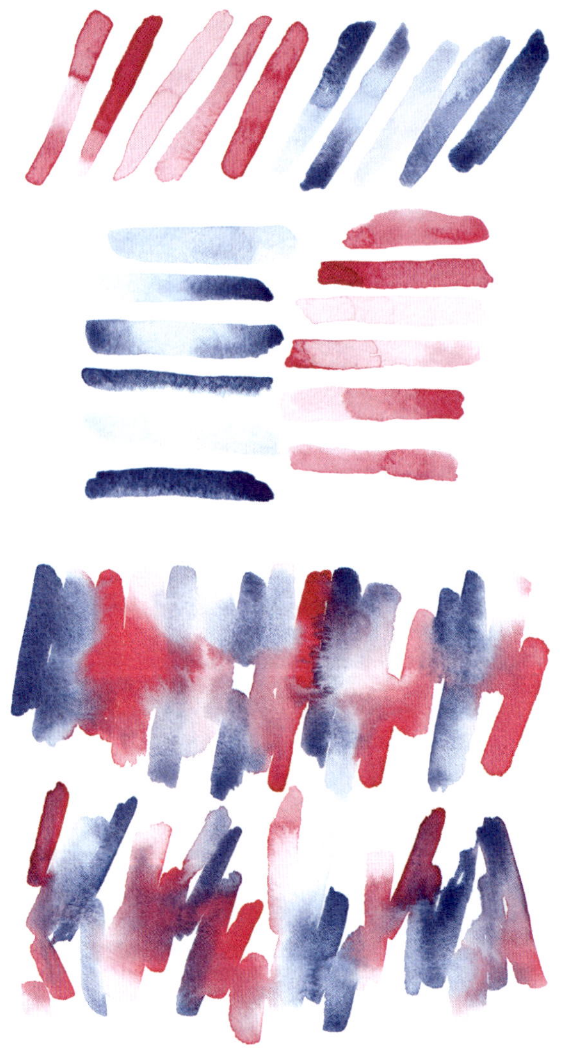

## 2/*Rounded shapes*

Load up a large round or a mop brush with a generous amount of water for a good flow, and saturated paint for vibrant colour. Make squiggly, rounded doodles, varying the ratio of water to pigment and pressing the brush down to make thick strokes.

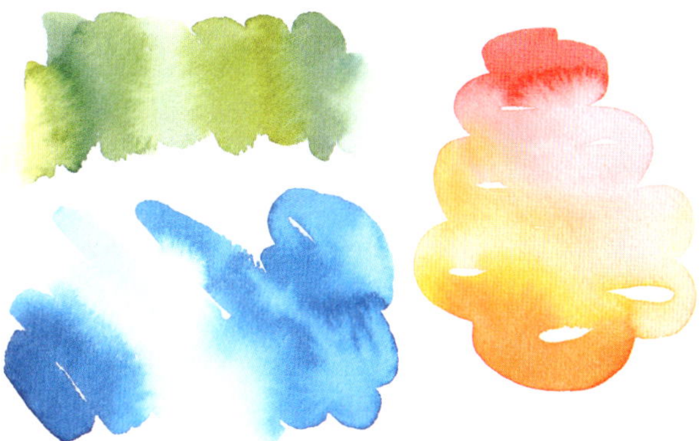

## 3/*Irregular teardrops*

Using the tip of your brush and two colours (here, primary yellow and secondary green), make irregular teardrop-shaped brushstrokes and fill a sketchbook page. You will find yourself going back and forth between the mixing palette and a water jar to adjust the saturation of each stroke.

## 4/*Long squiggly snakes*

Using a pointy round brush with a lot of colour and water, make continuous curving lines. Focus on not only varying the colours and saturation, but also changing the pressure you apply with the brush – the lighter you press, the thinner the lines, and vice versa.

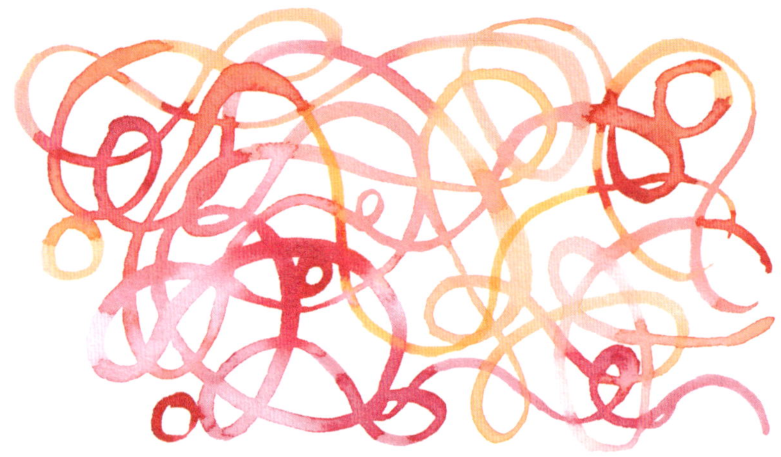

## 5/*Wet-on-wet horizons*

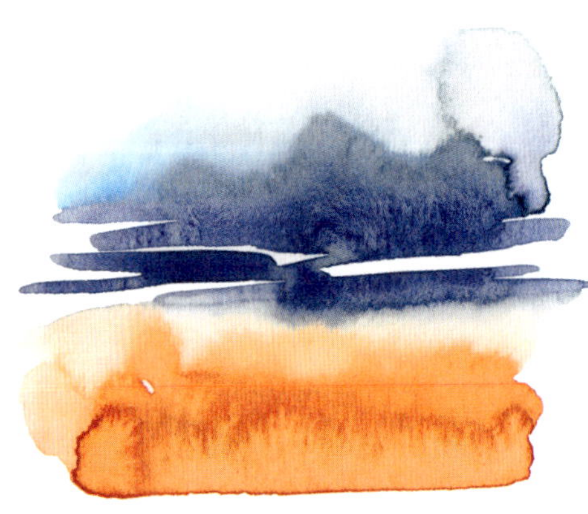

Pick any two colours of your choice. Load the brush with the first one (dark blue here) and make a few abrupt horizontal stokes, leaving empty gaps in between. Then clean the brush off completely and pick up a generous amount of clean water. Touch the lines and drag them upwards to soften the edges and create a blooming effect to imitate the sky.

Then clean the brush again and do the same at the bottom. This time, however, take it a step further and drop the second colour (orange-red) at the bottom of the wet surface so it can blend into the composition.

# 6/*Abstract patterns*

Pick up a large round or mop brush and mix two or three similar colours (here greenish yellow, green and bluish green) and one complementary colour (cool red). Make some crescent-shaped, rounded and squiggly brushstrokes using the green tones and varying the ratio of water to pigment. Then, introduce a few smaller strokes in the red tone. When working with a mixed colour palette like this, it is good to maintain an imbalance of colour to increase the 'pop' effect – here the red stands out because there is less of it than the yellows and greens.

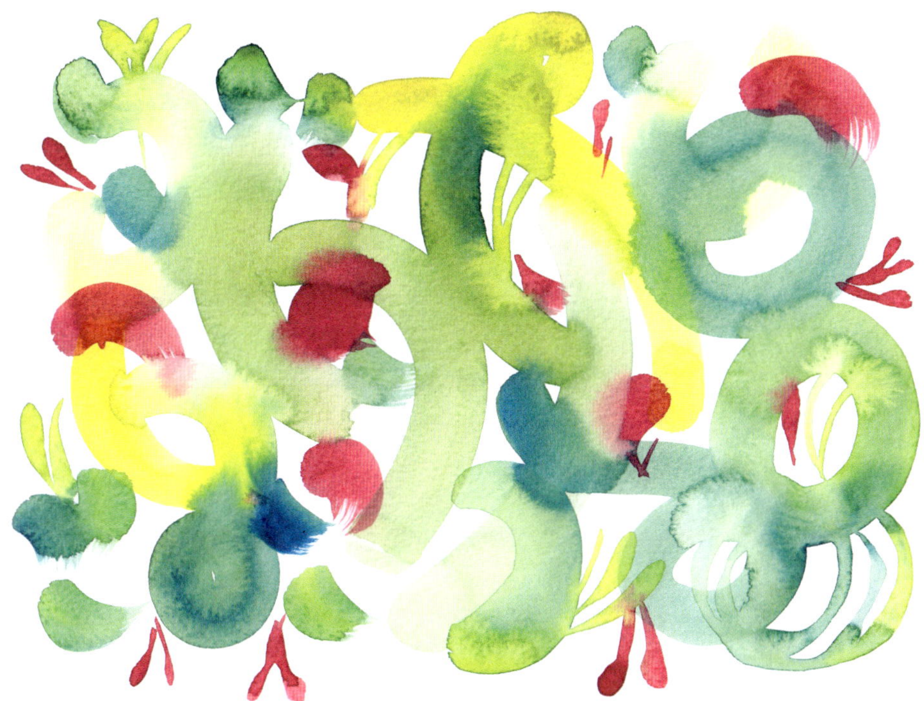

All of these examples are things I like to doodle when warming up, but I am sure you can come up with many more of your own simple exercises that serve the same purpose!

# Projects

# UP TO 35 MINUTES

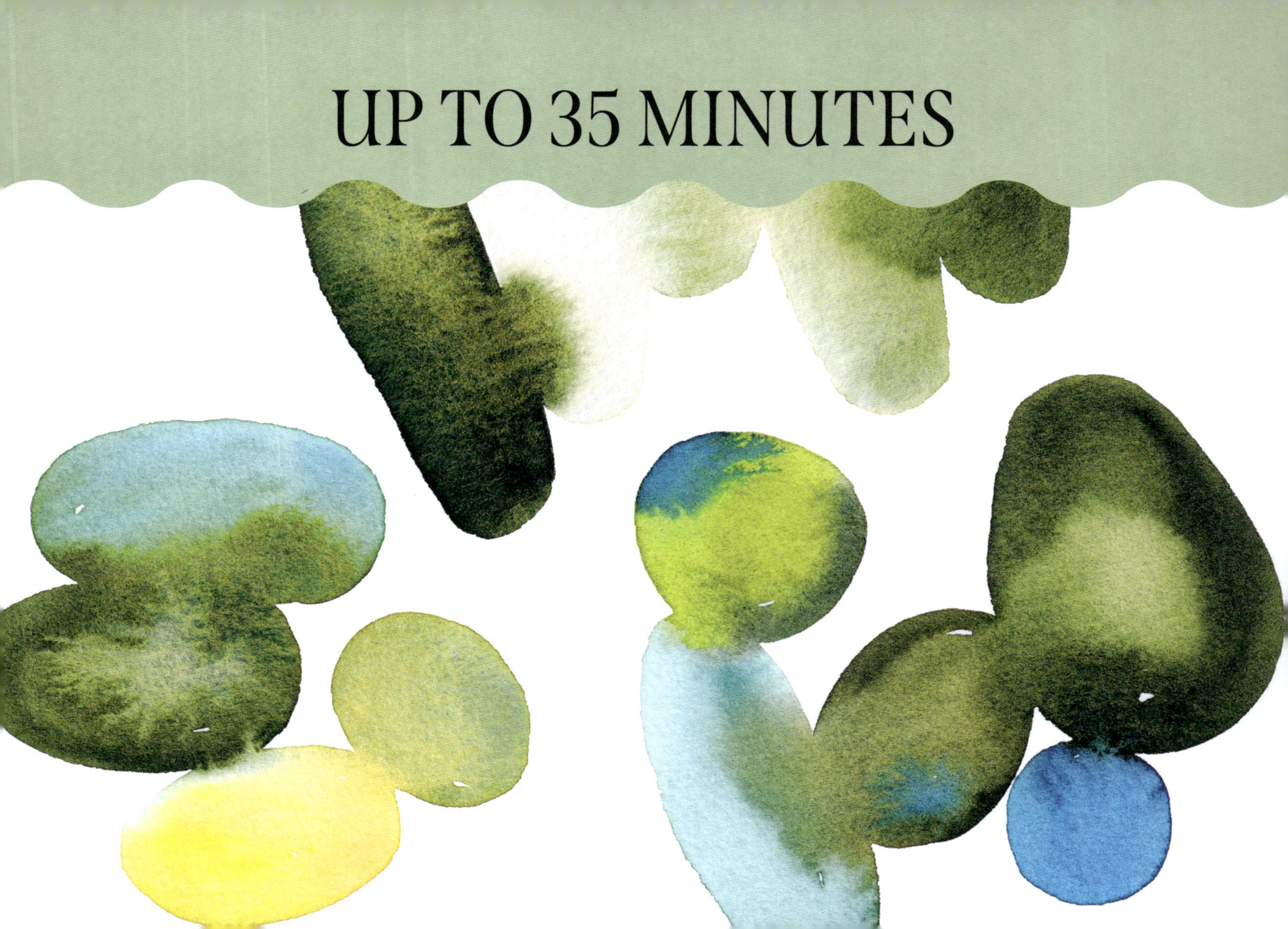

# 1/Duotone Abstract Pattern

The first exercise follows on naturally from the warm-ups. This unassuming loose pattern is simple but visually striking. The key is to vary the amount of water and pigment you apply to each brushstroke and to choose colours which, when mixed, produce an assortment of beautiful tones.

To create a double-coloured stroke, cover your brush in a generous amount of your base colour and dip the tip or the edge of the brush in the second colour. This will result in real-time mixing on paper, an effect difficult to achieve when blending pigments on a palette.

I used cool yellow as the base and introduced warm and cool blues to achieve secondary greens, but feel free to experiment with other colours! I used a large flat brush, which works very well for wide strokes, but the effect will work with a large round brush too.

SUGGESTED ART SUPPLIES: COLD-PRESSED PAPER, LARGE FLAT OR MOP BRUSH

UP TO 35 MINUTES

# Step 1

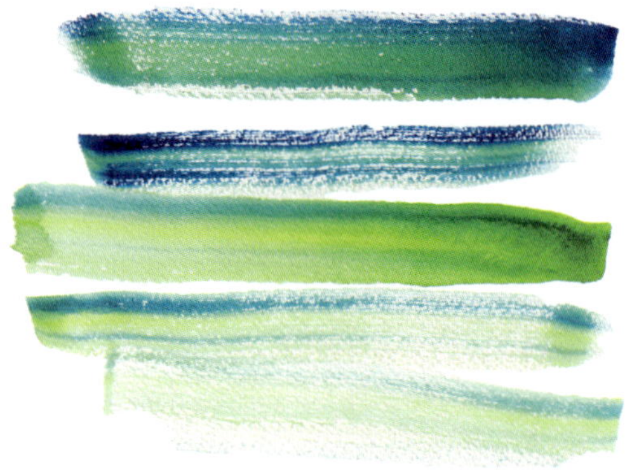

TRIAL 1

Before attempting the pattern, spend a little time practising the brushstrokes. Cover your brush hairs generously in cool yellow and then dip just its very tip in a mix of blue. If you are using a flat brush, you can dip both corners of the brush in the blue.

Practise loose strokes – both with lots of water for smooth lines, and with less water to achieve a dry brush effect. Get used to the feel and look of the duotone marks.

TRIAL 2

Practise loose strokes in the shapes of waves and arches. This is a solid warm-up exercise for your wrists, which builds your confidence to make brush marks quickly without overthinking. It doesn't matter which colours you use here – focus on loose hand movements and mixing up dry brush strokes with wetter ones.

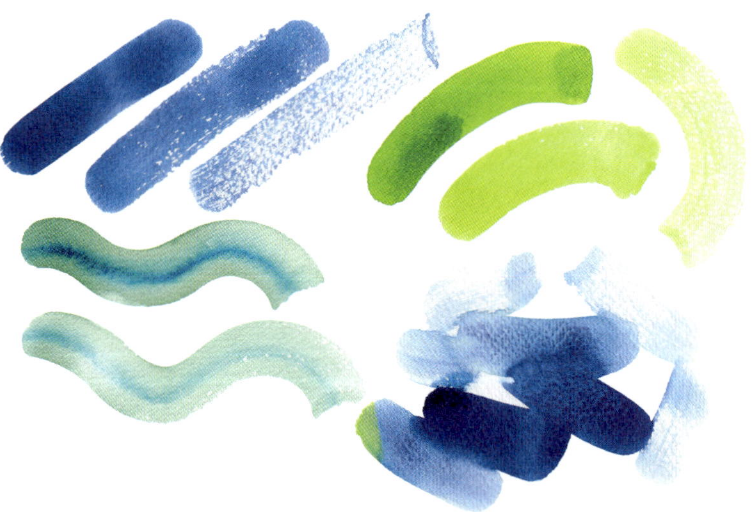

TRIAL 3

Try a few irregular strokes and start joining them together. Vary the amount of water and pigment you apply, either making the saturation higher or removing excess water to achieve drier strokes. The more variety, the more interesting the texture of the pattern.

# Step 2

Paint the patterns – create as many as you wish, in various overall shapes and orientations. Here, I painted two vertical stacks of strokes next to each other, as this shows how different the abstract shapes will look every time you attempt this exercise.

Because it is a free-flowing painting, your wrist will lead you to make slightly different brushstrokes each time, and the pattern will also be influenced by the amount of pigments and the quantity of water you apply. Experiment and have fun!

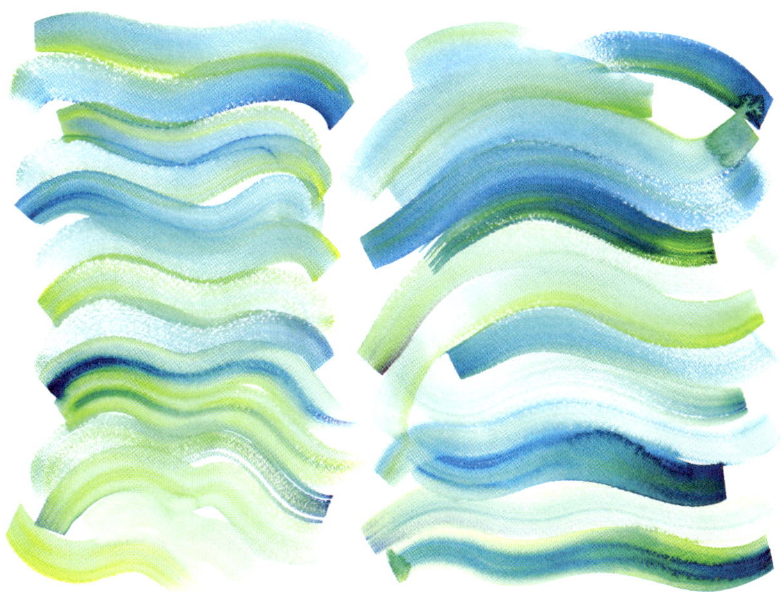

# 2/Beetroot

Beetroot is one of my favourites to paint quickly in watercolours. It's a charming vegetable with an earthy colourway and its rounded body complements the dark leaves wonderfully. Plus, it is such a healthy one to eat and sketching it may inspire a healthy meal. As my grandma used to say – beets are vitamin bombs!

SUGGESTED ART SUPPLIES: HOT-PRESSED PAPER, PENCIL, MEDIUM ROUND BRUSH, DETAIL BRUSH

## PREP

Mix a selection of earthy tones: reddish purple, pale pink, reddish brown, earthy greens. Lightly sketch out the beetroot with a pencil using sketch 1 on page 178 as a reference.

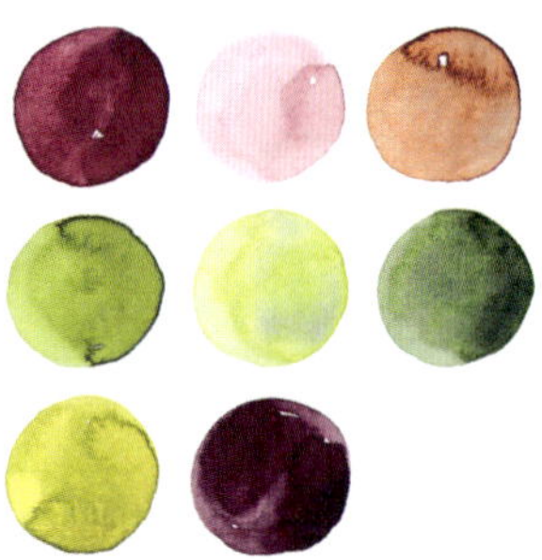

## Step 1

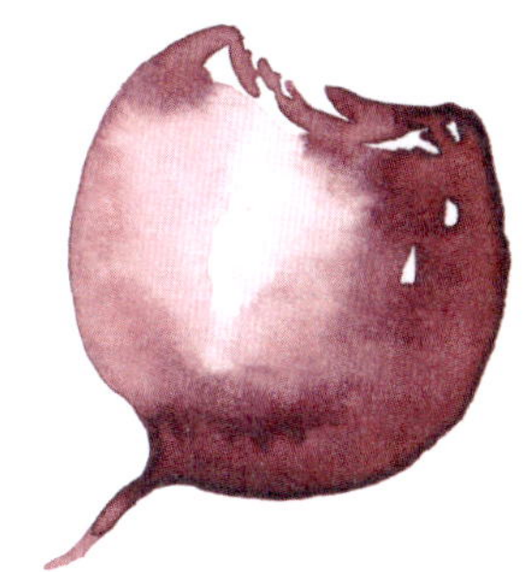

Using a purple with a red hue as the base, loosely paint the body of the beetroot bulb. Focus on creating depth by controlling the amount of pigment and water you apply. At the bottom right, use a lot of the deep purple and, as you move towards the top, middle and right, pick up a little more water to dilute the colour and reveal light pink values. Leave empty gaps between your strokes to create an irregular texture and accentuate highlights.

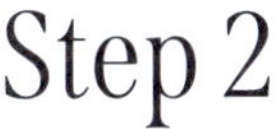

## Step 2

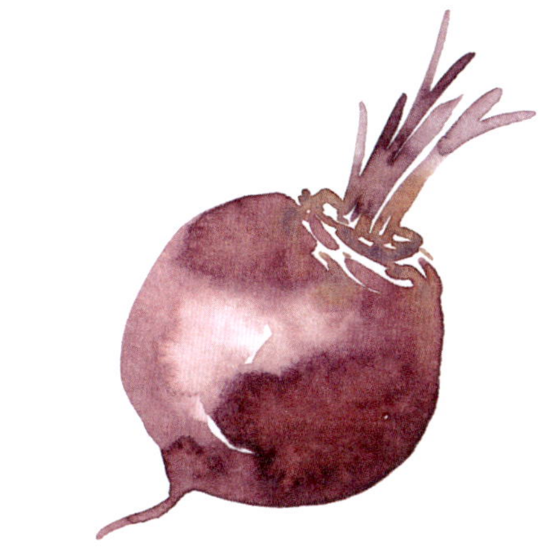

Add a little brown to your purple mix to loosely paint the stem base, and a few lines coming off it which will become the stems.

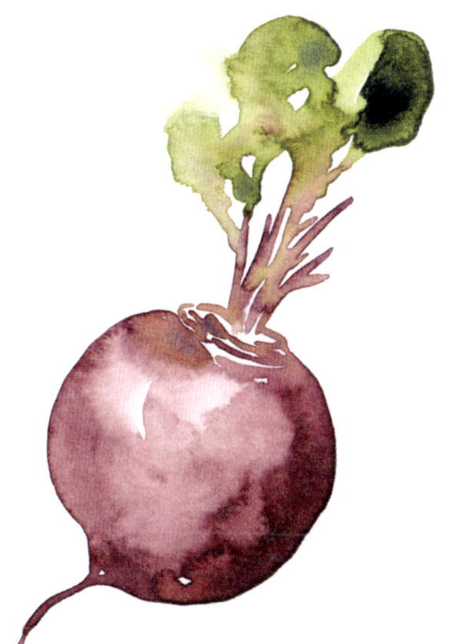

## Step 3

Without waiting for the stems to dry, clean off your brush a little and apply earthy greens. As in Step 1, the body of the leafy greens will gain volume by varying the amount of water and pigment you use. Paint some of the leaves in a dark green, then immediately apply some extra water to the brush and paint the next leaf.

## Step 4

Don't be afraid to mix colours quickly and spontaneously, as this will benefit the style of your loose botanical paintings. Add a little warm yellow to the green on your brush and paint another leaf, then quickly mix in a bit of warm blue to paint a further one. The pigments will engage in a somewhat unpredictable dance right in front of you.

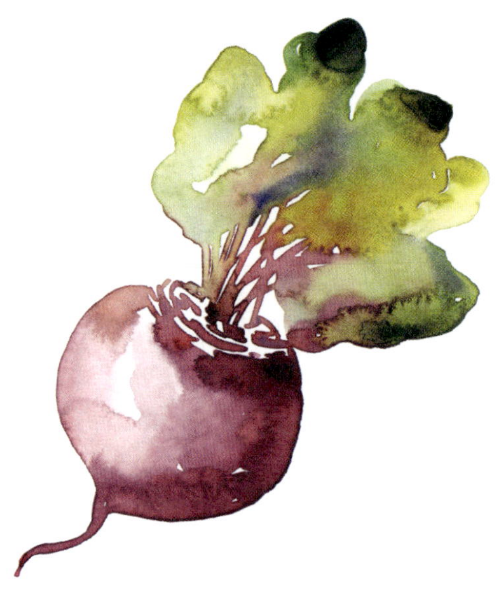

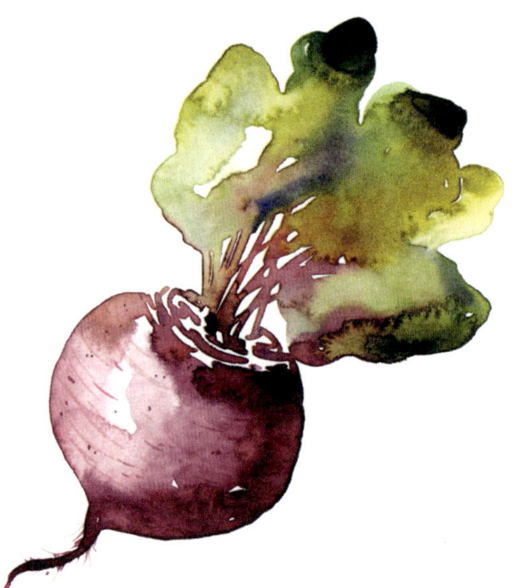

## Step 5

Let everything dry. Then, either with the very tip of your round brush, or with a smaller detail brush, delicately add a few thin purple strokes to the body and root of the vegetable. It is important to use a diluted colour and merely hint at the irregular bumps on the beetroot in order to avoid overwhelming the loose illustration with too much detail.

# 3/Snowy Tree

Painting an abstract winter tree can be surprisingly simple! You will need to apply a generous amount of water and light grey tones. This illustration relies on pigments merging to create a soft, cool-coloured look, which also requires us to paint fast – it is a splendid exercise for water control and timing.

SUGGESTED ART SUPPLIES: HOT- OR COLD-PRESSED PAPER, PENCIL, MEDIUM ROUND OR MOP BRUSH, DETAIL BRUSH

## PREP

Mix a selection of wintery tones: light greys, a greyish blue and a dark brown. Since we are depicting a snowy tree, we will not be using colours mostly associated with trees like greens and yellows. Focus on making your brushstrokes loose, using a generous amount of water and pigment on a round or a mop brush.

UP TO 35 MINUTES

# Step 1

Using a lot of water, apply a layer of very light grey on the paper where the tree crown will be using a medium round or a mop brush. It is paramount the water doesn't dry up quickly, so don't be afraid to make the mix very wet – most of the time it is better to use more water than too little when painting with watercolours.

Make sure the shape is irregular and asymmetrical. You only need to create a rough shape of a tree but remember to leave a few empty gaps within the shape as we will paint branches through them.

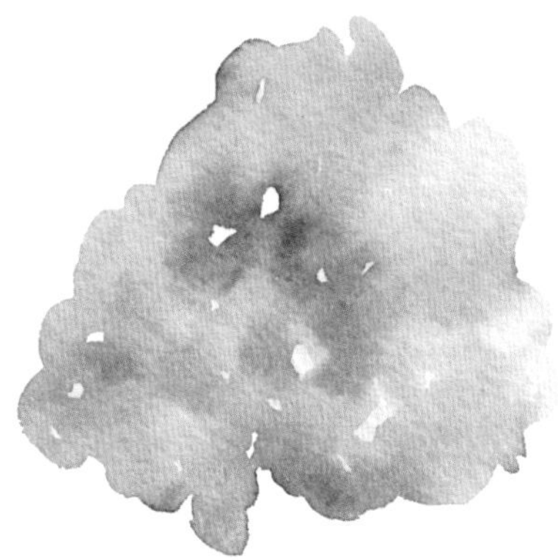

# Step 2

Without waiting for it to dry, add a little of a darker bluish grey to your mix and drop it unevenly into the wet shape of the crown. In some parts add a little more grey, while leaving other areas lighter.

# Step 3

Quickly load up a dark, pigmented brown and paint the tree trunk beginning by touching the crown at the bottom. You want the brown and the grey to merge. You can also add a small branch to elevate the composition.

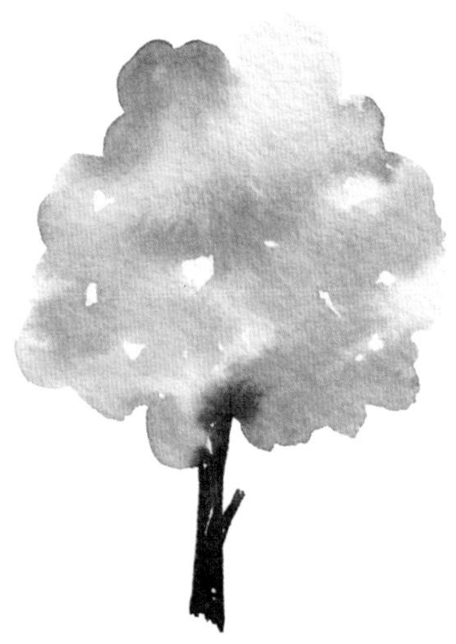

## Step 4

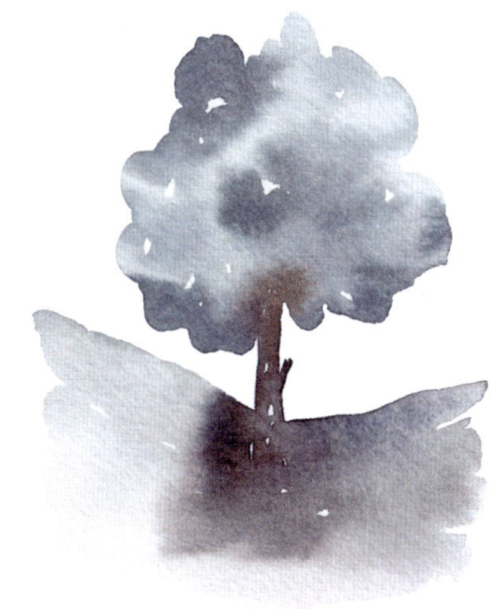

Remove most of the brown from your brush and quickly go back to a light grey with a generous amount of water. Paint the ground beneath the tree in large, loose strokes – notice how the brown trunk becomes lighter as we drag the pigment down into the ground.

I decided to paint a hilly landscape, but it is up to you to make it flat or not. Leave a few empty gaps between the brushstrokes to create highlights, and apply a darker grey to the right of the tree crown.

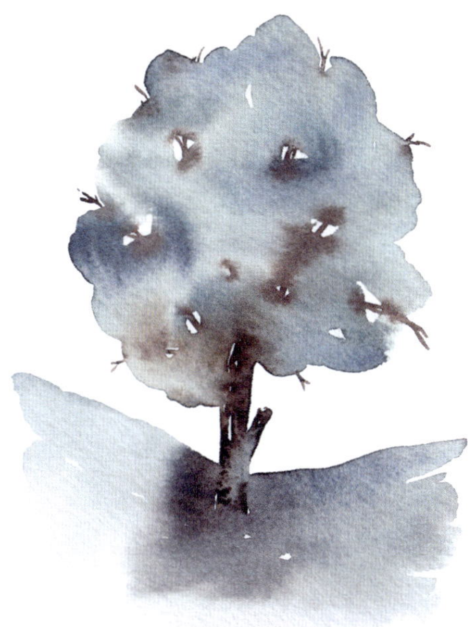

## Step 5

While the tree is slowly drying, pick up a smaller detail brush and load it up with the same dark brown you used to paint the tree trunk. Using small brushstrokes, fill in the empty gaps of the tree with hints of branches and add a few extra poking out of the crown, making them irregular for a spontaneous effect.

# 4/*Pebbles*

Painting stones and pebbles is a relaxing endeavour. There are so many rocks you can paint: if you are at the seaside, go for a walk and collect a pocketful of pebbles to paint from real life, or search online for images of beautiful stones to inspire your illustrations. The great thing here is that rocks come in all shapes and sizes, so you really can imagine all sorts of compositions and create a large, funky pattern!

SUGGESTED ART SUPPLIES: HOT- OR COLD-PRESSED PAPER, MEDIUM ROUND OR MOP BRUSH, DETAIL BRUSH

## PREP

Mix a selection of earthy tones such as light grey, dark muted green, mustard yellow, rust-like red, greyish blue and some brown-tinted black. This is my selection of colours, but feel free to experiment. Having colours ready in a palette is paramount to the success of this loose painting, as we will be switching from one tone to another quickly.

Have a few pebbles or stones in front of you for immediate shape reference or source images online. Don't get stuck wondering what shape of stone to paint next.

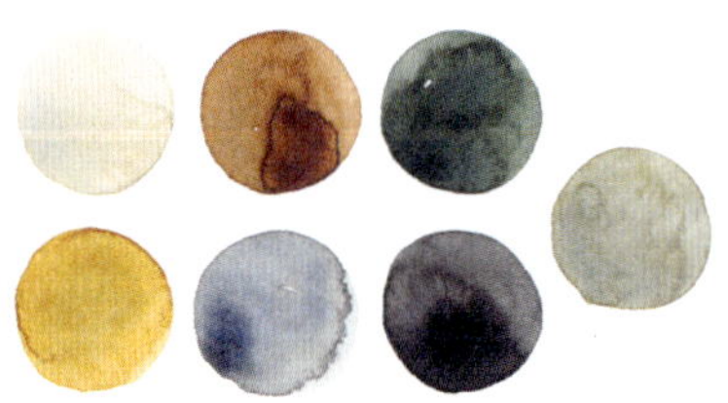

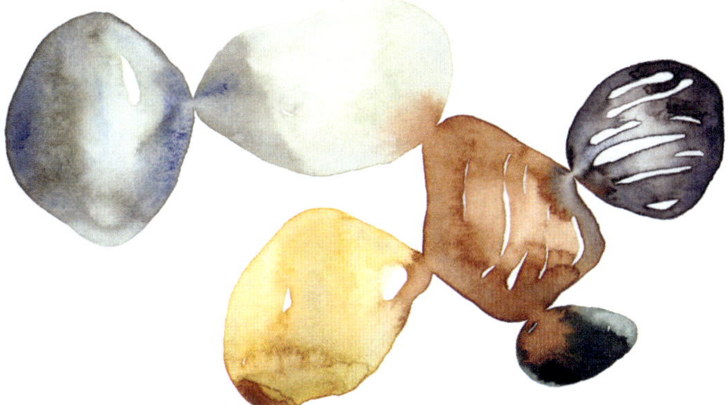

## Step 1

This step is all about painting pebble shapes fast and merging them together. I started with the greyish blue one on the left, then before it dried I quickly painted the light grey one, touching the first stone's side to achieve a wet-on-wet merging. Then I quickly picked up some rust red to paint the third stone, and so on. It is important to move on swiftly as we want the pigments to engage in a dance on the paper. Notice I left some generous empty gaps in some of the stones to create texture.

## Step 2

Wait for the pebbles to dry completely. Then pick up a fine brush and add various details to your stones. Try using curved lines, little faint dots and holes, and spiral patterns. Experiment to your heart's desire; this illustration has endless possibilities – all you need to do is to look at some beautiful rocks.

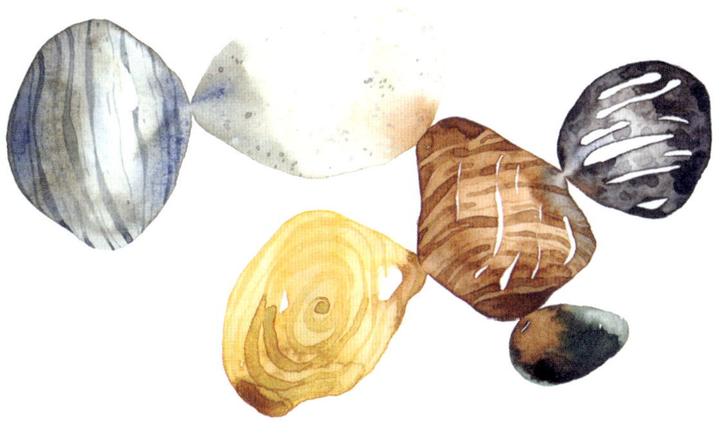

UP TO 35 MINUTES

# 5/*Tropical Fruit*

This pineapple, dragon fruit and papaya illustration feels like summer captured on the page. It is also the perfect watercolour exercise, as we are working with vibrant colours and a lot of water application, which allows the pigments to merge and create a stunning loose look, while preserving some of the realism of the tropical fruit cross-sections.

SUGGESTED ART SUPPLIES: COLD-PRESSED PAPER, PENCIL, MEDIUM ROUND OR MOP BRUSH, DETAIL BRUSH

## PREP

Prepare vibrant, summery colours such as a few bright greens, saturated orange, pink and yellow. Also prepare a muted grey, yellow, light brown, plus a very dark brown and a very dark grey (nearly black).

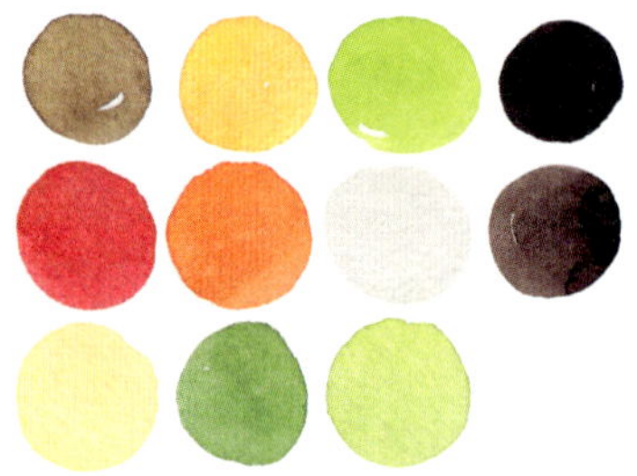

Lightly sketch out the three bodies of the pineapple, dragon fruit and papaya using sketch 2 on page 178 as a reference. I like to twist their orientations a little so that they are not all completely upright, to enliven the composition.

# Step 1

Sketch out the shape of the pineapple first, using a generous amount of water with a pale yellow. Without waiting for it to dry, clean off most of the yellow hue and load up a very faint grey to outline the dragon fruit next to it by touching the pineapple's side. Then quickly pick up a slightly more saturated yellow to outline the papaya on the right.

Notice that the pineapple and the papaya both have empty gaps between the brush strokes inside their flesh. The dragon fruit does not need them and can be painted as a flat wash.

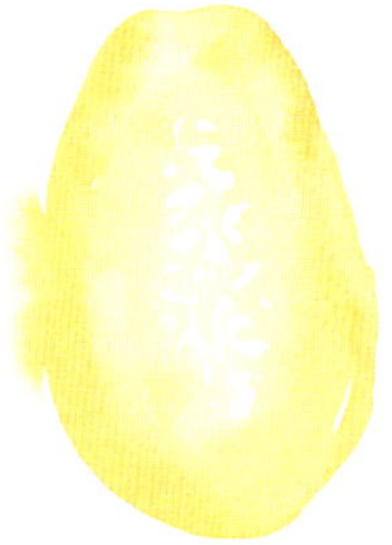

# Step 2

Without waiting for the base to dry, quickly move on to adding colour to the fruits' skin. For the pineapple, load the brush with a medium-light brown and add roughed-up brushstrokes to its edge, marking the bottom stem with a slightly darker brown – but don't put any brown where the pineapple meets the dragon fruit.

Use the same brown to paint a hint of the dragon fruit stem at its top. Then quickly wash off the brown entirely and load your brush with a saturated, hot pink to paint the skin – again, don't drop the pink on the meeting points of the fruits.

Quickly, remove the pink from your brush and load up a vibrant orange to apply it to the papaya's edges.

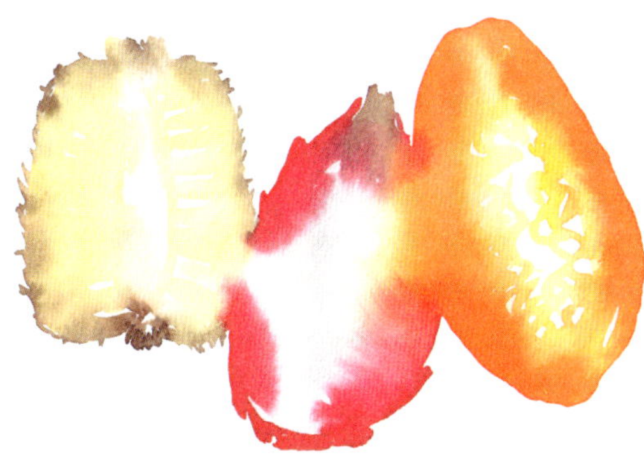

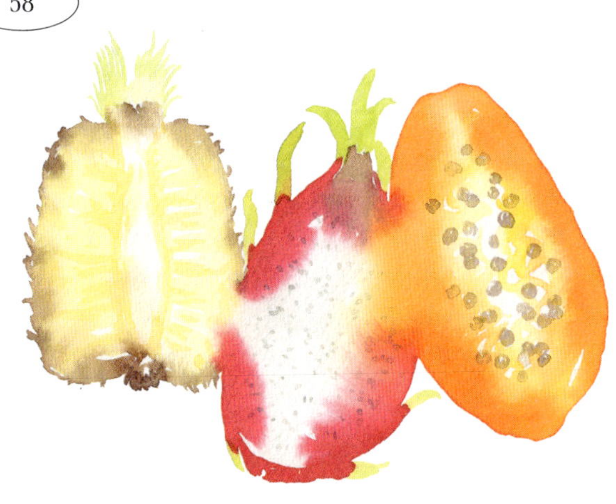

## Step 3

Now, breathe! Let the fruits dry completely before proceeding. It's time to start adding some details, and this process doesn't need to be rushed.

For the pineapple, go back to a pale yellow and lightly add some texture to the flesh, mostly accentuating the fibres. Then, pick up a little pale light green to add a few stems at the top.

Pick up a little more green pigment and paint the stems of the dragon fruit. Then, wash off the green and pick up very light grey to paint faint pips across the flesh as irregular dots.

Add a touch of diluted brown to paint some circles scattered across the middle of the papaya. Make sure you leave empty gaps in the shapes, to imitate light reflecting off the moist seeds.

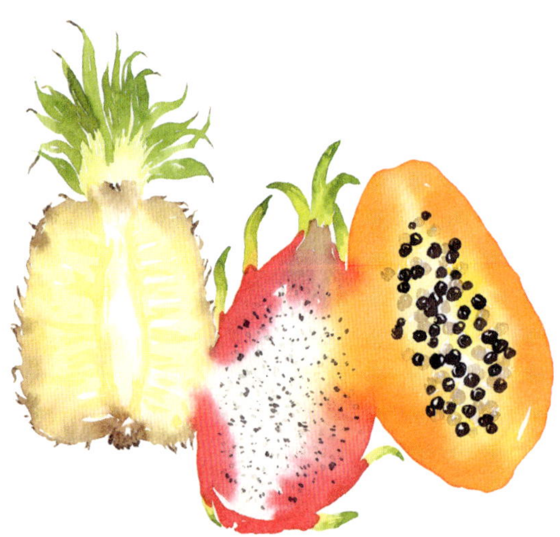

## Step 4

Wait for everything to dry, then it's time to accentuate the edges and add contrast.

Start with the pineapple. Mix a rich, earthy warm green to extend the sharp leaves at the top of the stem. Make some of them lighter than others to create dimension. Then, pick up some brown to darken the details on the stem and the skin.

For the dragon fruit, go back to a rich, vibrant green and apply it to the edges of the stems to add extra contrast. Then, mix a very dark grey (nearly black) to paint extra pips, which will pop against the faint grey ones underneath.

Using more of this dark, almost-black, paint more circular shapes on the papaya in the same vein, leaving empty gaps for highlights.

# Step 5

The last step is to add extra texture, which completes the delicate marriage of looseness and detail. Switch to a detail brush and pick up some dark green to accentuate the edges of both the pineapple and dragon fruit stems. With a dark brown, add a little more contrast to the rough edges of the pineapple, as well as adding tiny stems to the papaya at the very top.

The last step is to remove the brown from the brush and load up a faint orange. Add little circular strokes in between the papaya pips for added texture on its flesh.

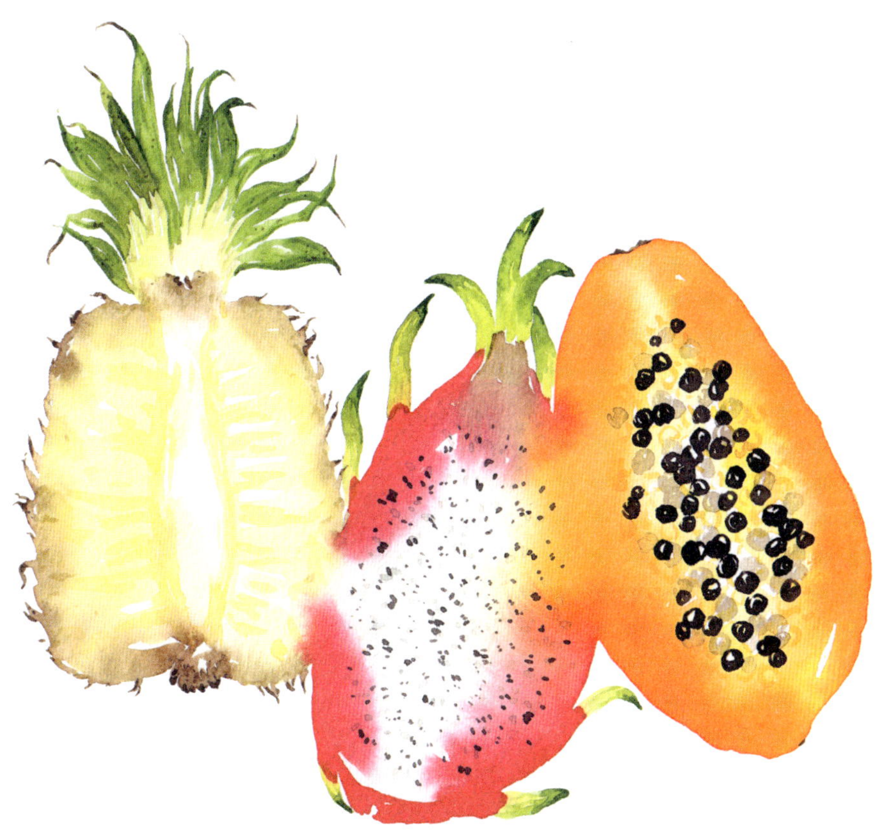

UP TO 35 MINUTES

# 6/Abstract Landscapes

This exercise is a quest to learn how to control watercolours by letting go. It requires the willingness to let the pigments and water work their magic without excessive brushstrokes. The main thing to keep in mind is that we want to lay down a generous amount of clear water on the paper and then drop in the colours, so they can explode in front of our eyes.

SUGGESTED ART SUPPLIES: COLD-PRESSED PAPER (100% COTTON), MOP OR A LARGE ROUND OR FLAT BRUSH

## PREP

Start off by mixing a variety of earthy, colourful tones. Think of autumn and winter landscapes, or a spring or summer day; imagine a beautiful sunset and a rainy afternoon. The colours in nature tend to be muted, so try to neutralise the tones by adding a little bit of a complementary colour to your mixes (refer to page 32 if you need a reminder). I opted for muted reds and pinks, pale blues, earthy browns and yellows and a couple of greens.

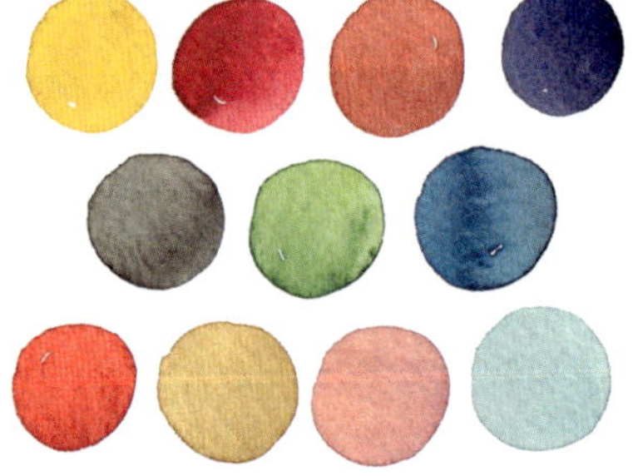

Note that high quality cotton cold-pressed papers will work best here.

# Step 1

<u>TRIAL 1</u>

Load your brush with a lot of clear water (without pigment) and lay down an uneven shape first. I opted for a wonky rectangle. While the shape is still wet, load your brush with a dark mix of any colour (I used dark blue) and practise laying down wonky lines. They will touch the bottom edge of the shape. Notice how the blue pigment erupted onto the 'rectangle'.

<u>TRIAL 2</u>

Try different configurations of the same concept. Make a few of the shapes with clear water and use different colours to drop in some pigment, starting from the edges. Usually, you need to wait for the shapes to dry completely before the final, often surprising, result reveals itself.

**TRIAL 3**

Be brave and try a different twist by making some squiggles instead of a rectangle. Also, it is important to experiment when practising and reverse the order of painting: try laying down a few lines of dark, saturated colour, then clear off your brush and load it up with plenty of water to lay down a wash of clear water starting off by the edge of the coloured line. Drag the wash away from the stroke.

Another fun exercise is to combine two or three colours in one abstract wash, and leave an empty circular shape by the darkest, bottom line to imitate the sun setting (bottom right).

# Step 2

Let your imagination run wild and imagine some dramatic landscapes. Use your own photos or simply search in picture books or online to find inspiration for intriguing colour palettes, then experiment with plenty of water application and vibrant colour mixes. It is best to use three, maximum four, colours within one abstract loose landscape to avoid colours turning muddy.

The great thing about this exercise is that the looser and more accidental the sketches, the more fun effects you can achieve. Sometimes, the pictures that were mere trials end up being more beautiful than the more considered attempts. That is because these abstract landscapes benefit most from letting go of expectations and control.

UP TO 35 MINUTES

# 7/Blueberries

This cheerful blueberry pattern is one of the most relaxing themes to paint in this book, but simultaneously it will really strengthen your colour mixing skill.

SUGGESTED ART SUPPLIES: COLD OR HOT-PRESSED PAPER, MEDIUM ROUND BRUSH, DETAIL BRUSH

## PREP

Prepare a selection of colours: a few shades of cool and warm purples (varying from reddish to blueish purples), light and dark blues, muted yellow-greens and reds. It will be handy to have a variety of tones available in your palette as it will allow you to quickly switch between them.

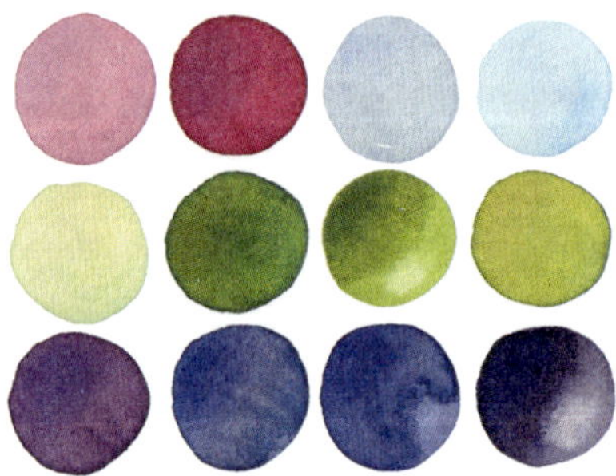

# Step 1

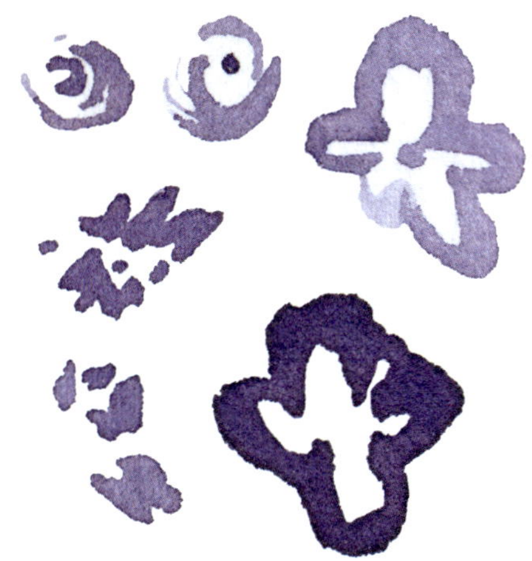

## TRIAL 1

The key is to familiarise yourself with the brushstrokes necessary to produce plump, colourful blueberries. The fruit's shape isn't difficult to master, but the stems can seem tricky to paint, so focus on sketching some out before you tackle an entire blueberry. The elements are shaped like wonky flowers and little circular buttons.

## TRIAL 2

Let's move on to the round blueberry bodies. Take some time to practice different sizes of the oval shapes, with some of them plumper and some smaller or wonkier – the more variety the better. Try different colours and pigment saturation levels. Notice that I sketch them in several positions – facing up, sideways or lying flat. I like to paint a round shape and leave an empty gap in each blueberry for its stem, but also to imitate light reflecting off their surface.

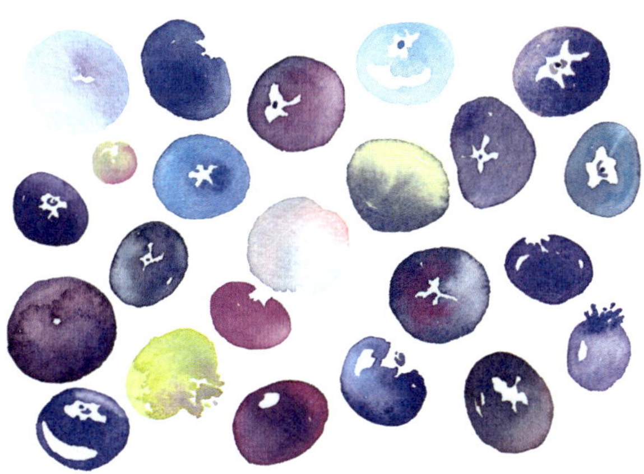

UP TO 35 MINUTES

## TRIAL 3

One way to add the stems is to mix a darker colour after you have painted the circular shape, and add it to the blueberry as short, rough brushstrokes.

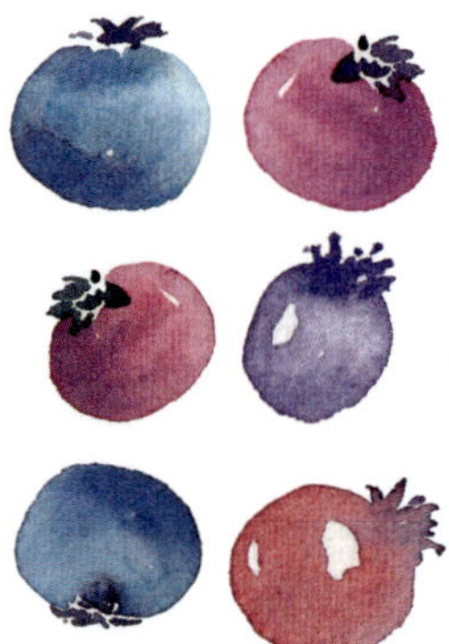

## TRIAL 4

The last thing to practice before you fill the page with the fruit pattern is to test painting clusters of blueberries. Once you paint one, don't wait for it to dry but continue adding a few more blueberries by touching them at the sides and allowing the pigments to merge on paper. It will be important to switch from one colour to another swiftly, as well as adding or removing water and pigments from the brush to create tonal variety.

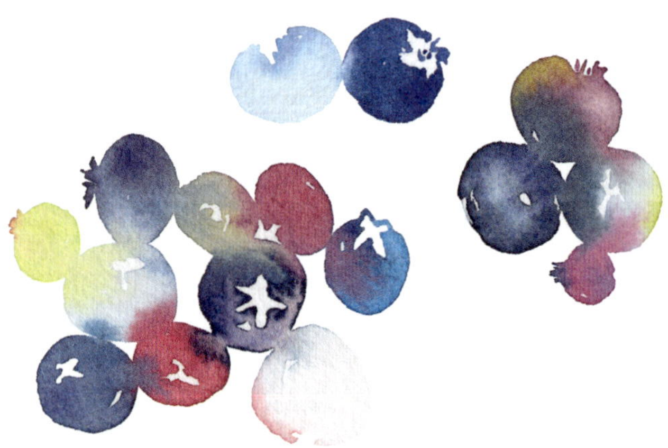

# Step 2

Having practiced all the individual elements, it's now time to get lost in the blueberry watercolour heaven! I recommend not planning the composition too much and simply filling an entire sheet of paper with this loose, free-flowing pattern. The way the fruit is scattered is not the focus here, but rather it is the colours; the variety of earthy blues and purples mixed in with muted yellows, reds and some greens. Remember to change up the amount of water and pigment you apply to each fruit.

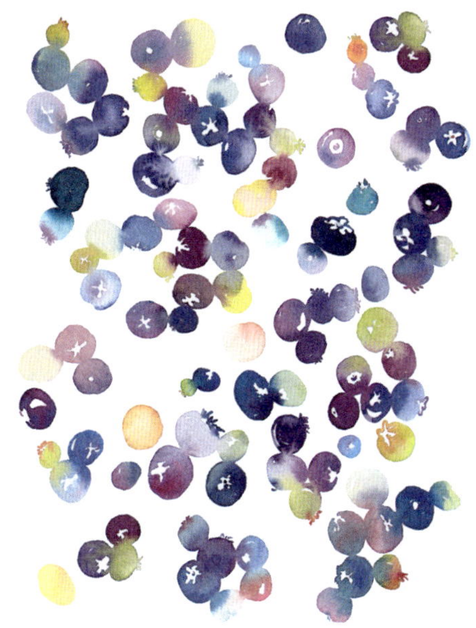

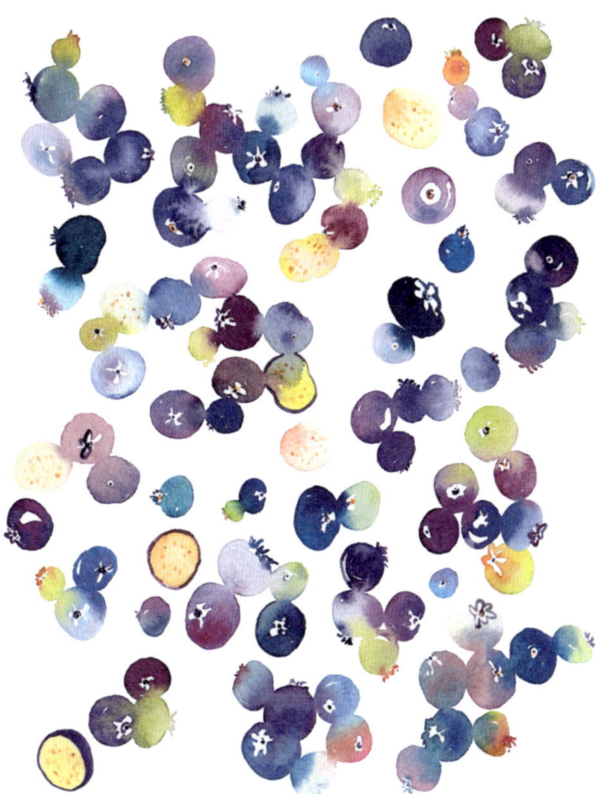

# Step 3

Once your blueberry shapes are dry, you can use a detail brush to add some texture: little red seeds on the blueberries cut in half, dark outlines around the pale-yellow ones to add the fruit skins and tiny dark brushstrokes to accentuate some of the stems.

# *8/Fish, Shells and Seaweed*

This vibrant, playful and loose pattern of sealife is a fantastic way to train your wrist to paint with more ease and speed without worrying too much about precise shapes and shading. Instead of painting in traditional brushstrokes, we use the tip of the brush as if it were a crayon or marker by focusing on the outlines of the shells, fish and seaweed. However, we must work fast as we need the individual elements to merge while the paint is still wet.

SUGGESTED ART SUPPLIES: HOT-PRESSED PAPER, MEDIUM ROUND BRUSH

## PREP

Prepare quite a few different colours on your palette so you don't need to interrupt the flow of painting when you are in the thick of it. I opted for vibrant greens and blues, shades of yellows and oranges, and some purples as well as paler grey and brown. You can find inspiration by looking up images of fish species, types of seaweed and various seashells.

I opted to work on hot-pressed watercolour paper as the smooth texture allows for a cartoon-like feel to the illustration.

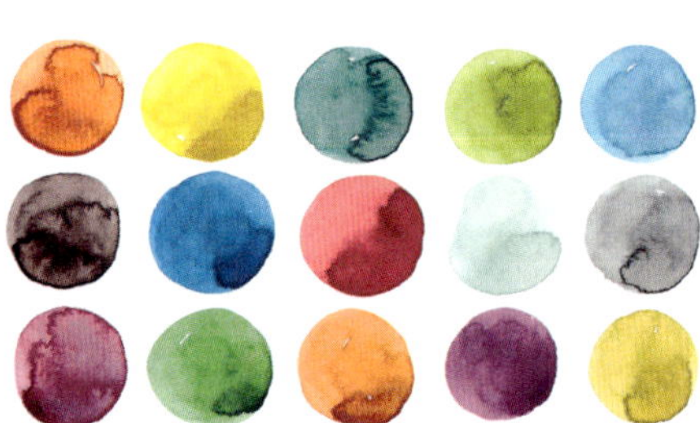

# Step 1

**TRIAL 1**

I encourage you to spend some time studying the shapes of shells. You do not need to worry about naturalistic colour palettes (it is up to you if you would prefer more muted colours), as the vibrant mixes lend themselves so well to any sea-related theme and give a nautical feel.

A pointy round brush will work well here. Using a variety of colours, practise outlining the shapes of shells as if you were drawing rather than painting. This involves focusing on the edges of your subjects and leaving a lot of empty gaps between brushstrokes. Keep varying the saturation of your colours by adding or removing water with each stroke, to add depth and dimension to the sketches.

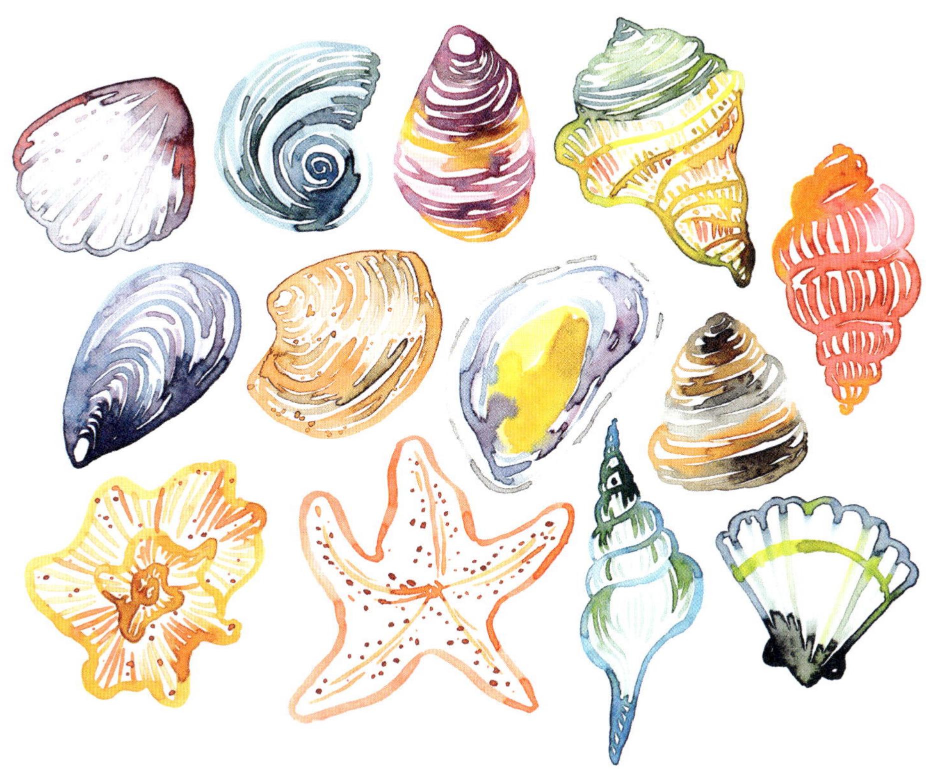

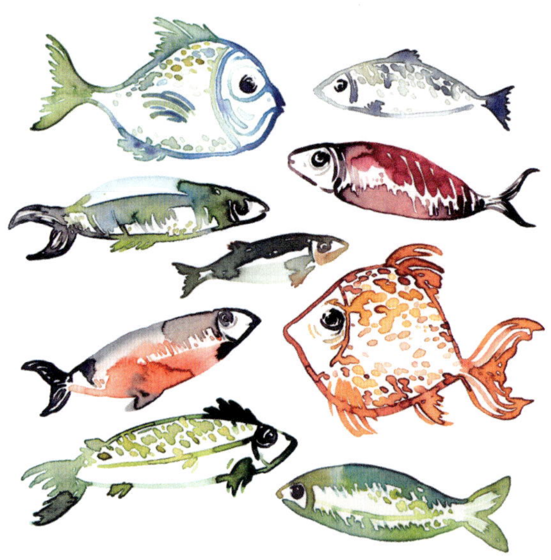

## TRIAL 2

Now practise sketching some fish in a similar loose manner. You can go crazy with the colours and invent fish that don't exist! A good tip is to focus on the eyes – using a dark value of brown or black, accentuate the eyes to give the creatures a life-like look.

## TRIAL 3

Finally, try sketching seaweed forms in a variety of colours. I do encourage you to research different types of seaweed – there are more than you may think, and some of them look really charming.

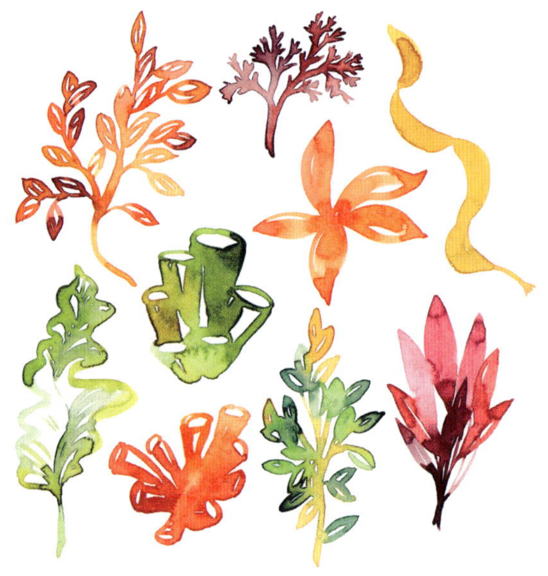

# Step 2

Let's work on a loose pattern where fish, seaweed and shells engage in a lively, funky dance! You do not need to use all of the shapes we have practised, but you can use them as inspiration.

Don't worry too much about all the elements merging together – hot-pressed paper dries up faster than textured papers, so we do have to paint fast. However, this illustration will work well even if there is hardly any wet-on-wet colour merging, because of its child-like drawing style.

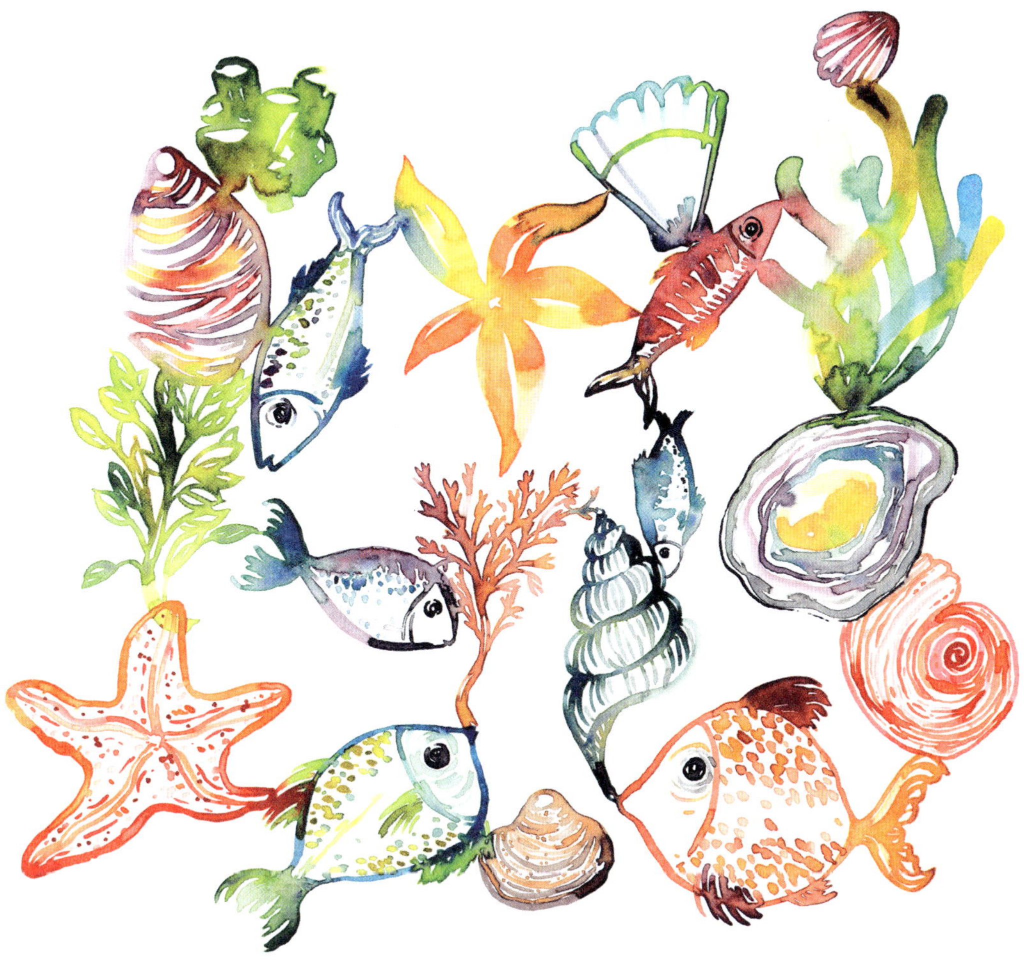

UP TO 35 MINUTES

# 9/*Cucumbers*

Cucumbers make me think of summertime and bring back the sensation of eating them with a bit of salt and pepper seasoning for a quick, refreshing snack on a hot day. The colour scheme of this pattern is cool and vibrant, and the semi-transparency of sliced cucumbers lends itself well to watercolour painting.

SUGGESTED ART SUPPLIES: HOT- OR COLD-PRESSED PAPER, PENCIL, MEDIUM ROUND BRUSH, DETAIL BRUSH

## PREP

When mixing your colour palette, focus on various shades of green, but prepare one very diluted, muted yellow as well. You can adjust the temperature of your mixes depending on whether you use cool or warm blues and yellows. As always, it is up to you to experiment and see what shades feel appropriate to you!

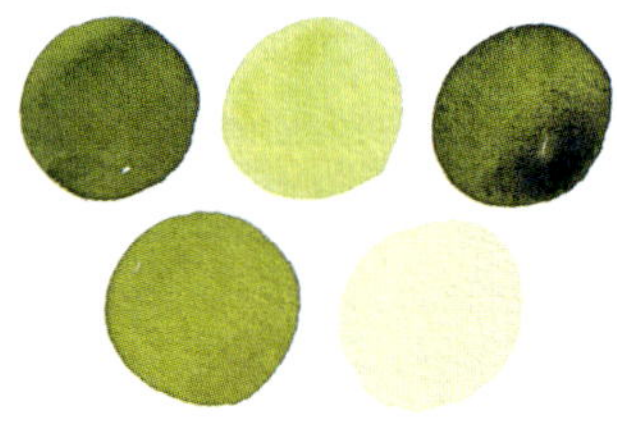

# Step 1

## TRIAL 1: WHOLE CUCUMBERS

Familiarise yourself with the cucumber shapes and the rhythm of painting them. To sketch the sliced cucumber, apply a layer of the pale yellow in the correct shape. Quickly add dark green to your brush and apply it on the very edge.

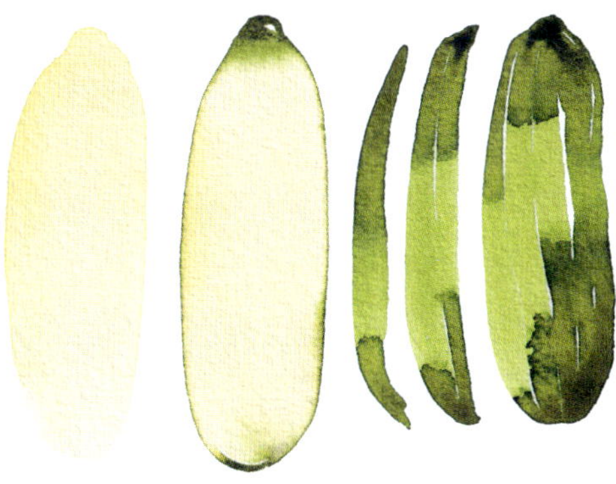

As for a whole cucumber, a quick and fun way to paint it loosely is to compose it with a set of individual, slightly curved vertical lines. Paint one, then couple it up with the second one immediately, and add a few more until you have made the shape of a cucumber. It is important to leave some empty gaps between the vertical strokes to preserve luminosity. You should also aim to apply darker values of green at the top and bottom of the vegetable, while the middle should be a mid-green – this transparency variation will enhance the contrast and dimension.

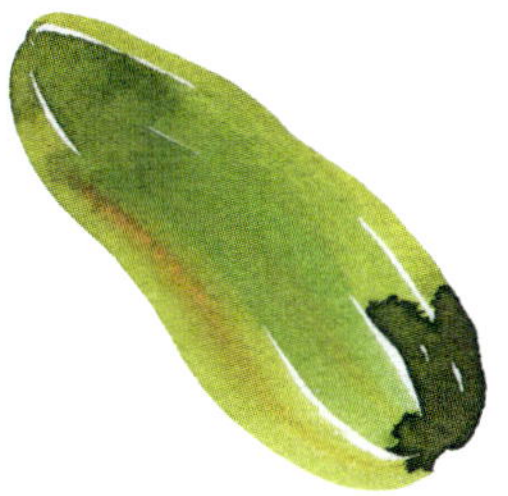

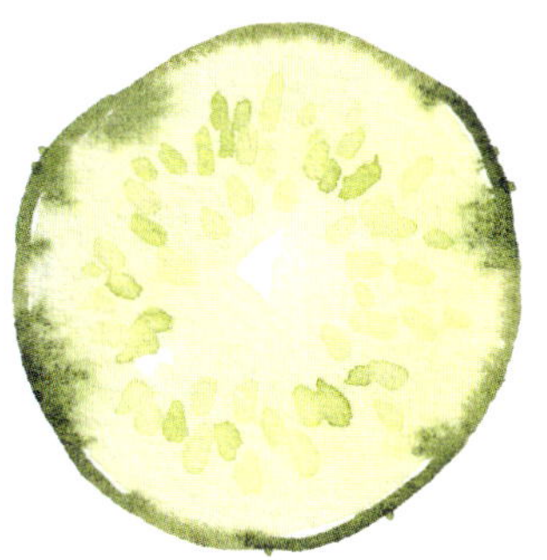

## TRIAL 2: CUCUMBER SLICE

Now sketch out a circular shape using the pale yellow. Before it dries, apply a dark green outline to paint the skin. Wait a few minutes for the layers to dry a little, then pick up some pale green (diluted with water) to add the cucumber seeds around the slice, making some of them a bit more saturated than others for added texture.

<u>TRIAL 3: STEMS AND SEEDS</u>

A great way to practise adding details and texture is to sketch out scribbles like these. Using the very tip of your brush or a detail brush, make irregular dots, varying the colour saturation – these will become the bumps of the cucumber skin.

Then practise painting the stems, which can range from flat rounds to cylinder-like shapes.

Mixing in a bit of warm yellow, try loosely painting uneven dabs that will become cucumber seeds.

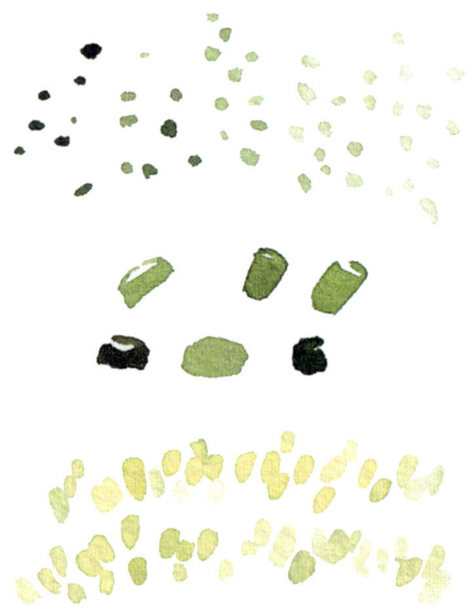

# Step 2

Lightly sketch out the cucumber shapes using sketch 3 on page 179 as a reference – remember you don't need to follow my placement of the elements specifically, though!

The illustration will require working quickly before the initial layers dry up, so we can make the most of the wet-on-wet application.

Start with the first whole cucumber on the left by painting it in dark green. The second shape will be a sliced cucumber, so pick up a bit of pale yellow and paint its shape by touching the first cucumber on the side. Now quickly get back to green and paint the third cucumber right next to the second.

The fourth one is also a cross-section, so go back to the pale yellow to add it to the third cucumber's side.

The other three pieces of cucumber are separate. Paint the circular slice with a green outline in the same way as in Trial 2. The last two shapes will be cucumbers sliced at an angle: paint a cylinder shape and leave it to dry completely without skin. Paint a second cylinder shape and before it dries, load up your brush with dark green and add paint the remaining skin with the kind of strokes shown in Trial 1.

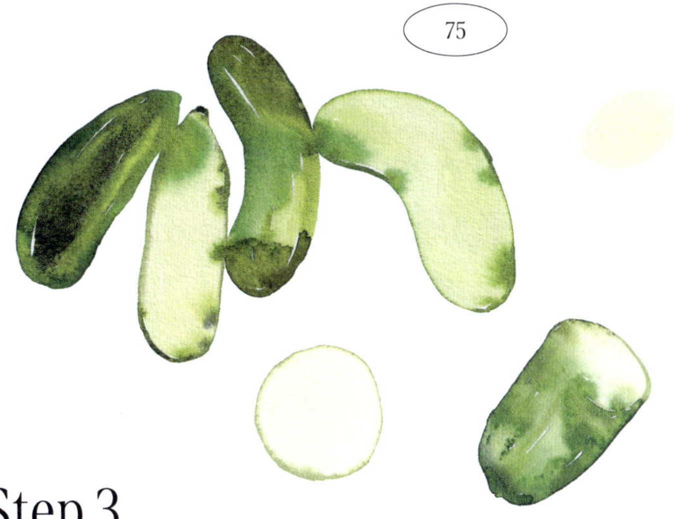

# Step 3

Wait for everything to dry. If your round brush comes to a fine point, you can use it to add the remaining details, or else pick up a detail brush. Load it with a dark green to add scattered dots around the cucumber skins. I used the same green to add skin to the cucumber sliced at an angle to add an extra dimension to the composition.

Switch to a pale yellowish green to paint some faint, irregular seeds on the sliced pieces. I decided to add another round slice on top of the existing one, layering one third of it over the top to showcase transparency.

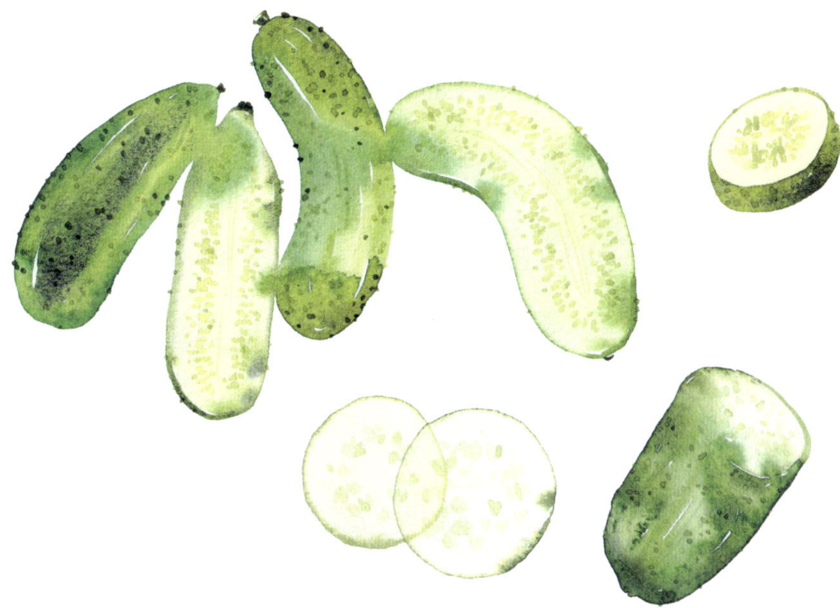

# 10/*Flowers at Dusk*

We usually focus on painting specific subjects, but how about illustrating a soft shadow instead? We can call this a 'reverse method' – we are looking at an ethereal imprint of a flower vase standing by a window at dusk, with no hard lines to determine details. It feels like painting a romantic feeling or a nostalgic sensation, rather than a particular object.

SUGGESTED ART SUPPLIES: ROUGH OR COLD-PRESSED PAPER, PENCIL, LARGE FLAT OR MOP BRUSH, ROUND BRUSH

## PREP

Watercolour shadows look wonderful when they are shades of blue and purple. When preparing your palette, keep in mind the complementary colour rule. If the shadows will predominantly be bluish purple, the complement will be a warm yellow.

Notice how my purple mixes granulated – you can see that both warm blue and cool red are visible within the swatches. I personally adore this unique textured effect.

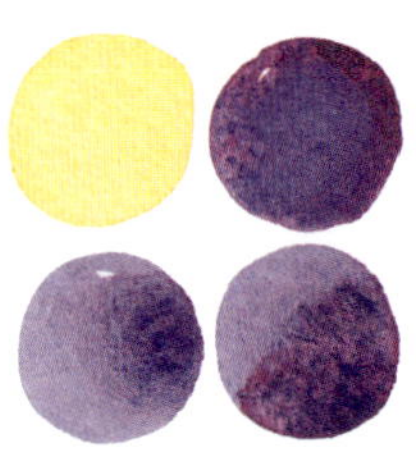

# Step 1

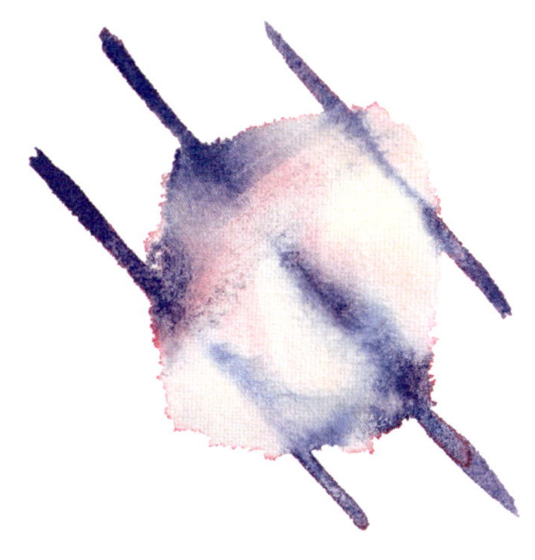

## TRIAL 1

First, practise the technique on a smaller scale. Load your brush with a watery mix of yellow and lay down a shape (mine was a wonky square). Then, quickly wash the yellow off and pick up a dark, blue-purple.

Make some straight vertical lines starting from the outside of the shape, then going right through it, and finishing off on the other side of it. This is to familiarise yourself with the way the colours will blend.

## TRIAL 2

Now, be more specific about the shapes you are sketching. Lay down a rectangular wash of yellow, then go back to the dark purple and quickly paint one vertical and one horizontal line over the yellow background like a cross. Then paint a shape roughly resembling a flower vase beneath and, using wet-on-wet, drop in the outlines of a few leaves and flowers across the yellow shape.

We need the pigments to merge and blend, but don't add too many flower elements; we don't want to lose all the yellow background underneath the purple.

# Step 2

It's time to paint the final piece. Make a light pencil sketch, using sketch 4 on page 179 as a reference, to mark the window frame and a rough outline of the flowers in a vase.

Choose between a flat or a mop brush and load it up with lots of clean water and lay down an even wash on the entire area of the window and a little bit extra beyond.

While it is all wet, pick up some warm yellow and drop it onto the wet shape using wet-on-wet. Focus the yellow where the pencil lines are – the window frames and the flowers. Try to leave some white areas where the four windowpanes are.

# Step 3

Move on quickly to the bluish purple – we must act fast before the yellow wash can dry up.

With a round brush, drop in the dark colour using wet-on-wet again, following the sketch. Notice we are dropping in the purple exactly on top of the yellow background wash. I started with the cross to create windowpanes, then added four straight lines to outline the window – you will need to use a generous amount of the purple to achieve a dark enough frame.

I painted the vase and the flowers last. At this point the initial yellow background wash is a little bit drier, which allows for the flower and leaf shapes to show up gently without the colours exploding in random directions.

This exercise requires patience and you may need to try it a few times before you achieve a desired effect – it is a learning curve!

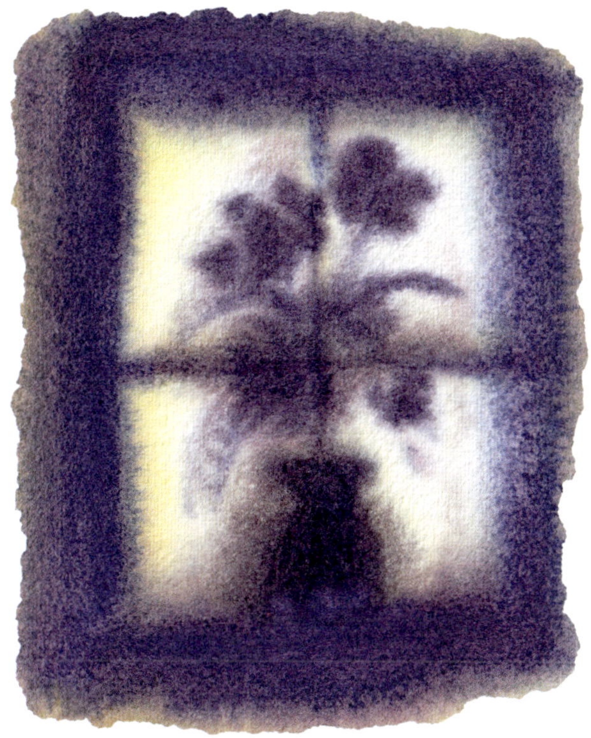

UP TO 35 MINUTES

# UP TO ONE HOUR

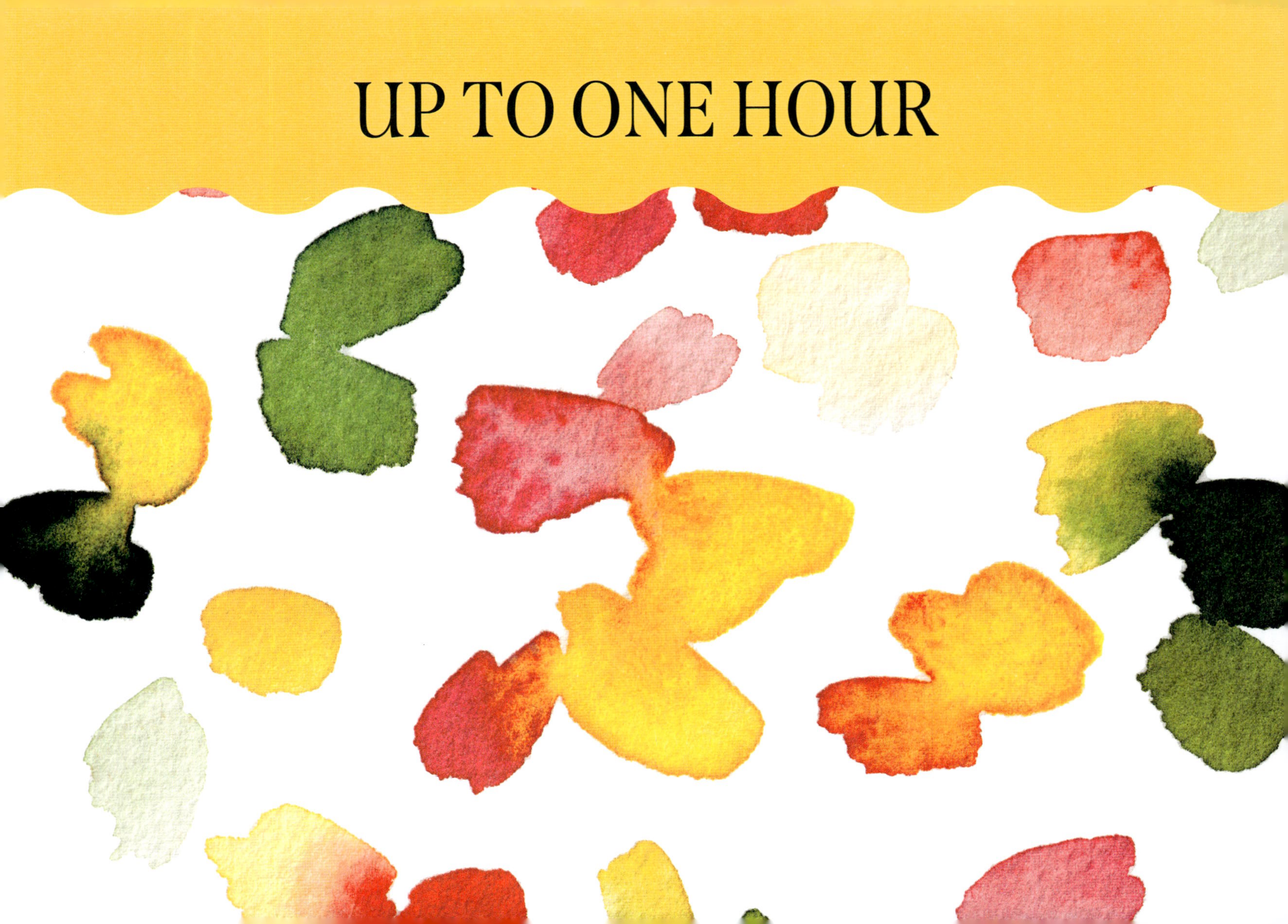

# 11/*Autumn Leaves*

The variety of colours within mature autumn leaves can be surprising. Their wilted shapes with holes and folds make for a really enticing topic for botanical art. Try painting these three leaves, which hopefully will spark inspiration in you to look out for them every autumn from now on!

SUGGESTED ART SUPPLIES: COLD-PRESSED PAPER, PENCIL, SMALL OR MEDIUM ROUND BRUSH, DETAIL BRUSH

## PREP

Prepare a selection of muted and vibrant colours: yellows, oranges, reds, purples, greens and browns. There is a great variety of possible tones here.

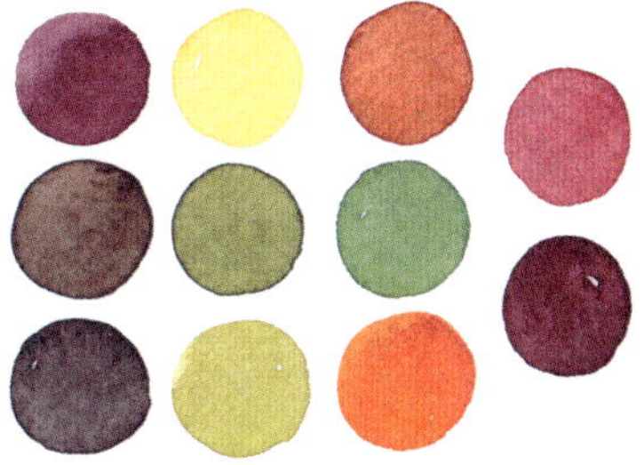

UP TO ONE HOUR

# Step 1

Sketch out the trio of leaves lightly with a pencil, using sketch 4 on page 181 as a reference.

For each one the method will be similar: lay down washes of colour straight onto the sketch (this is why pre-mixing colours is paramount for quick transitions), while leaving empty gaps between some strokes to accentuate leaf veins. Each leaf will have a thin stem at the bottom.

The maple leaf on the left features various tones. Start from the bottom left and continue filling the surface with changing tones of red, brown, orange and green. Continually get rid of excess water, then add more water; dilute excess pigment, then add more pigment onto your brush; continue in this rhythm until the leaf is covered completely.

The second leaf will be monochromatic, so cover the area with a muted yellow with a hint of brown or green.

The third one is rounder and leans towards reds and purples. Its top edge is ragged and it has an uneven hole in the middle, so avoid putting down colours in those areas.

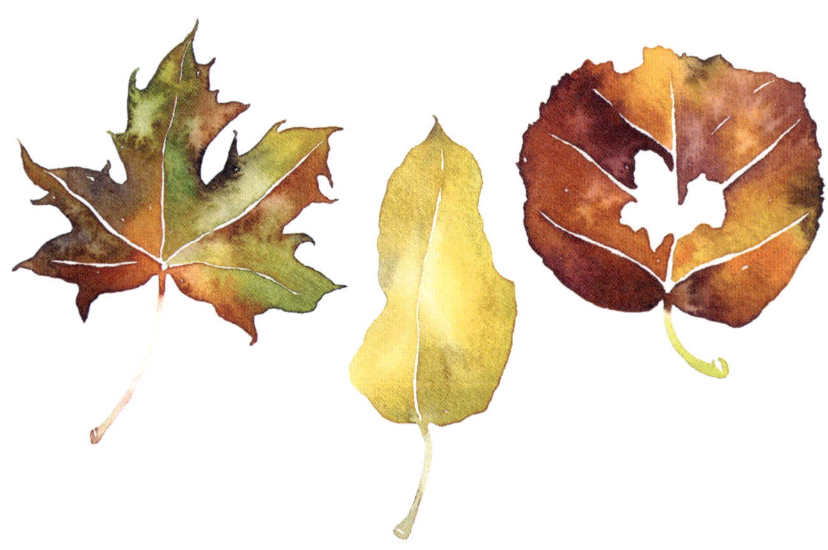

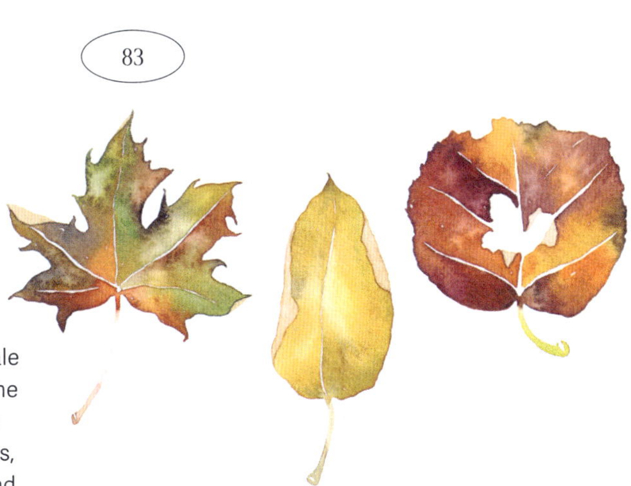

## Step 2

Let everything dry. Mix a muted, pale orange-brown and paint some of the tiny folded edges on the leaves: on one of the maple leaf's sharp points, on both sides of the middle leaf, and around the round one's ragged hole.

## Step 3

Let it all dry again and pick up a detail brush. Start by loading it up with some brown and add faint lines and irregular dots to the folds of the leaves. Paint veins across the body of the middle leaf using the same colour.

Then pick up a range of colours such as browns, dark oranges and dark greens. Scatter dots and ragged brushstrokes on the leaf surfaces to add texture, and shade the stem of each one to give it a little extra dimension.

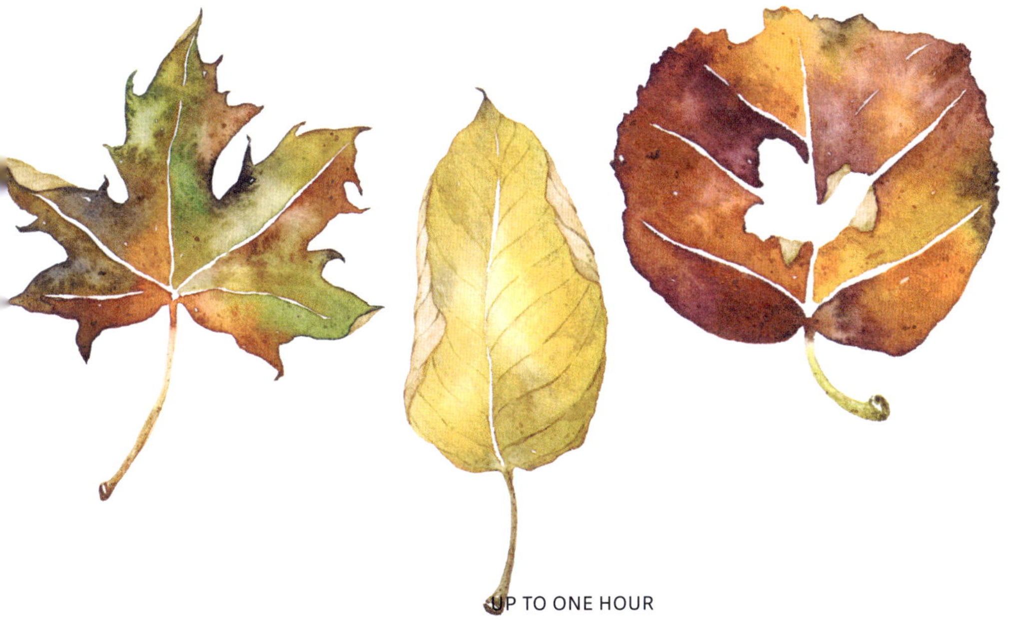

# 12/*Leaf Vine*

This leaf vine is a free-flowing, loose composition that I would encourage you to try and paint without excessive pencil sketches, to train your muscle memory and start trusting your gut when it comes to making decisions about composition. You could adapt the concept and change the foliage to different kinds of leaves, or introduce some flowers or fruit – it is up to your imagination.

SUGGESTED ART SUPPLIES: HOT- OR COLD-PRESSED PAPER, POINTY ROUND BRUSH, DETAIL BRUSH

## PREP

Mix a few shades of green and yellow in your palette. I opted for dark, cool greens, a few brighter greens in cool and warm shades, and a brownish green to paint the stems.

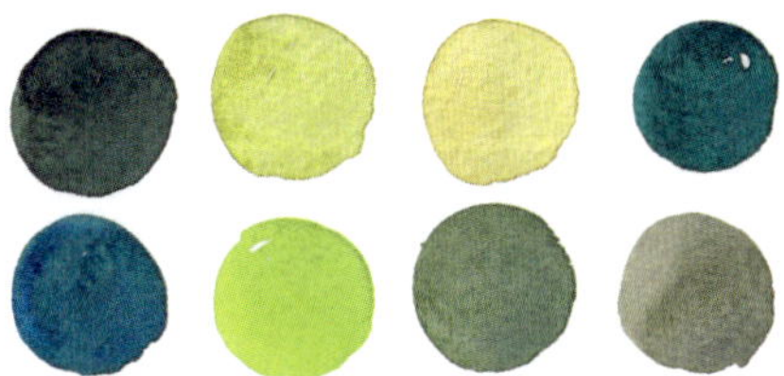

# Step 1

I encourage you to take a little time to study the angular shapes of the leaves and sketch them out repeatedly on a spare sheet of paper, loosely with a brush. I like to paint them by mixing a couple of shades of green within one leaf and by adjusting the saturation of the paint.

If I'm painting a cluster of leaves, I want a couple to be saturated and dark, and others pale and diluted. Remember to leave empty lines and marks in the middle of the leaves to create luminosity and contrast.

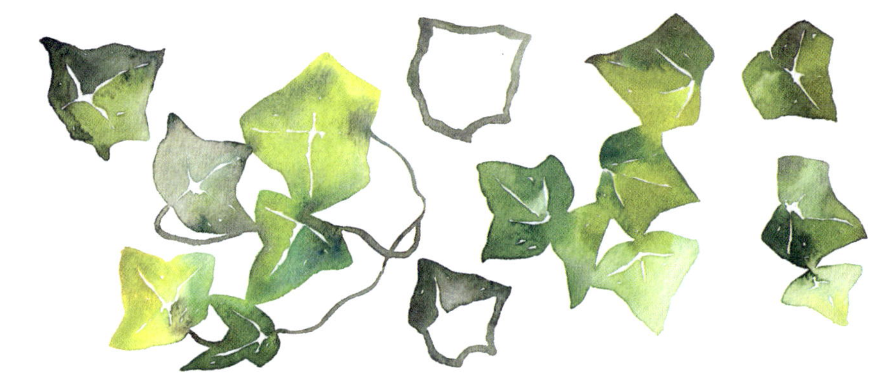

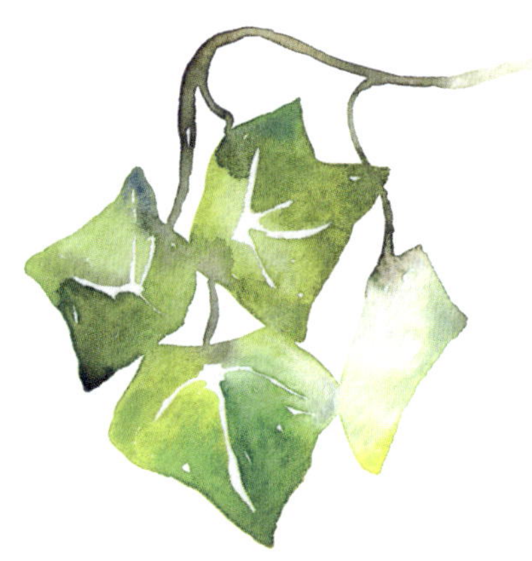

# Step 2

Now that you have got your wrist used to painting the leaf shapes, let's start the vine. Paint a cluster of a few leaves touching each other, using various shades of green and adjusting the amount of water and pigment constantly. Once the cluster is complete, add a little curved stem with the brownish green.

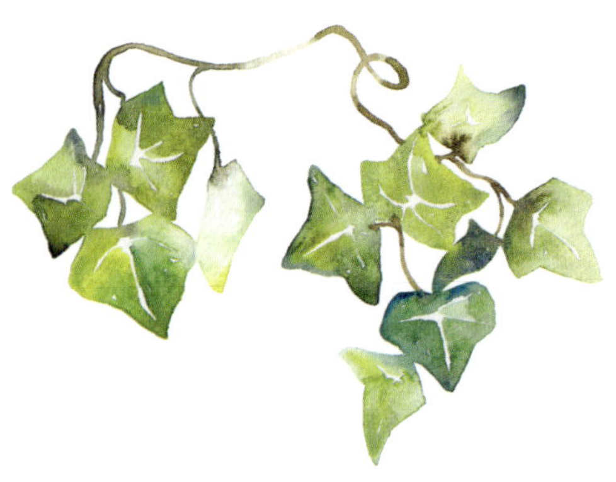

## Step 3

Follow the stem and extend it, making a little spiral bend – you do not need to follow my composition to the letter.

Add another cluster of leaves hanging from the new stem. This will become a rhythmical way of painting after a while. Just keep in mind that it is good to vary the angles of the foliage – some can be facing forward, some can be seen from the side, facing upwards or downwards, and so on.

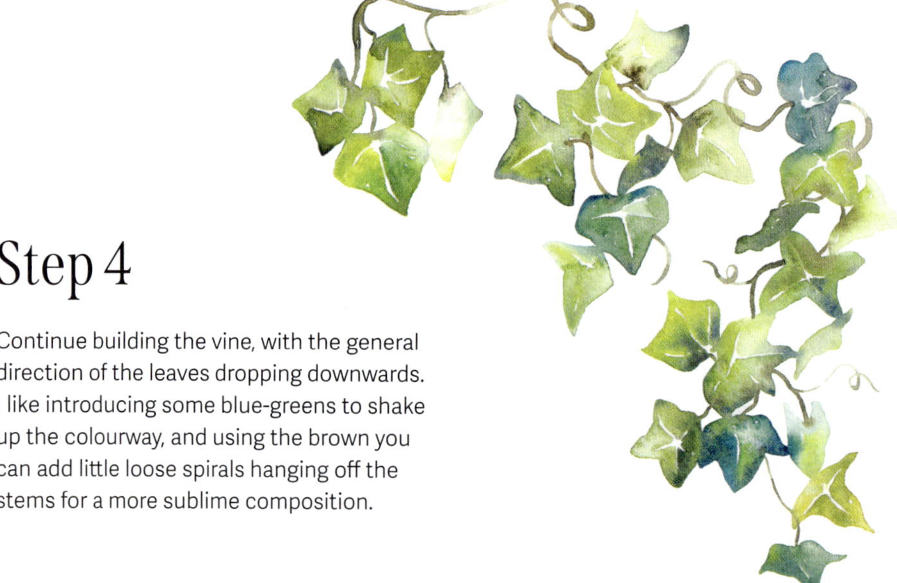

## Step 4

Continue building the vine, with the general direction of the leaves dropping downwards. I like introducing some blue-greens to shake up the colourway, and using the brown you can add little loose spirals hanging off the stems for a more sublime composition.

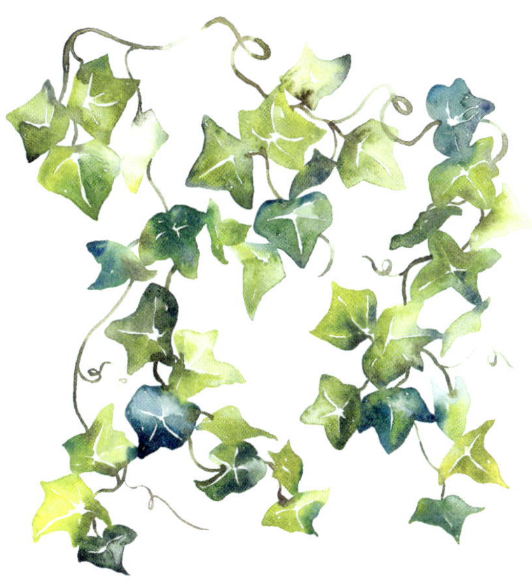

## Step 5

Fill the entire sheet of paper with this dancing vine. Notice how I placed the leaves irregularly, without any symmetry – this is intentional. The less rigid the composition of a loose painting like this, the more natural it will look.

## Step 6

The last step is to add some details and texture. Add some more swirly stems hanging off the sides; it is a good idea to use a diluted colour for this so that they are merely an accent.

Pick up a detail brush and load it up with some midtone green to add little irregular dots scattered around all the leaves.

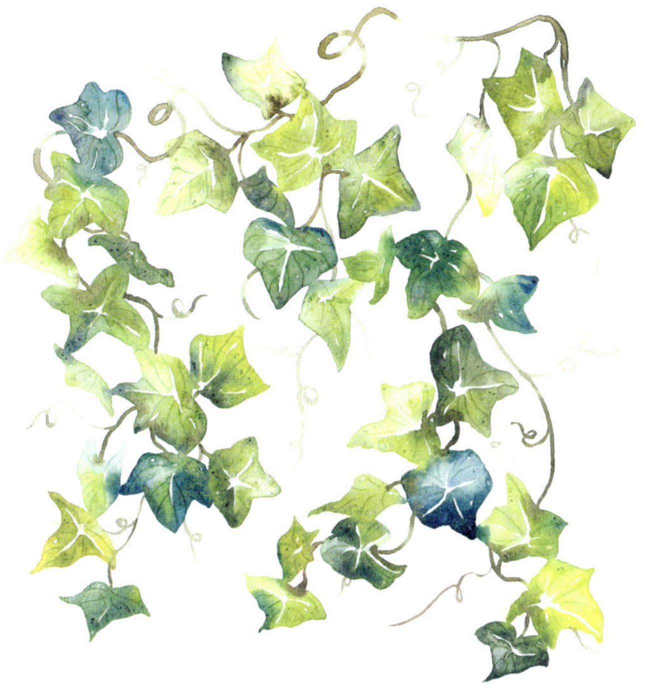

# 13/*Moon*

I absolutely love the moon – there is something mystical and timeless about it as it looms over us at night or softly decorates the sky in early morning. Recreating it in watercolours is a great pleasure, and a neat exercise in wet-on-wet painting.

SUGGESTED ART SUPPLIES: ROUGH OR COLD-PRESSED PAPER, PENCIL, MOP OR LARGE ROUND BRUSH, DETAIL BRUSH

## PREP

You won't need a great variety of colours for this exercise, but do mix a few shades of grey: pale greys with varied levels of blue in them, a brownish grey and a very dark brown, nearly black. Using ultramarine blue (warm shade) in this mix can give you great granulation, which suits the moon very well.

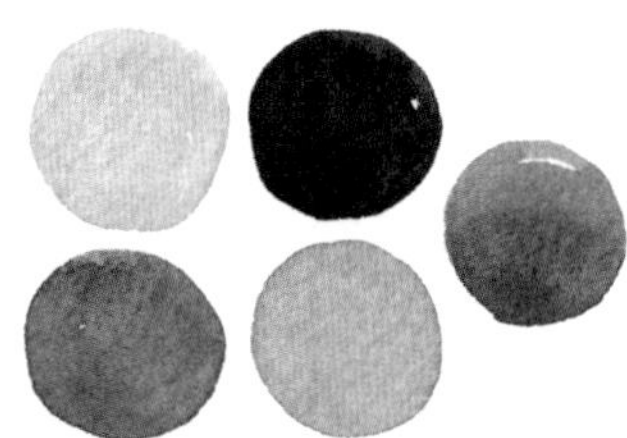

# Step 1

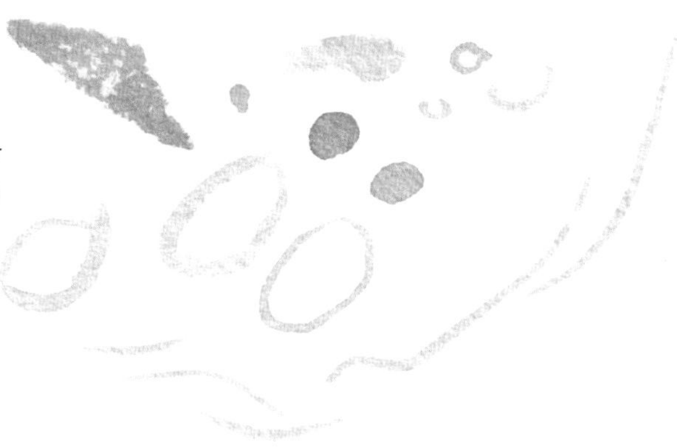

## TRIAL 1: ROUGH DETAIL STROKES

I want you to pick up a detail brush and practise some irregular brushstrokes, which you will need at the end to add textures after painting the final piece. Using watered-down grey, make rough marks – curved lines, flat oval shapes, dots and some wonky marks.

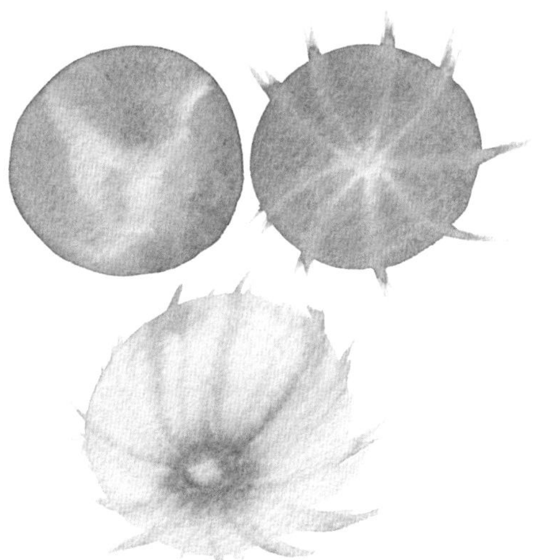

## TRIAL 2: DRAGGING LINES

To get a feel for adding the distinctive 'dragging' lines to the moon's surface, sketch a few circles with a lot of water. Then with the tip of your brush, start lifting some of the excess colour and water to reveal highlights and drag out the curved lines.

## Step 2

It is time to paint the moon! Sketch out a perfect circle (using compasses or sketch 2 on page 184 as a reference) and lightly draw the craters. Pick up a large or medium brush and load it up with a very diluted grey. Lay down an even wash of the watery grey within the circle without leaving any gaps.

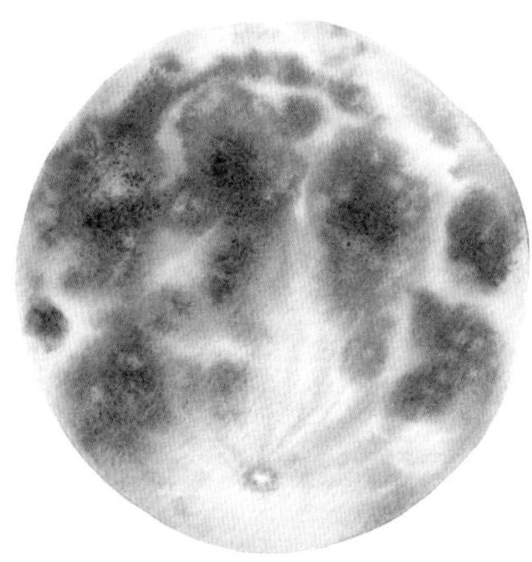

## Step 3

Without waiting for the first layer to dry, immediately remove excess water from your brush and load it up with values of dark grey. Using a wet-on-wet technique, drop the colour around the surface in various spots. Be careful to leave some areas of the moon brighter – don't drop excessive pigment across its entire body.

At this point you may already start to notice the ultramarine blue pigment granulating, if you used it in your colour mixing.

After a few minutes, when the moon is still damp but not entirely wet, use the tip of your brush to lightly paint a circular shape at the bottom of the moon to indicate a crater. Then drag some lines out of it as you practised in Step 1, Trial 2.

# Step 4

Wait for the entire surface of the moon to dry. Pick up a detail brush and load it up with a diluted grey. Using the techniques outlined in Step 1, Trial 1, add faint lines, circles and dots across the surface to accentuate textures and add little craters and irregularities.

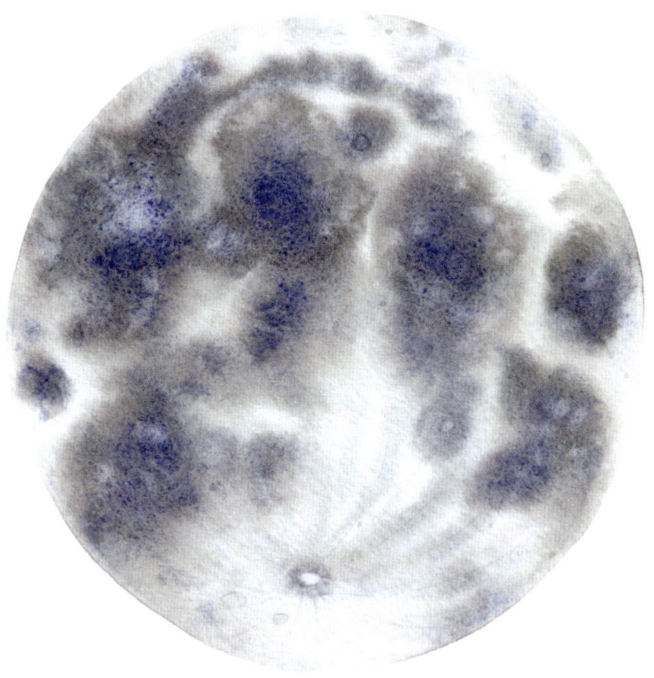

# 14/*Stork*

White stork birds are extremely close to my heart: they populate my country of origin, Poland, in the summer, where they nest and raise offspring, then migrate to Africa every autumn. Spotting them is a special sight. They are so distinctive looking with their white-red-black colouring, which lends itself well to painting.

SUGGESTED ART SUPPLIES: COLD-PRESSED PAPER, PENCIL, MEDIUM ROUND BRUSH, DETAIL BRUSH

## PREP

Mix a couple of shades of dark brown and black, some very diluted brown and faint yellow, and a few shades of warm red – a dark one, a medium tomato shade and a pale, soft red. Lastly, prepare soft warm greens, one darker and one more watered down.

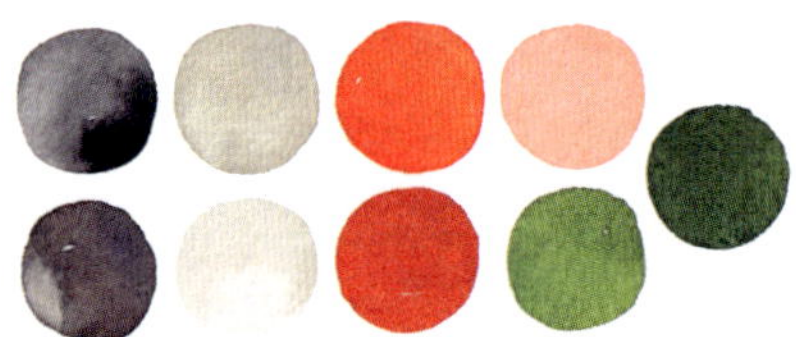

# Step 1

Lightly sketch out the shape of the stork with a pencil, using sketch 2 on page 180 as a reference. Load up a pointy round brush with the muted yellow or brown to lay down a wash over most of the bird's body. Try to drop in a slightly darker value at the ends of the feathers and on the left-hand side of the long neck, to start building dimension.

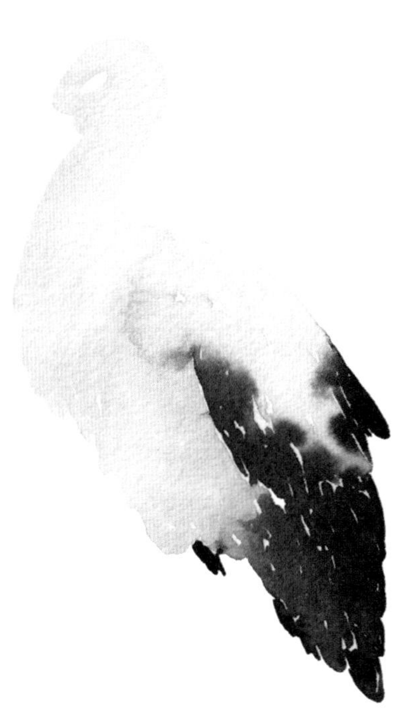

# Step 2

Without waiting for the first wash to dry, load your brush with a very dark brown to drop in some black feathers. You want some of them to merge with the initial pale wash. Paint the feathers with individual rough strokes using the tip of your brush, leaving some empty gaps between them to preserve luminosity.

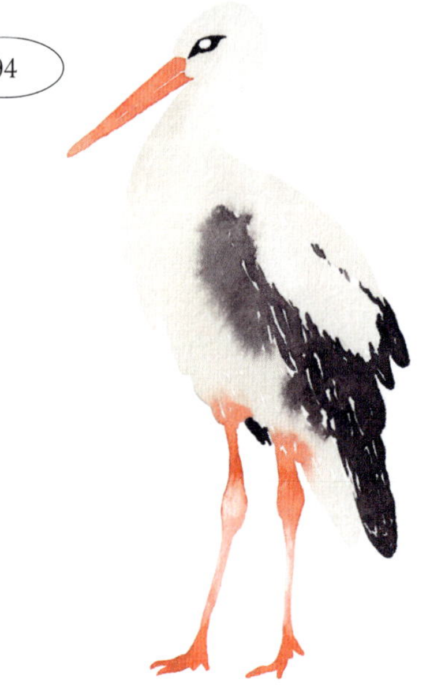

# Step 3

If your round brush comes to a sharp point, keep using it now and load it up with a warm red – if not, switch to a detail brush to do this. Starting with the legs, painting them at the bottom of the belly so the red can merge a little bit with the base colour.

At this point, wait for the bird's head to dry before you paint the long red beak with the same warm red. When you are sure the head is dry, pick up a detail brush and load it up with a very dense black to add the small eye outline.

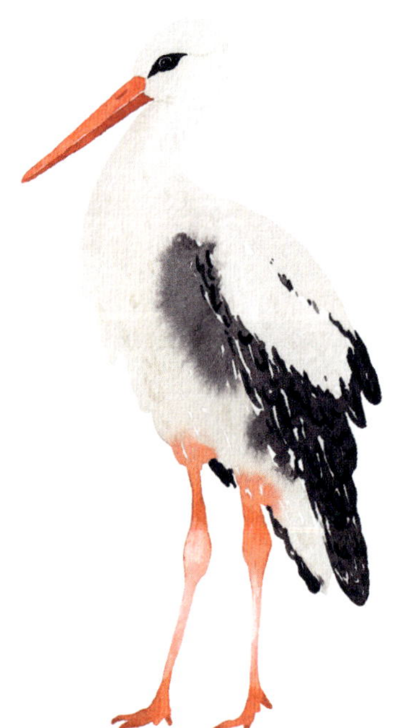

# Step 4

It is time to start adding details. Fill in the eye shape with the eyeball, leaving a tiny empty gap within that circular shape – this tiny detail is what gives the bird more personality and liveliness!

Stick to the dense black and add some rough strokes on the dark feathers to create texture.

Wash off the black completely and pick up a little diluted brown (the same colour we used for the base in Step 1). Add some faint rough strokes across the bird's body to add texture to the light feathers too.

Now load up the brush with a little darker red to add a layer of colour to the bottom of the beak, which creates dimension and contrast. Use the same red to add a little texture and shading to the legs and feet, especially at the bottom of the belly and the feet.

# Step 5

Let the bird dry completely before switching to the green. Using a detail brush or the tip of a round brush, add rough brushstrokes underneath the stork to paint a grass base. Once the initial light green base dries, add a few further strokes in darker green around the bird's feet to create shadow.

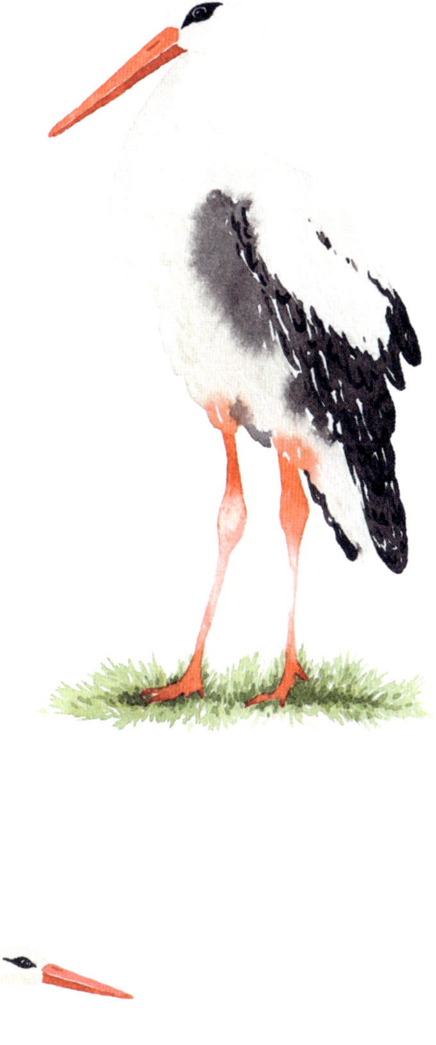

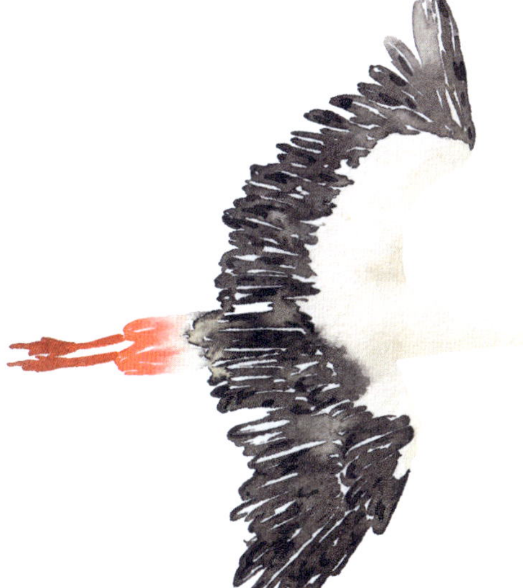

Optional extra challenge: Paint a stork in flight if you are up to it. The steps are very similar, but the bird's pose is different.

# 15/*Apples and Pears*

Pears and apples are two of my favourite fruits to sketch. The rounded shapes and a variety of warm colours allow for a relaxing, albeit challenging, watercolour exercise. I like to include slices of fruit too, to create a dynamic composition.

SUGGESTED ART SUPPLIES: COLD-PRESSED PAPER, PENCIL, MEDIUM ROUND BRUSH, DETAIL BRUSH

## PREP

Prepare warm colours: a few oranges, yellowish greens, muted reds, a watered-down warm yellow and some very dark brown.

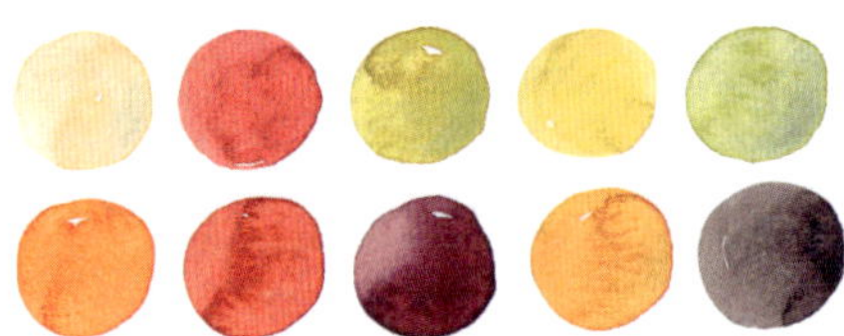

# Step 1

Lightly sketch out the shape of the pattern if you wish (see sketch 3 on page 181), but if you are feeling confident, you can paint the fruit freehand and change the composition to make it your own.

To start, load up your medium round or a mop brush with a diluted yellow and paint an outline of a pear cut in half, leaving some empty gaps in the middle. Quickly, load up your brush with a muted red and add a crescent shape by the bottom of the pear, and introduce a drop of yellowish green. This crescent will become an apple slice.

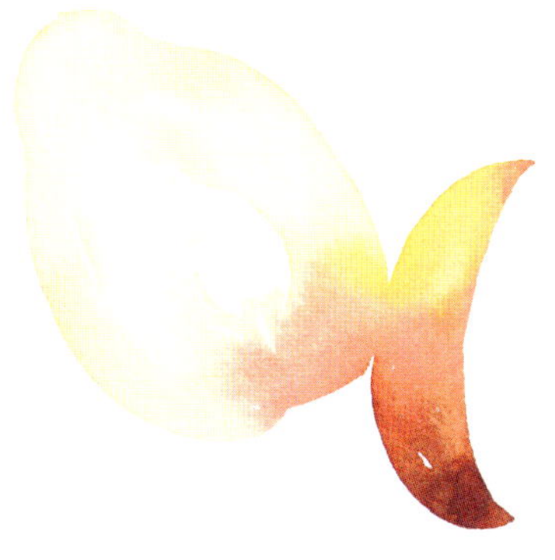

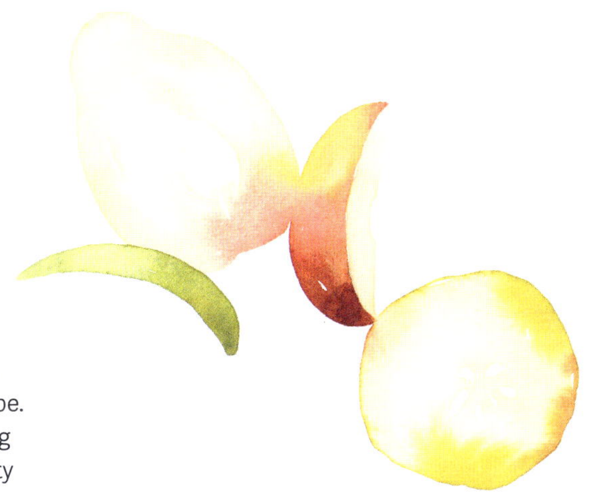

# Step 2

Wait for the shapes to dry. Go back to the diluted yellow to fill in the latest slice shape. Immediately paint a circular shape coming off the crescent, again leaving some empty gaps in the middle, which will be spaces for pips. Pick up a little warm yellow and orange to outline this shape and give the fruit its skin.

Next load up the brush with some muted green and add another crescent by the bottom left of the first pear shape.

## Step 3

Wait for everything to dry. Go back to the diluted yellow and fill in the green crescent shape, and then quickly paint half an apple touching the green crescent shape. Again, leave an empty gap in the apple's core. Pick up a little warm red or orange to add a skin outline.

## Step 4

Leave the cluster of apples and pears to dry and paint a second one to the right of it.

Pick up a purplish red and paint a whole apple outline, dropping a little muted yellow onto its skin. Before it dries, quickly switch to a warm green to paint an upside-down pear coming off the side of the apple. Adjust the saturation of the paint by adding or removing excess water. When the green pear is still wet, go back to the muted yellow base and add another pear slice. Then pick up a little warm orange and drop it onto its skin.

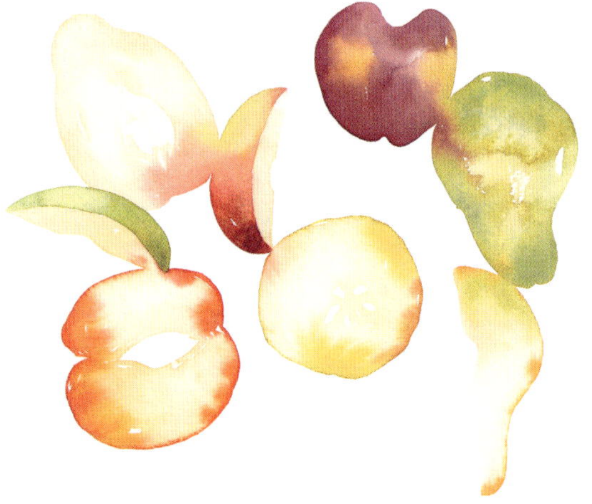

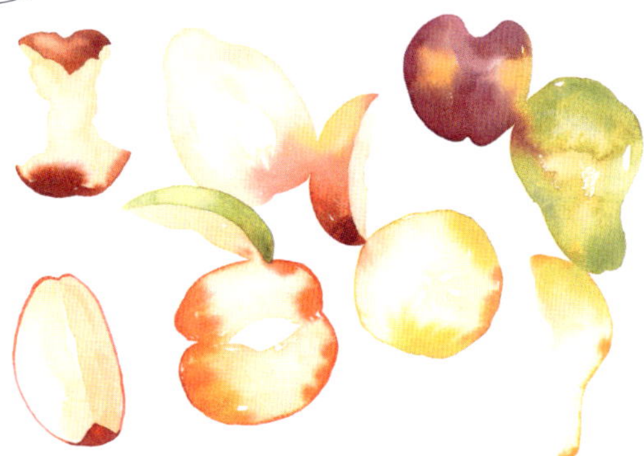

# Step 5

While the second cluster is drying, add two more apple shapes to the left: a core with bite marks, which is an unexpected funky detail, and a quarter sliced at an angle.

The apple core is a somewhat wonky cylinder shape, painted in the muted yellow. Make sure you include uneven edges to indicate the bite marks. Leave it to dry a little, and in the meantime paint the remaining apple quarter using the same base yellow – it is made up of two rounded elongated shapes, with the right one being a little more saturated, indicating a shadow. Leave an empty gap in between.

Go back to a dark red and add the remaining skin of the eaten apple – a little at the top, and a bit at the bottom and, using the same colour, add the outline of the quartered slice.

# Step 6

Let everything dry before you add the details with a small brush. Load it up with very dark brown and add all the stems. I use the same colour to fill in the empty gaps across the fruit pieces with little dark pips. A bonus element is to add some loose pips across the composition – make some of them darker, and some lighter in value.

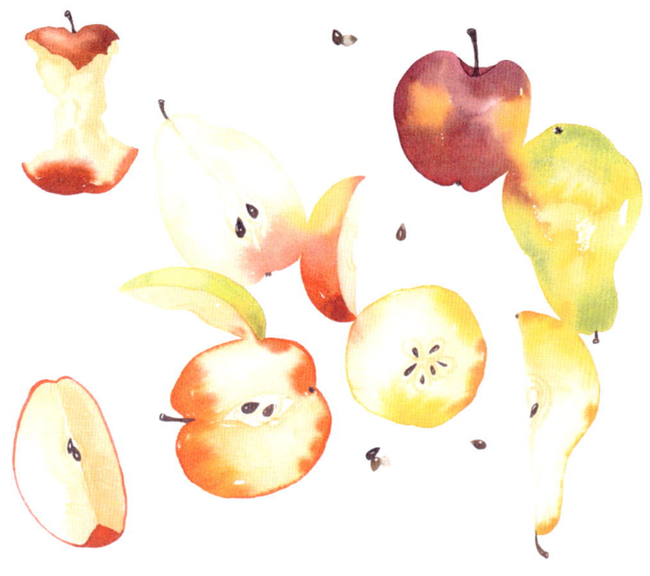

# 16/*Countryside Flowers*

Picture the scene. It is a warm spring day and you are going for a walk in the countryside. Stepping out of a lush forest, you are going to meet a friend who lives in a small cosy cottage. The front garden of their porch is beautifully lined with fresh, scented flowers and you lean down to smell them.

SUGGESTED ART SUPPLIES: COLD- OR HOT-PRESSED PAPER, PENCIL, SMALL OR MEDIUM ROUND BRUSH, DETAIL BRUSH

## PREP

Mix an assortment of vibrant colours, thinking of a wide variety of wildflowers. I prepared a deep blue, muted yellows, red and pinks, some purple, muted browns and a couple of warm shades of green.

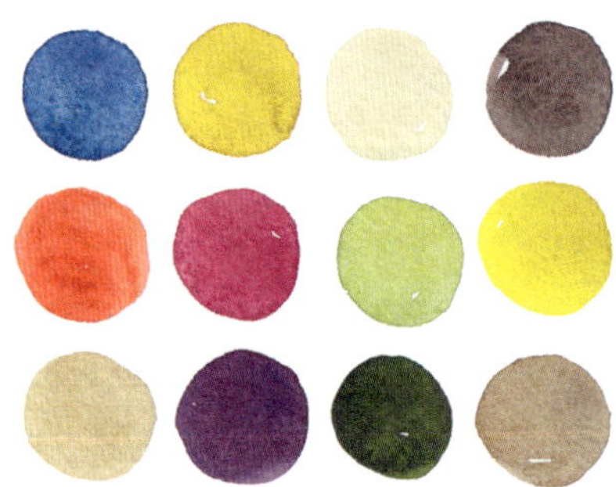

# Step 1

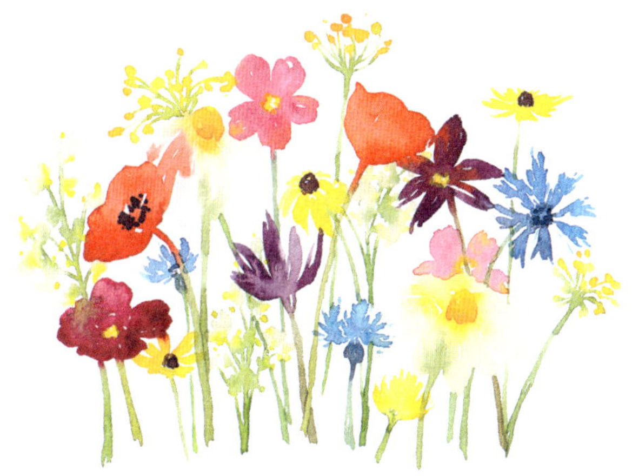

Make a light pencil sketch using sketch 1 on page 182, focusing mostly on the fence behind the flowers because it is the most rigid element of the composition. I encourage you to sketch the flowers loosely and place them intuitively – wildflowers grow informally.

Start the illustration by painting an assortment of flowers of different heights. I included some dainty yellow daisies, two poppies, a few cornflowers, a couple of pink ones, plus some tall cow parsley.
Pick up a bit of green on your brush and paint the stems.

# Step 2

Let the flowers dry completely, then add grass around the stems to make the composition denser.

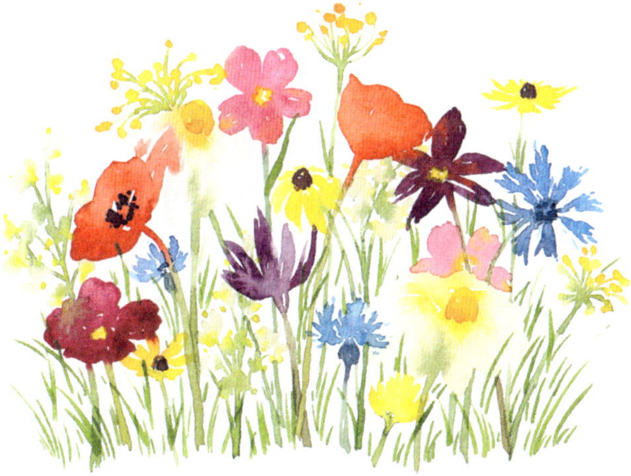

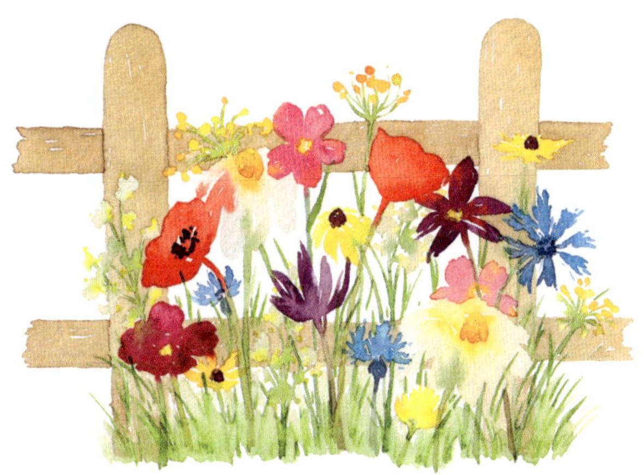

## Step 3

Switch the colour on your brush to a soft, muted brown in a midtone to paint the background fence. I left tiny empty gaps between the brushstrokes to evoke the texture of wood.

Afterwards, pick up a diluted green and smooth down the green grass by putting down a layer of light green on top of it. This will give your flowers a base.

## Step 4

Let everything dry. Pick up a detail brush and load it up with a medium dark brown to add irregular strokes across the fence to imitate a rough wood texture.

Then mix up a bit more dark green again and scatter a few more sprigs of grass on the ground, for extra layering and depth.

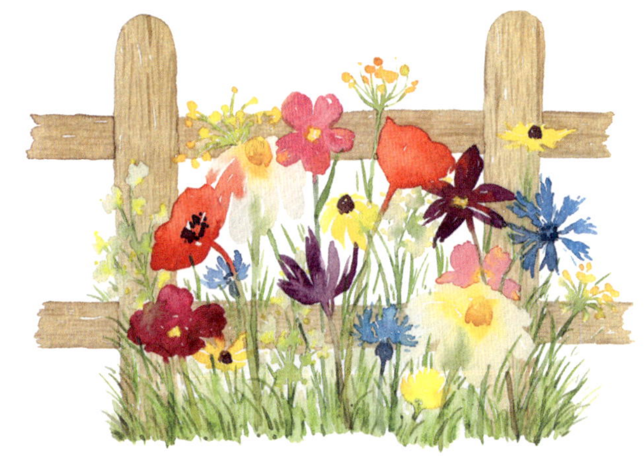

# Step 5

Lastly, go over the fence with a detail brush once again to elevate the wood grain texture even further. I mixed some more dark brown and painted little bolts and nails in the fence and added a bit of shading to its edges.

I believe this necessary, albeit repetitive, detail ties the illustration together and creates the rustic feel of a cosy cottage.

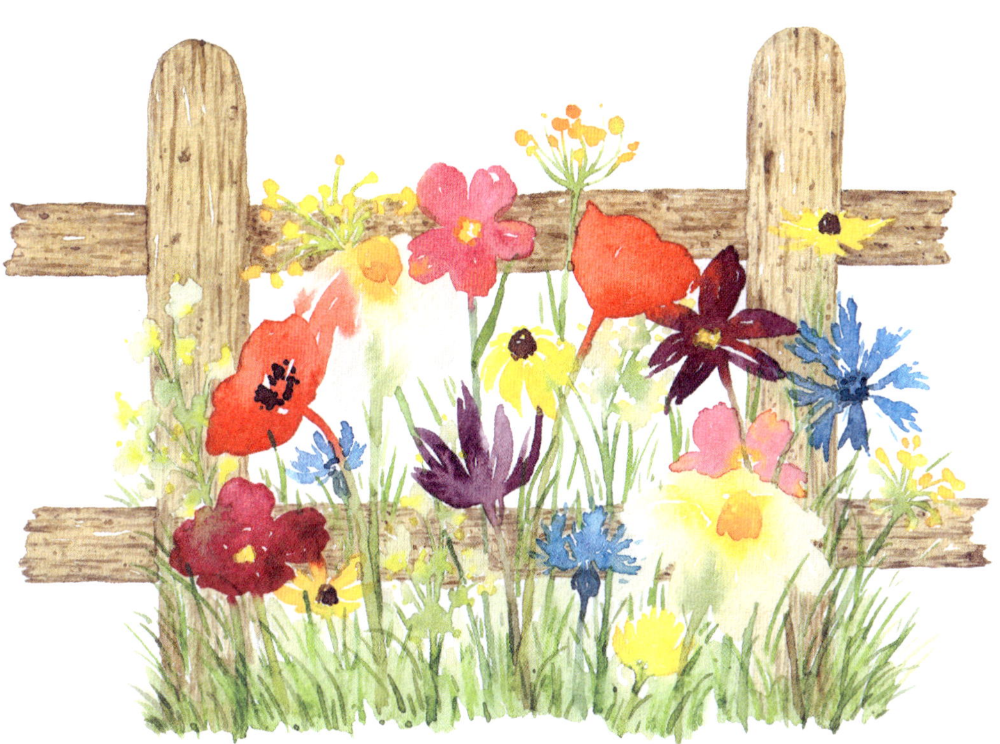

# 17/*Milky Way Sky*

For many of us, it is quite rare to see a clear night sky with bright stars illuminating it and a vibrant milky way leading the way. These jaw-dropping scenes require low light pollution, so it is tricky to witness such sights if you live in a city. I encourage you to attempt painting it in watercolours in the meantime – it is a mesmerising process, much like watching the night sky itself.

SUGGESTED ART SUPPLIES: COLD-PRESSED OR ROUGH PAPER (100% COTTON), LARGE FLAT OR MOP BRUSH, ROUND BRUSH FOR SPRINKLING, TABLE SALT, OPAQUE WHITE WATERCOLOUR ('BLEED-PROOF WHITE')

## PREP

You will need an assortment of dark, rich colours ranging from deep purples to intense blues and heavy black. Unusually, we will be using an opaque white gouache-style watercolour paint called 'bleed-proof white', which I recommend you add to your art supplies collection, as it is a very useful tool at times.

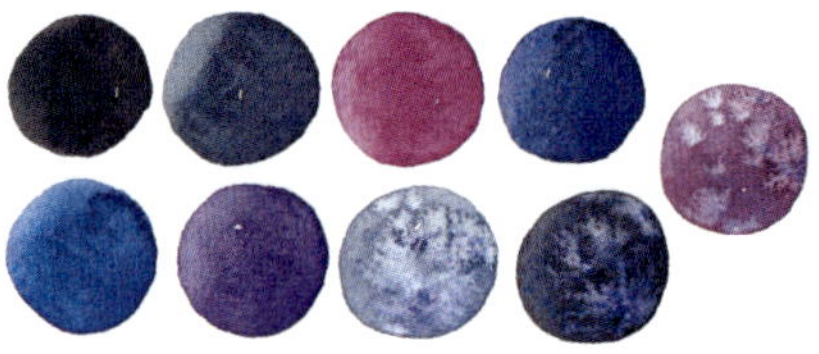

Prepare some table salt as well – we will be seasoning our night sky to achieve some fantastical effects.

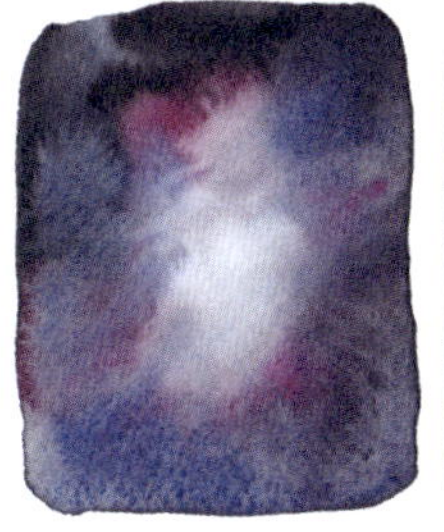

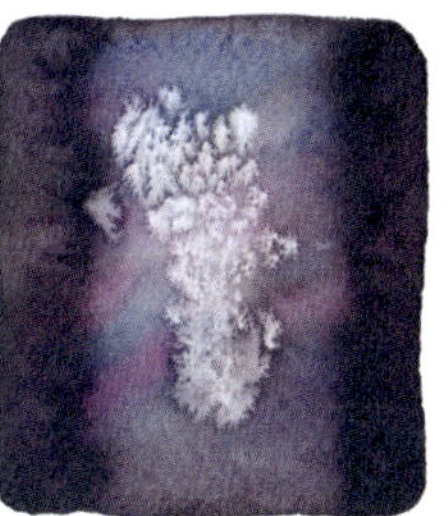

# Step 1

TRIAL 1

Before committing to painting a big sky scene, first sketch out a few frames and fill them in with the rich colours you just mixed. Do this by laying down a flat wash of water on your paper, and immediately dropping in the black, purple, blue colours, especially focusing on the edges. Try to leave the middle of the frames brighter by not dropping the darkest pigments in those areas.

It is also an opportunity to test the salt method, as seen in the image on the right. Drop just a few grains of salt onto a wet surface and patiently wait for it to dry naturally. The salt will create blooming effects that cannot be replicated with a paintbrush!

TRIAL 2

Next sketch three very dark shapes using a fair amount of pigment and let them dry completely.

Then, pick up some bleed-proof white paint and test various ways of splattering it to create distant stars in the sky. To make the image on the left I splattered the white paint from a round paintbrush from close up, hence the marks are quite large.

For the middle image, I splattered the white from higher above the paper, which created smaller marks.

Lastly, in the third image I used a flat brush, dunked it in the white paint, then used my fingers to flick the fibres of the brush to achieve very fine, delicate splatters.

Experimenting like this will enable you to build a multi-dimensional starry night sky.

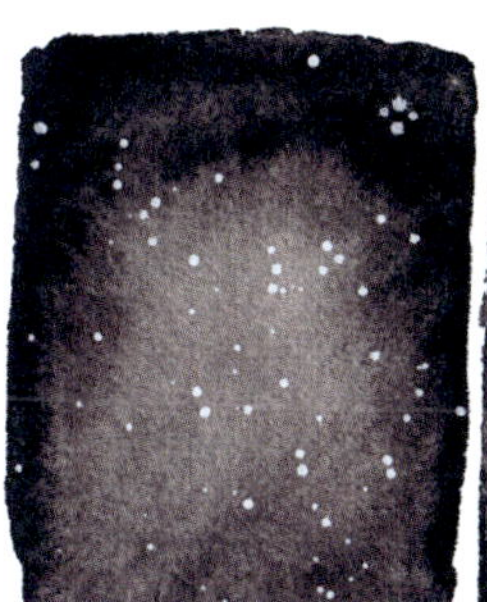

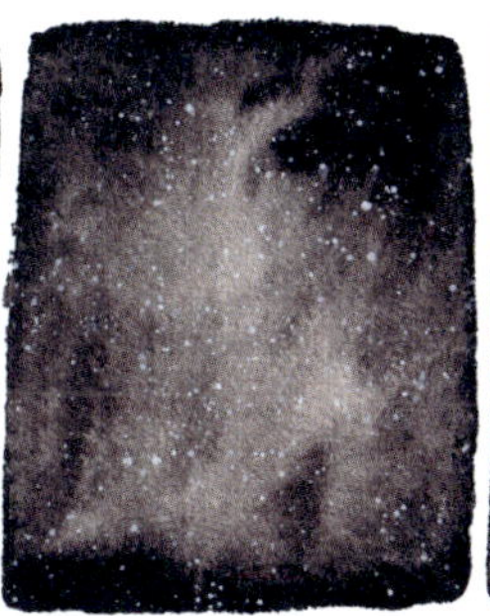

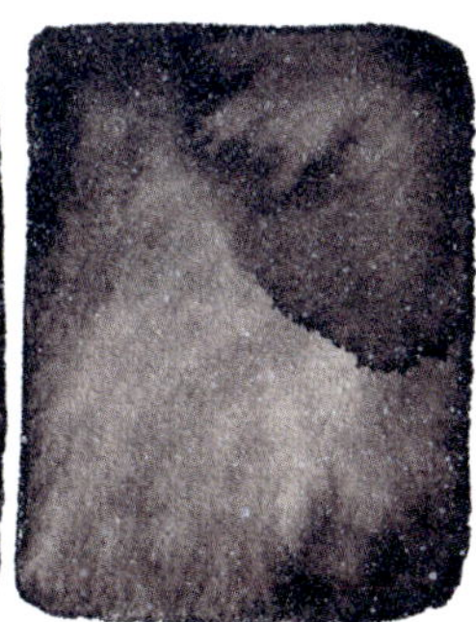

# Step 2

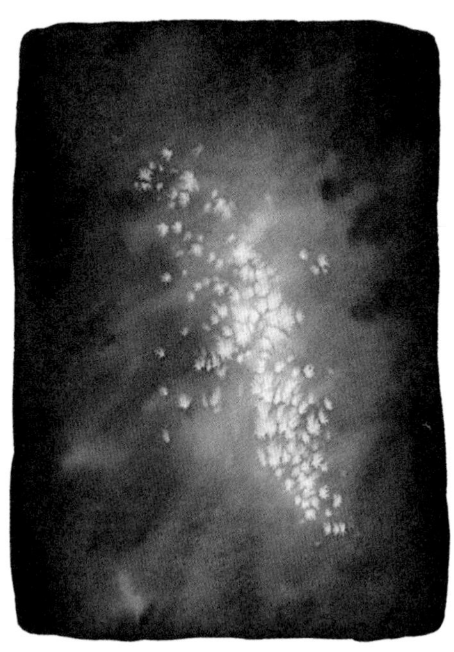

Now that you have experimented with the techniques, it is time to paint our milky way scene.

I recommend using an entire large sheet of paper, preferably of high quality, which will allow you to apply a great amount of both water and pigment.

First use a large brush loaded with heaps of clean water to cover your paper entirely in an even layer. There is a happy middle ground for how much water to apply – you don't want the water to dry too quickly, but you don't want to create puddles on the paper either. The more you practise, the more you will gain muscle memory for the quantity of water necessary.

Quickly load up your brush with very generous amounts of pre-mixed colours. Using wet-on-wet, I apply the darkest tones such as blacks and deep blues on the very edges of the paper, then push the pigments into the middle. The colours you apply in the middle should be a little more diluted, to leave space for the milky way to shine.

Don't be afraid to drop in the shades of pink and blue as loose strokes scattered around the sky.

When you are happy with the dark-coloured sky, make sure it is still very damp and drop in a few drops of salt in a diagonal line.

# Step 3

Let this layer dry completely on its own – don't use a heat tool or a hairdryer here, as it may affect the way the salt reacts. The drying will take a little while due to the amount of water we applied, so leave it for a few hours or come back the next day to discover what the salt grains have come up with!

When it is completely dry, gently sweep the surface with a paper towel without scrubbing, to remove any salt residue. Then pick up a detail brush and load it up with some bleed-proof white opaque paint. Using just the tip, make little dots scattered around the sky, mostly around the milky way.

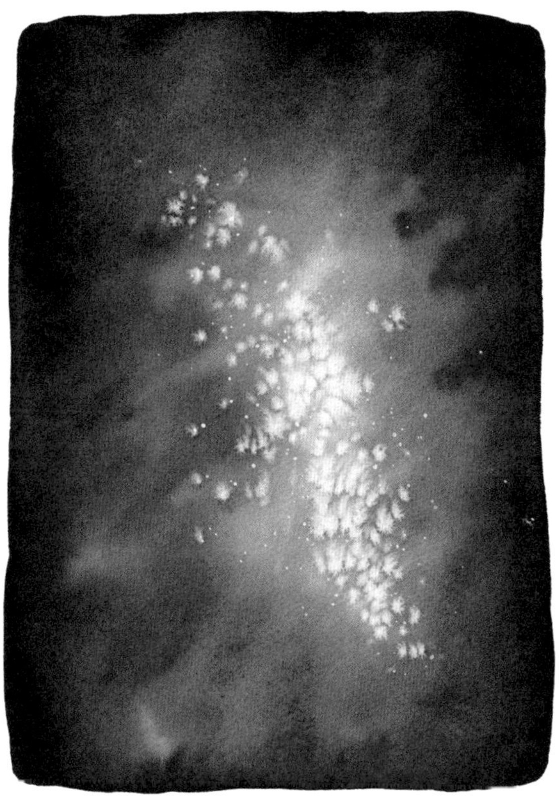

# Step 4

Finally, pick up a bigger brush and load it up with the bleed-proof opaque white to start splattering the paint more generously around the night sky. As practised in Step 1, Trial 2, change the distance from which you splatter the gouache, then grab a flat brush and flick the paint around the milky way with your fingers. This way you will create stars of different sizes and really illuminate the night sky.

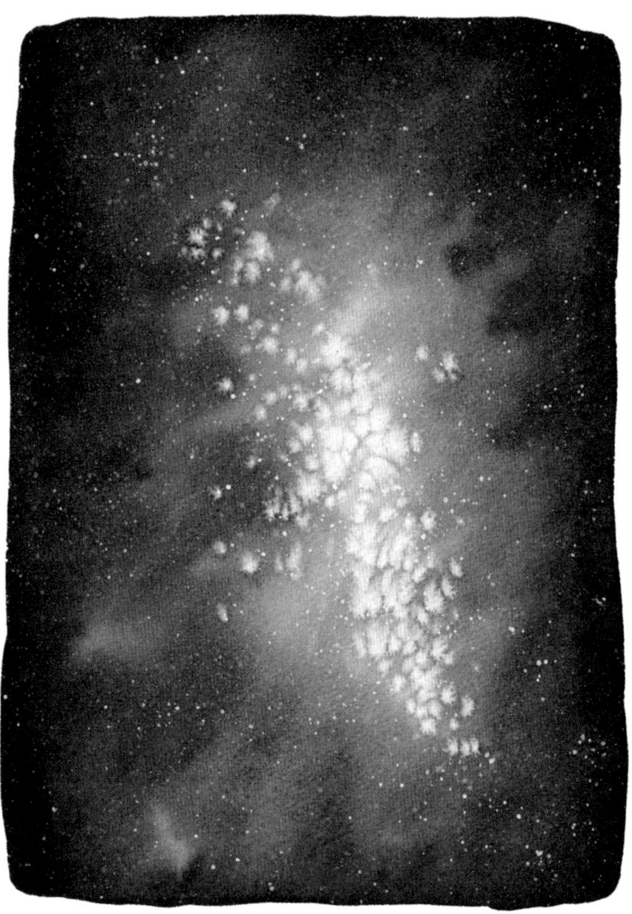

# 18/*Glass Flower Vase*

When it comes to painting glass in watercolours, I think the best approach is a loose one. The luminosity of watercolour paints should elevate its transparent quality. Work with the contrast between light and shadow to create dimension in this flower vase, and do not worry much about symmetrical lines and rigid proportions.

SUGGESTED ART SUPPLIES: COLD-PRESSED PAPER, PENCIL, MEDIUM ROUND BRUSH, DETAIL BRUSH

## PREP

Feel free to paint a different flower to mine! I opted for a rich red one. I also prepared shades of warm yellow, rich greens, a deep dark blue and purple for the shadows as well as a diluted, pale blue for the glass.

UP TO ONE HOUR

# Step 1

Make a very light pencil sketch of the vase using sketch 2 on page 182 as a reference, or skip the sketch entirely if you wish to try painting freehand.

Load up a round brush with a very diluted greyish blue and go over the edges of the vase, including rounded shapes to accentuate the base of the vase and the water's surface.

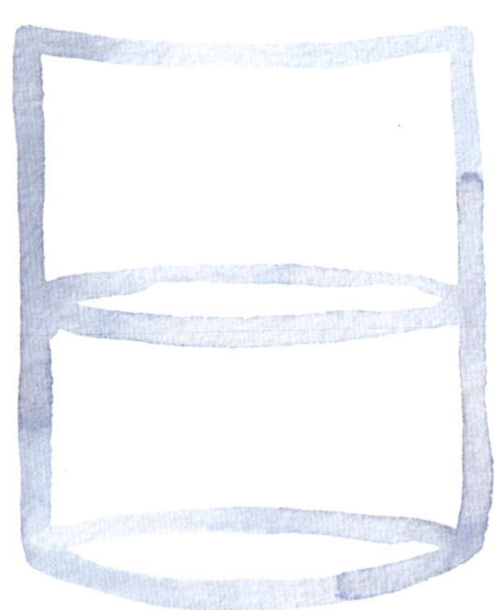

# Step 2

Immediately, add even more water to your brush and add large flat brushstrokes from the top of the vase to the bottom on either side, to create glass reflections. With that watery application, add the remaining rim on the top of the vase. Then, swiftly before it all dries, pick up a bit of soft pale green and run a single vertical brushstroke from the top to the bottom of the vase, and watch the green merge with the pale blue.

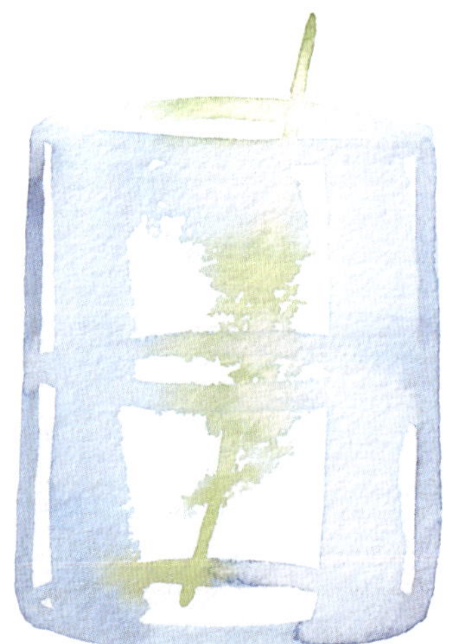

# Step 3

Darken the stem of the flower with a richer mix of green while it is still wet. Now, pick up deep blue and lay it down around the vase, especially on the right and bottom right, leaving just a sliver of empty space between the vase and the shadow. Without cleaning the brush, pick up a little cool red and drop it into the blue, which will result in purple being mixed straight on the paper. This will create immense contrast between the transparent glass and the deep blues and purples. Once you lay down the dark strokes, quickly load up your brush with extra water to dilute the intense pigments and soften the edges of the shadows as you move outwards (this is feathering, as shown on page 20). We want the darkest values to be concentrated around the edges of the glass.

Notice I left some empty gaps in the shadow wash and introduced a little dry brush technique – this creates captivating textures.

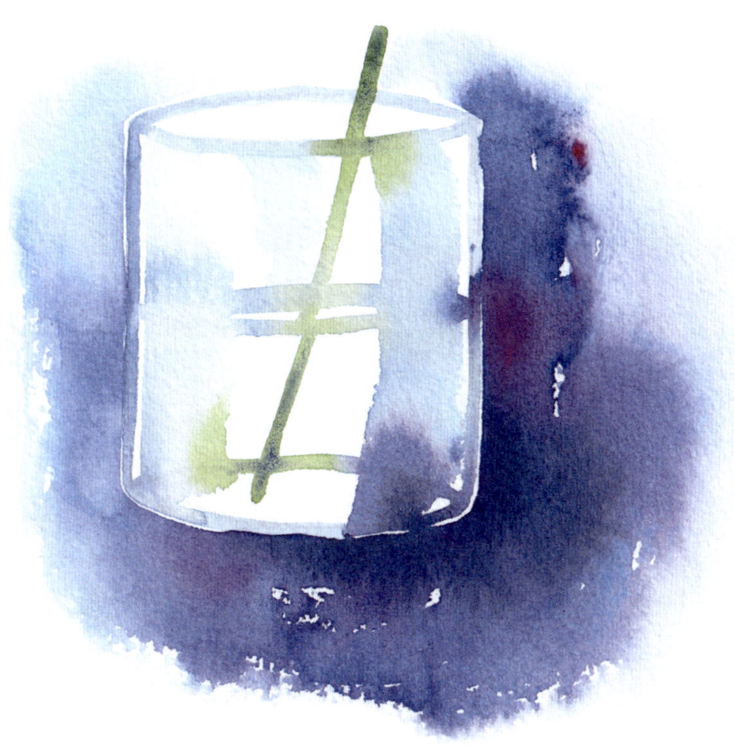

## Step 4

Let the painting dry. In the meantime, pick up the colour of your flower of choice and paint the petals using a small, pointy round or a detail brush. Do that by starting in the heart of the flower, making slightly curved brushstrokes which go outwards. Leave a few empty gaps between each stroke to preserve texture and highlight.

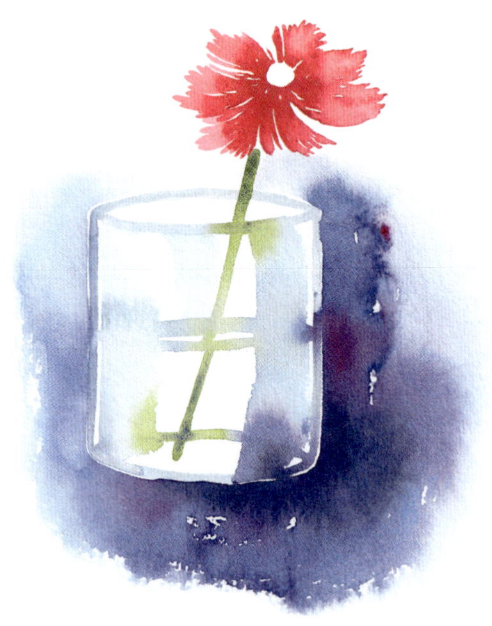

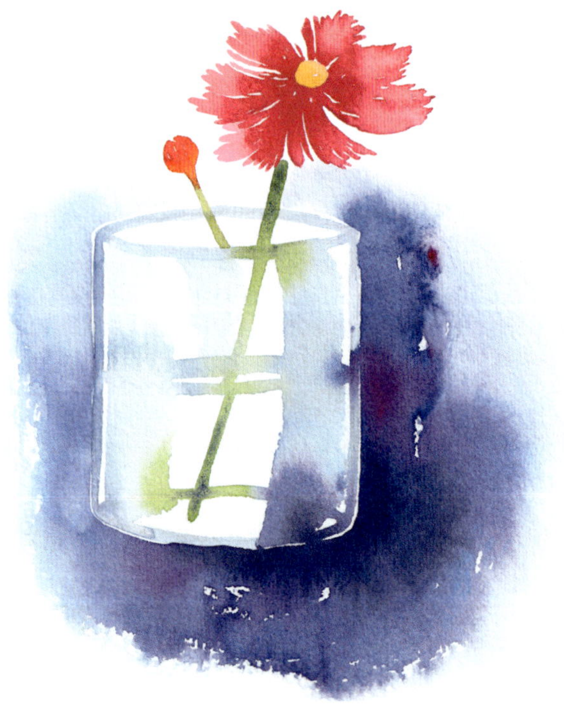

## Step 5

Fill in the middle of the flower. I used a warm yellow. You can also add another flower; I opted for a little unripe bud.

# Step 6

Lastly, add a few details and textures. Using a detail brush, accentuate the petals with scattered rough lines and dots. Add a bit of contrast to the heart of the flower and some dark green shadow to the stems. I included tiny leaves coming off the flower bud and extended its stem to touch the base of the vase.

Go back to a greyish blue (just don't make it too dark) and add some fine hairline strokes on the top and side edges of the glass to give it more of a pop.

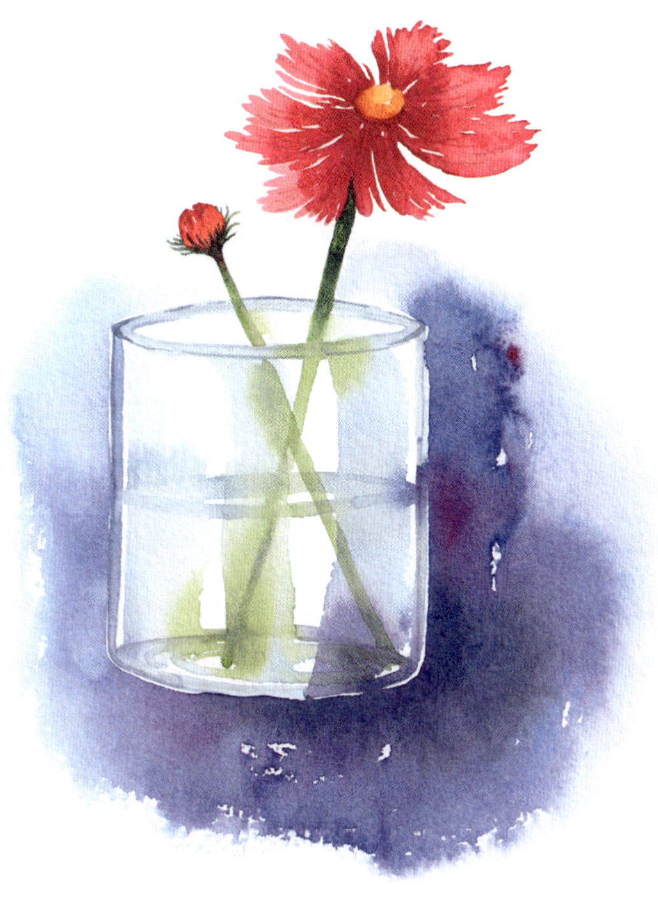

# 19/*Artichoke*

There is one greatly overlooked vegetable which looks stunning as a watercolour illustration – the mighty artichoke. Its colourful layers push us to paint as if we were putting together puzzle pieces. You will require a little patience, so you need to trust the process.

SUGGESTED ART SUPPLIES: HOT- OR COLD-PRESSED PAPER, PENCIL, MEDIUM ROUND BRUSH, DETAIL BRUSH

## PREP

Mix a range of warm, earthy tones: a variety of greens, muted yellows, a purple, a pink and a dark brown.

Sketch out the artichoke cross-section gently with a pencil, using sketch 1 on page 180 as a reference.

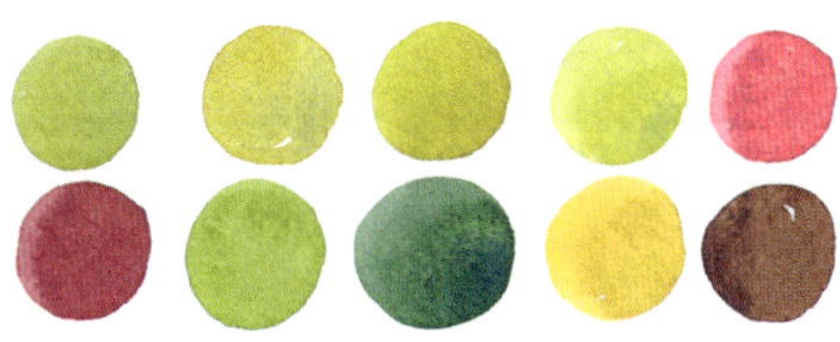

# Step 1

Using a fine point of your brush, lay down the first artichoke textures with a muted warm yellow, as in the example below. I used loose, rough strokes and left plenty of empty gaps. The citrus segment-like shape needs a little darker yellow at its base to create contrast.

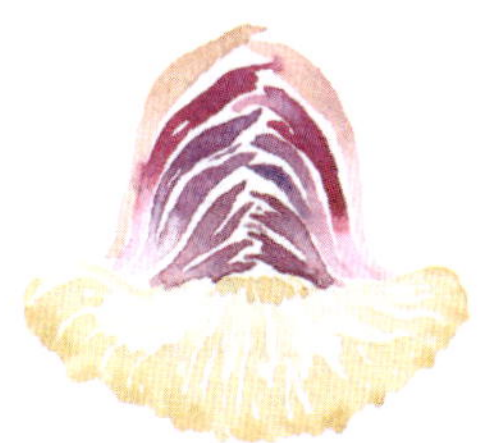

# Step 2

Go back to the palette and switch between pinks and purples to start adding the artichoke 'puzzle' pieces. The bent and curved lines all need a space between them to preserve the unique structure.

# Step 3

As you move outwards building the artichoke body, switch colour to a muted yellow and paint a few curved lines. Gradually add a bit of green to your brush to paint the longer ones as you move further out. Remember to vary the amount of water you use to dilute your colours, keeping the bottom edges of the curved strokes a little darker.

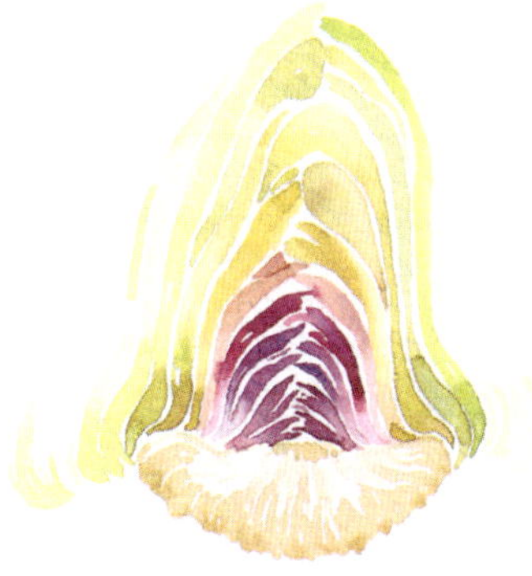

## Step 4

Gradually mix in more green until the colour on your brush is a vibrant darker green for the outer layers of the artichoke. The darkest layers now start peeling off from the main body of the artichoke, which creates a lovely dynamism.

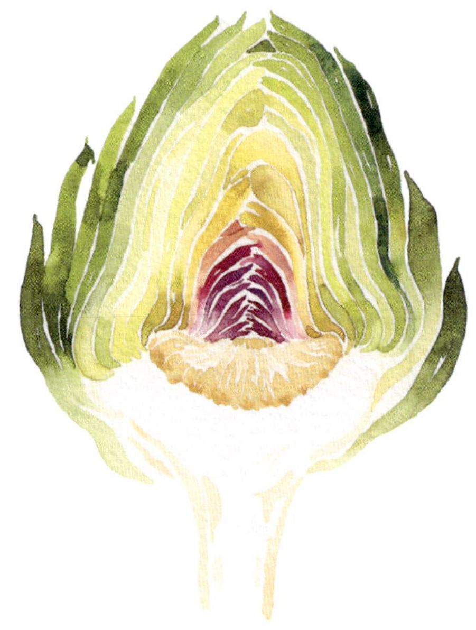

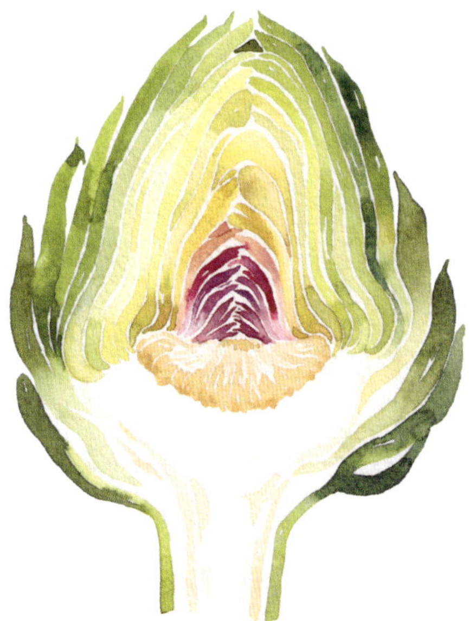

## Step 5

Continue using the dark green value and paint a thick outline around the stem at the bottom.

## Step 6

The last steps are all about adding texture. Let everything dry before picking up a detail brush. Using the muted yellow you started with, add rough, uneven strokes across the middle of the stem to accentuate delicate details.

## Step 7

Then switch to muted green and yellow and add little dots and faint lines across the artichoke layers. The image to the right shows the kind of strokes that work best for building gentle textures.

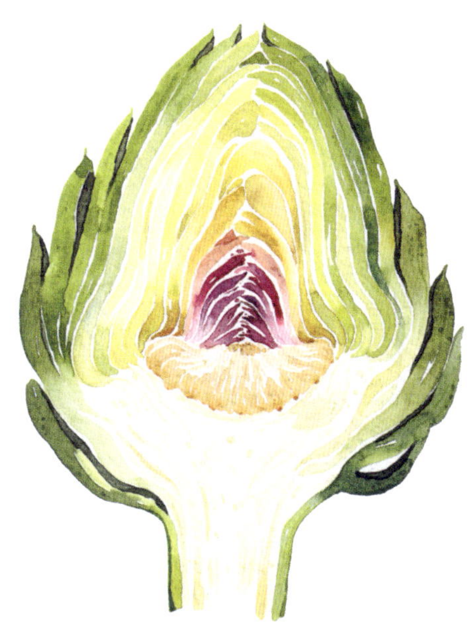

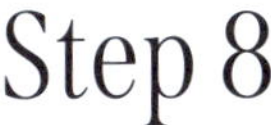

## Step 8

Finally, use the darkest brown to paint tiny shadow areas in between some of the outer layers and add a darker outline to the stem. This really accentuates the depth of the illustration.

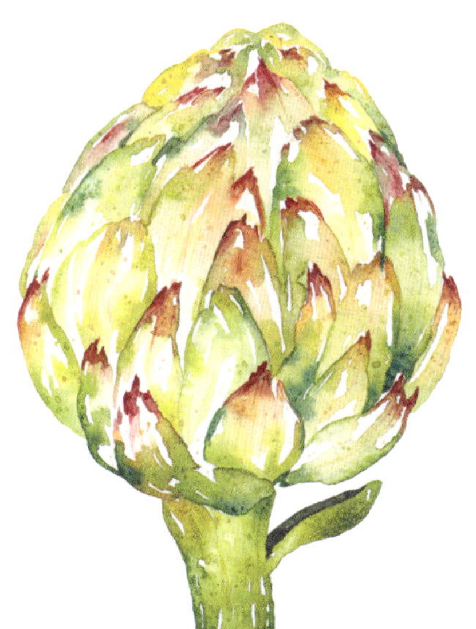

Optional extra challenge: If you enjoy painting artichokes as much as I do, try to paint a whole one using the same colour palette!

# 20/*Sea Waves*

Dreamy seascapes are one of my favourite visual images, which I often call to mind when falling asleep. Such scenes evoke the soft sound of crashing waves, a gentle breeze and bare feet on a soft sandy beach. Painting this seascape is quite an ethereal experience.

SUGGESTED ART SUPPLIES: COLD-PRESSED PAPER, IDEALLY 100% COTTON, LARGE FLAT OR MOP BRUSH, MEDIUM ROUND BRUSH, TABLE SALT

## PREP

You will mostly need shades of muted yellow and oranges along with some cool, green-tinted blues for this ocean colourway. Mix quite a bit of paint, especially the blues, as you will use a generous amount of pigment in this exercise and the last thing you want is to run out of the perfect mix in the middle of the process.

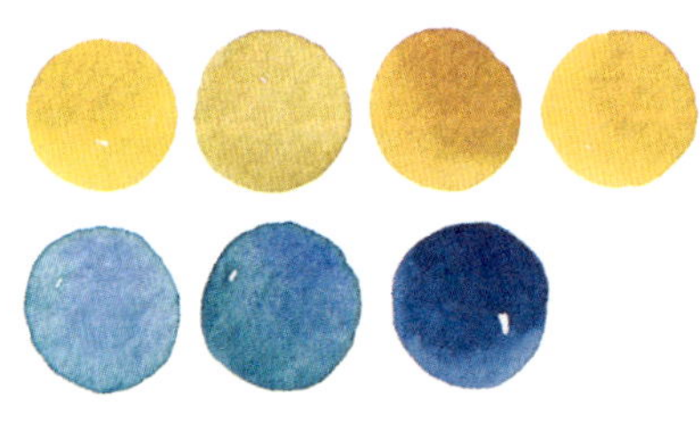

# Step 1

Before we commence, refresh your muscle memory about how to create a gradient wash as it will be necessary to paint the deep blue sea. Start with a very dark saturated blue, gradually adding more water to dilute it until you reach a faint blue.

We will also implement the dry brush technique at the bottom of the sea gradient, so try that again in a sketchbook. It is also a great time to test the way salt works on watercolour paper – make a few swatches and before the paint dries, and drop a few grains. Wait for it to dry and observe the beautiful blooms.

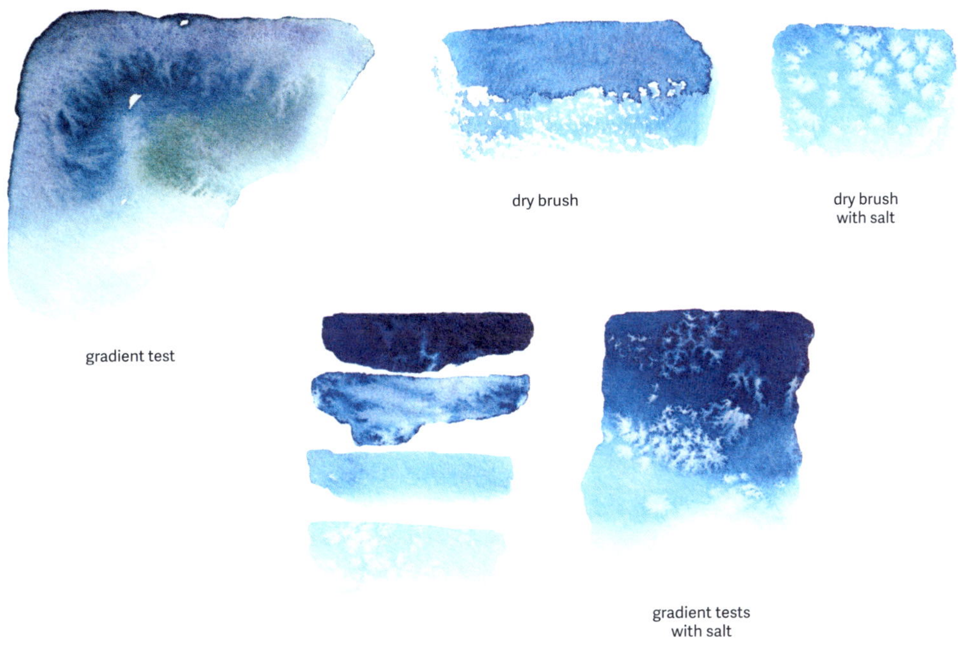

# Step 2

I recommend working on a decent sized sheet of high-quality cold-pressed paper, so you have enough space to make large, bold brushstrokes.

Pick up a flat brush and load it with the muted yellow. Starting from the bottom, apply a midtone value in a sweeping hand movement. As you move towards the seashore, gradually add extra water to dilute the sand colour.

At the very top, dry the brush off a bit on your paper towel to remove excess water and apply the dry brush technique to create a ragged edge to the sand.

Before the sand dries completely, drop just a couple of grains of salt on it.

# Step 3

Let the sand dry. Clean off your brush from the yellow and pick up a tiny bit of light blue. Again, you want the brush to be semi-dry at this point. Make a few sweeping dry brushstrokes. These will be the foundation of the crashing sea waves.

# Step 4

Now, get ready for intense water and pigment application! Load your large brush with a generous amount of water and darkest blue pigment. Starting at the top of the paper, begin building the gradient. The first strokes will be the richest blues, then as you move down towards the sand, gradually add more water to dilute the colour. As you are laying down this wash, remember to vary the colours you use; include different shades of blue and bluish green.

When you get closer to the sand, get rid of excess water and apply some dry brushstrokes again to reinforce that texture.

Before the sea water dries, grab the table salt and apply a few grains at the top of the painting. Add slightly more at the point where the sea starts meeting the sand. The salt will soak up the pigment and create beautiful explosive blooms which imitate the sea foam, so it is good to concentrate the salt a bit lower down.

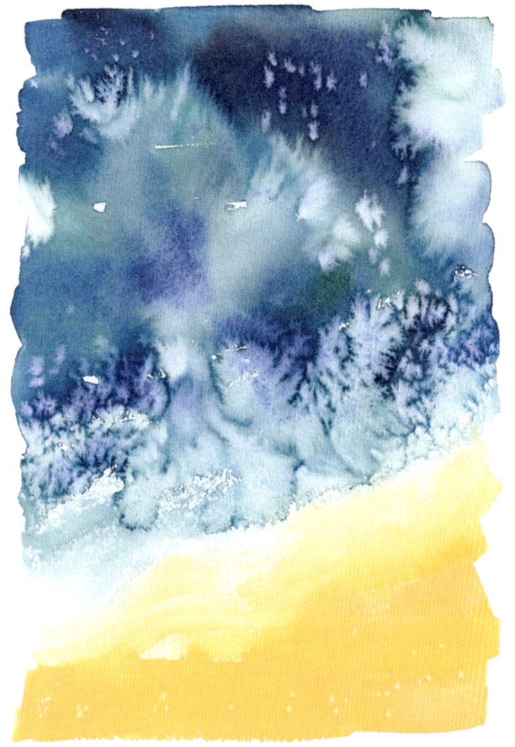

# Step 5

You can stop painting here if you like, as it is already a charming scene. However, I was unsatisfied with the flatness of the sand, so I went back to my large brush and picked up a little more muted brownish orange and added a further layer onto the beach. The visible, ragged brushstrokes work well with the uneven textures of sand. Try to concentrate the dark value just at the bottom of the frame however, to avoid overwhelming the paler seashore itself.

Before the sand layer dried, I applied a few grains of salt onto it. Wait for the painting to dry completely – it may take several hours depending on the size of the paper. Gently sweep all the salt particles with a clean hand or a paper towel without scrubbing.

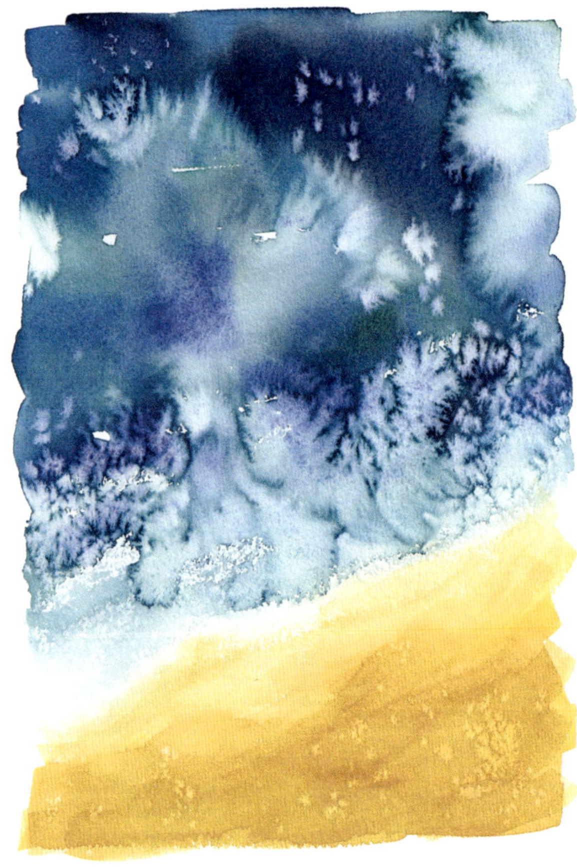

# 21/*Forest Mushrooms*

To me, one of the most potent and fresh natural scents is the smell of rain in a forest and the wild mushrooms poking out of the ground after a dense rainfall. I like to transport myself to a scene like that in my imagination sometimes – and being able to paint an earthy mushroom pattern loosely, but with a little botanical detail, is one of the ways to do it successfully.

SUGGESTED ART SUPPLIES: COLD-PRESSED PAPER, MEDIUM ROUND BRUSH, DETAIL BRUSH

## PREP

Mix a selection of muted earthy colours – pale, subdued yellows, browns, some greys, purple and red.

Sketch out the mushroom composition lightly with a pencil using sketch 1 on page 184 as a reference.

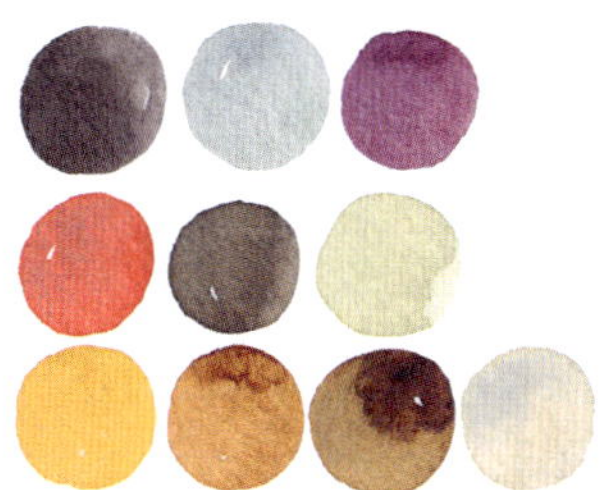

UP TO ONE HOUR

## Step 1

Switching swiftly between colours, use a medium-sized brush to start painting the pattern, joining the mushroom elements at their sides.

I started off with dark brown for the large mushroom cap in the middle, then quickly loaded up the brush with muted yellow to paint a thin bent stalk to the left of it. Then I cleaned off most of the pigment and with a very faint yellow-grey, I added the upside-down sliced mushroom to the right of the first item. While the slice was still wet, I went back to the palette to pick up a warm brown and added another mushroom cap touching it.

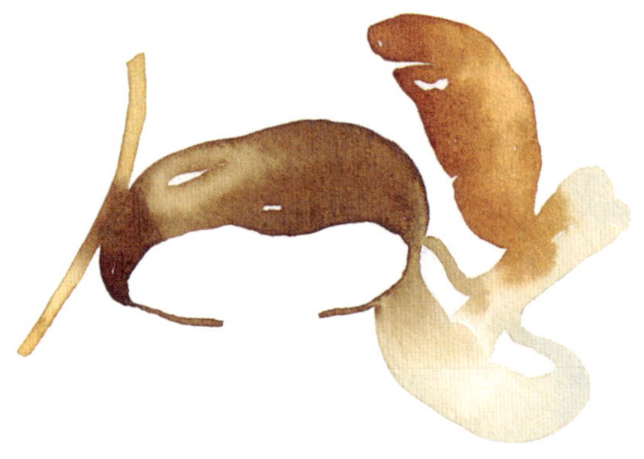

## Step 2

Let the first cluster of mushrooms dry. Pick up a muted yellow-brown mix and paint the stalk of the first mushroom, making it wider and slightly darker at the bottom. Quickly switch to a warm deep brown to outline the cap of another mushroom at the bottom of the composition – this one is upside-down.

While it is still wet, remove the brown from your brush and pick up a watery mix of grey to add parallel brushstrokes to make the gills, dragging the strokes from the edge of the mushroom outline onto the stalk in the middle. Now pick up a little extra warm brown and add another little mushroom cap to the right.

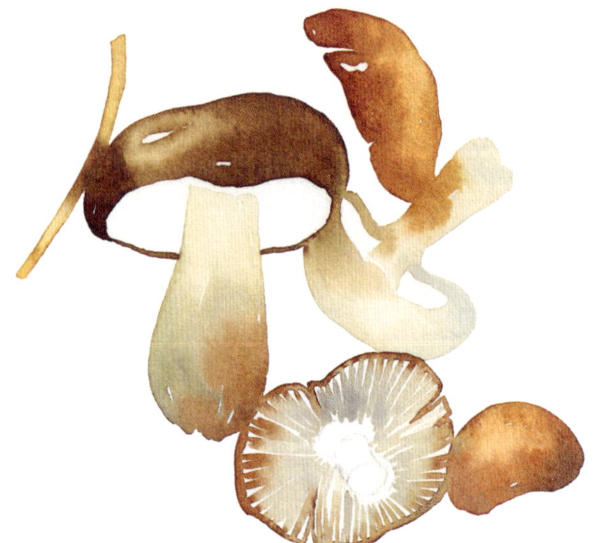

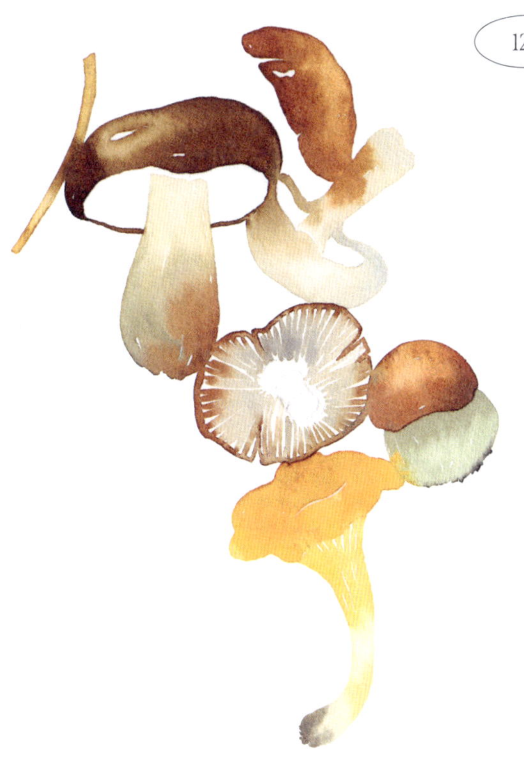

## Step 3

Let that dry again. Mix a very muted green-grey and add a bulky body to the latest small mushroom, dropping a tiny bit of dark brown at the bottom.

Now switch colours quickly to a warm yellow to paint a chanterelle mushroom, starting with its saturated cap and then diluting the yellow a little to add its wonky stalk. When it is still wet, pick up a little dark brown and drop it at the end of the stalk to imitate soil.

## Step 4

Pick up a slightly muted yet still vibrant red to paint the cap of a toadstool on the other side. Be careful to leave plenty of empty gaps within this shape to give it its iconic spotted surface.

Get rid of excess red from your brush and pick up a very diluted mix of brown. Paint another upside-down mushroom stalk coming out of the toadstool hat, dropping in a little darker brown at its bottom.

Add a tiny bit of red back to your brush and add a faint little pink mushroom cap to the left.

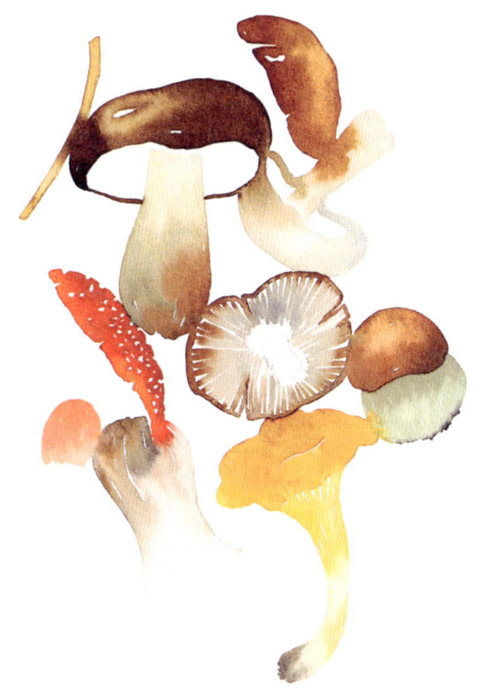

# Step 5

The composition is nearly finished! It is time to add some remaining elements.

The upside-down mushroom by the toadstool needs a cap – use dark brown to add a wavy shape. The thin stem by the side of the first mushroom we painted needs a cap. For variety, I chose a soft purple for this, painting it in parallel strokes and leaving some empty gaps in between.

The tiny pale red mushroom by the side of the toadstool needs a thin, muted yellow stalk. The toadstool itself needs a leg to stand on – use a muted pale grey-green to paint it in, dropping in some darker brown at its bottom.

Add two grey brushstrokes to the middle of the sliced mushroom. Using the same dull grey with a little cool blue, paint the very end of the mushroom whose stalk is pointing towards you – the base of its stalk should be of darker value.

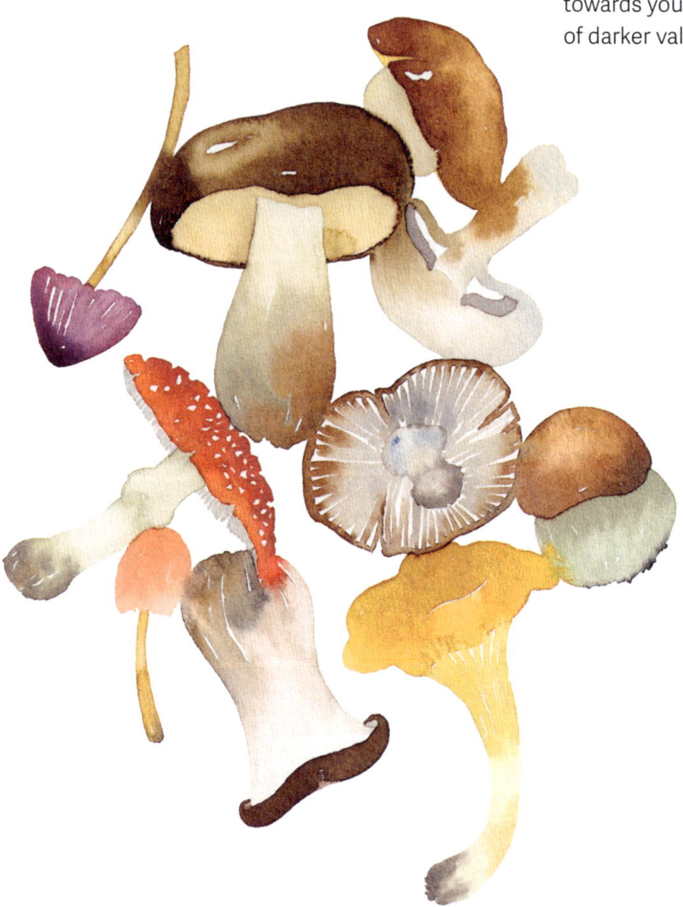

# Step 6

Finally, switch to a detail brush to add texture and irregularities.

Mix a very dark brown, nearly black, to fill in the empty gaps in the sliced mushroom. Use the same colour to add more soil to the bottom of most of the stems.

Pick up some pale grey again to add tiny strokes underneath the cap of the toadstool, and use it to add tiny dots in the middle of the sliced mushroom.

Using pale, diluted colours, add wonky lines and dots scattered around all of the mushrooms to elevate their imperfections and add subtle shading wherever you deem necessary.

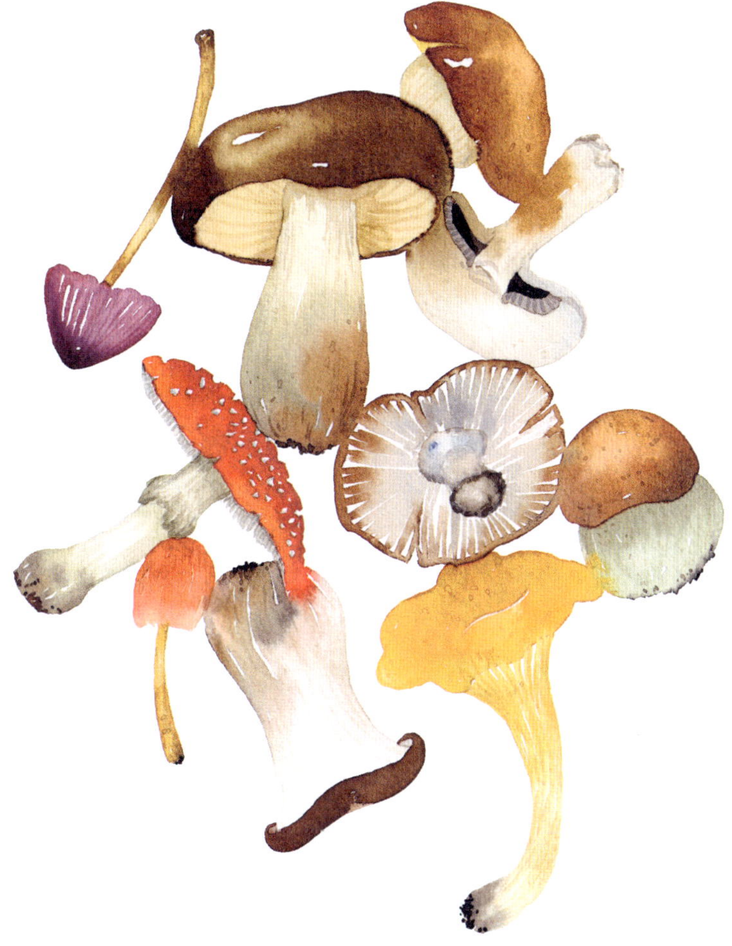

UP TO ONE HOUR

# 22/*People*

Painting people realistically is arguably one of the most difficult skills. An approachable way to attempt illustrating human figures is to focus on their outlines, hairstyles and clothes without excessive detail and particular facial features. The key is to mix appropriate colours to match realistic skin tones and sketch out natural poses before applying paint.

SUGGESTED ART SUPPLIES: COLD- OR HOT-PRESSED PAPER, PENCIL, SMALL OR MEDIUM ROUND BRUSH, DETAIL BRUSH

## PREP

I encourage you to revisit the section on Skin Tones on pages 35–36, where I outline how to mix realistic shades to match every complexion to suit your subjects.

Note I have not included colour mixing suggestions for the figures' clothing and accessories – I would like you to make your own fashion choices here and have fun with dressing the people up!

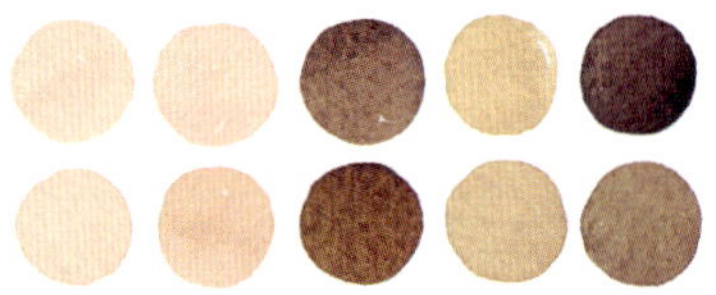

# Step 1

Using sketch 3 on page 183 as a reference, draw the human figures lightly with pencil. I opted for people doing everyday things – walking the dog, cycling, sitting, walking. After you have mixed your skin tone colours of choice, start by painting each person's complexion. Don't worry about painting the entire body – most of it will be covered by clothing in Step 2.

When painting the skin, take your time. Apply slightly diluted colours on the highlight points such as foreheads or the tops of arms. Drop in darker values at shadow areas, for example the neck or the meeting points right next to where clothing will be painted.

## Step 2

Let the skin washes dry completely. Now is the time to choose your clothing colours – this is entirely up to you, so I did not include reference swatches for that.

I like to include denim, cotton trousers, dresses, coats and t-shirts in a variety of colours. I admit this feels like creating characters in *The Sims* computer game!

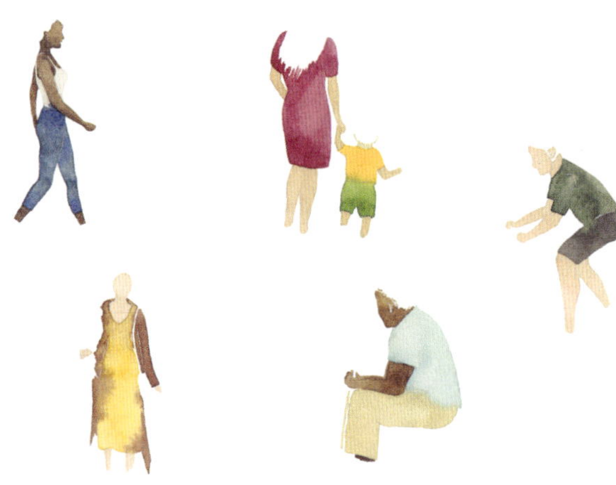

## Step 3

Let the clothes dry. We will now add the hairstyles and further details. Mix black colour to paint three of the figures' dark hair – one curly, one straight and a child's short hair. One figure will have blond hair, which requires muted yellow. Another one will have grey hair, so a very diluted black will come in handy. Another one of my characters has red hair.

Now analyse each figure and add details such as shoes, handbags, a balloon, a bicycle, a bench, a dog lead, a walking stick and any others you come up with.

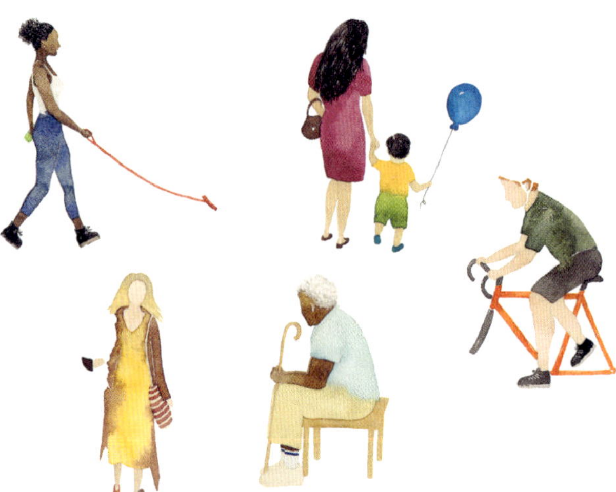

# Step 4

The final step is to add details to make the humans pop with personality. One lady is now walking a dog, the cycling man has gained a helmet and bicycle wheels, the older sitting man is wearing trainers, and the walking lady is carrying a bouquet of flowers.

Go over every illustration and add any relevant detail or shading you think necessary. I applied a little lip line and cheek colours to the two walking ladies, darkened the mother's hair, added a small beard to the cyclist's chin and added some texture to the sitting man's clothes and walking stick.

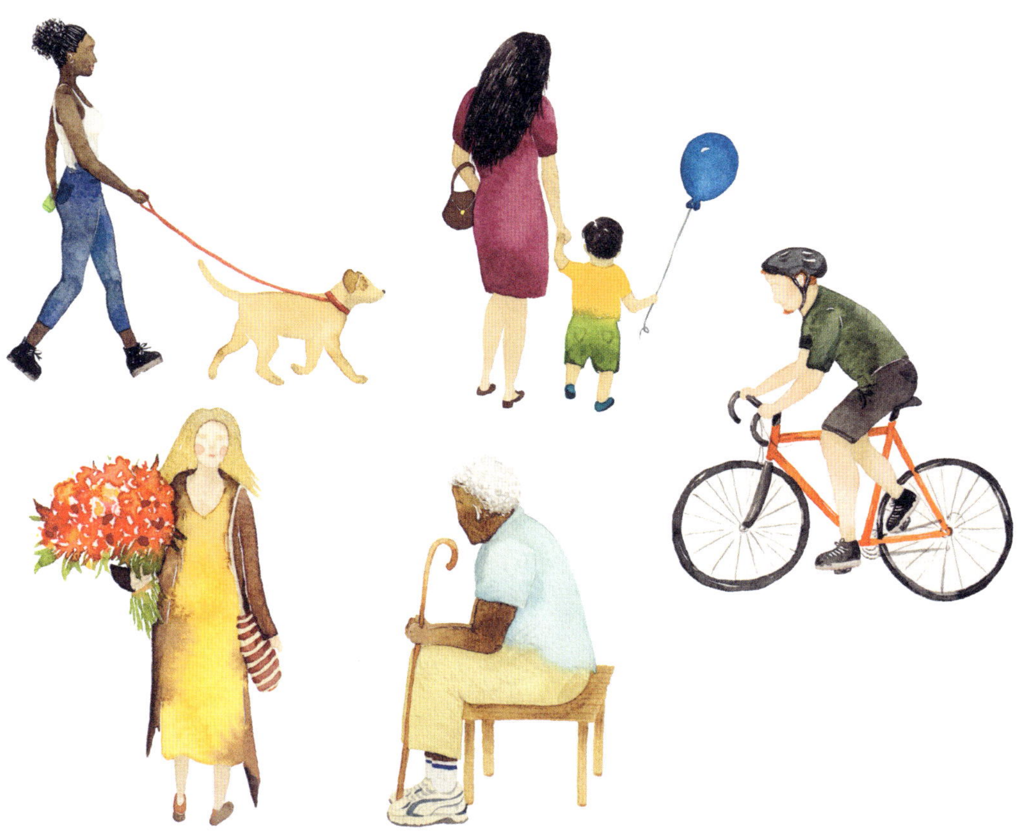

# MORE THAN AN HOUR

# 23/*Winter Landscape*

There is something serene about painting snowy landscapes, because it seems as if the snow and ice transmit a special kind of intimate silence and stillness. I like to think this scene shows a frozen lake – as if time had paused and was due to resume only when the ice started melting in spring.

SUGGESTED ART SUPPLIES: ROUGH OR COLD-PRESSED PAPER, IDEALLY 100% COTTON, PENCIL, LARGE ROUND BRUSH OR MOP BRUSH, DETAIL BRUSH

## PREP

Prepare a selection of earthy, muted tones of dark blue, grey, warm brown and subdued oranges.

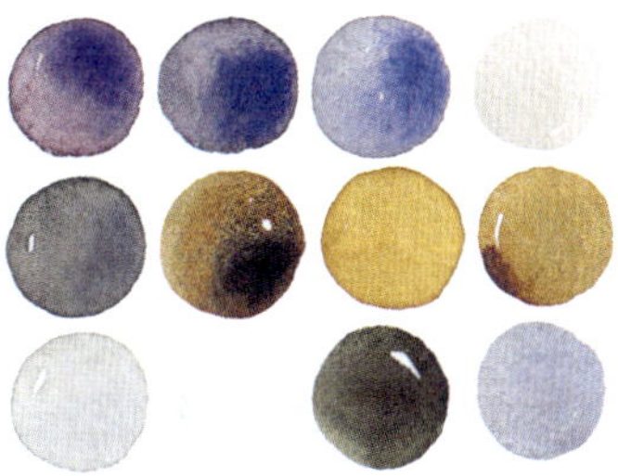

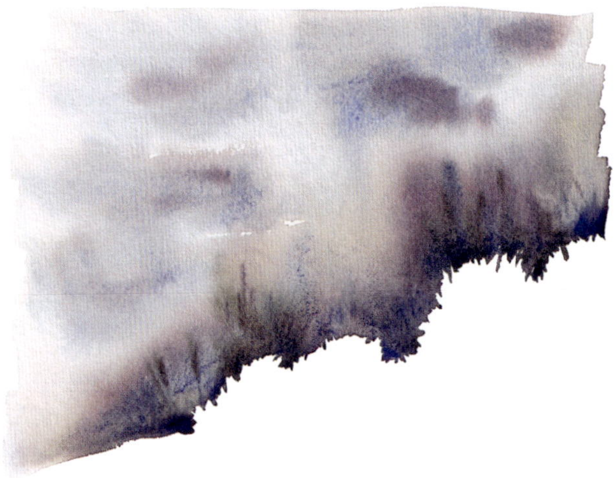

## Step 1

Sketch out the landscape using sketch 2 on page 189 as a reference.

Using a large mop or a round brush, load it up generously with clean water and lay down an even wash across the sky area. While it is still wet, quickly pick up the soft dark purples and blues and drop them onto the sky using wet-on-wet, creating clusters of colours to imitate a moody, cloudy winter sky.

Pick up a dark brown and drop it down in short, uneven brushstrokes to create a ragged edge at the bottom of the sky, thereby painting the outlines of snowy bushes.

## Step 2

Fill in the first two layers of snowy bushes with a wash of pale grey, then gently drop in earthy muted yellow using wet-on-wet.

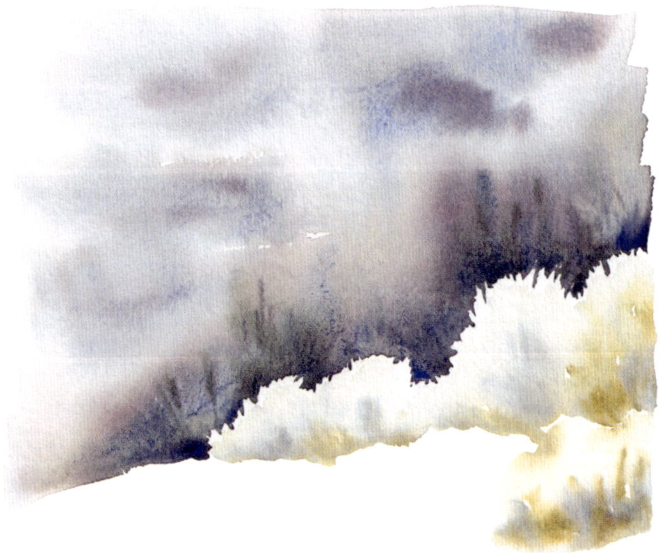

## Step 3

Continue the method from Step 2 to expand the bushes. Those in the foreground are more defined and a bit darker than the ones in the background, keeping to the rules of perspective painting.

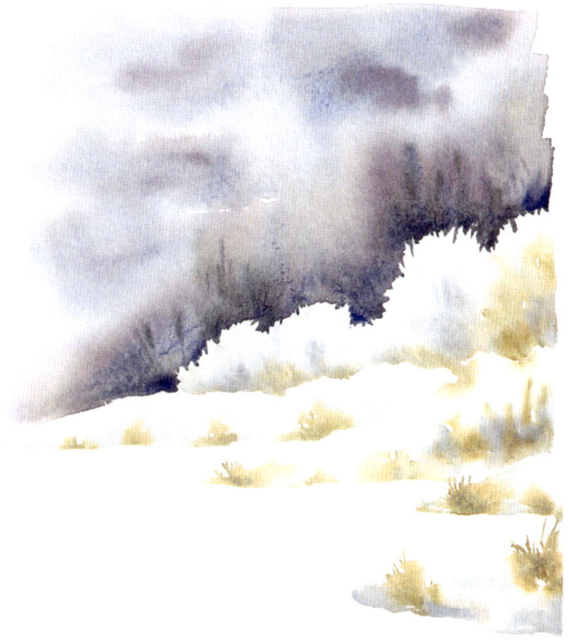

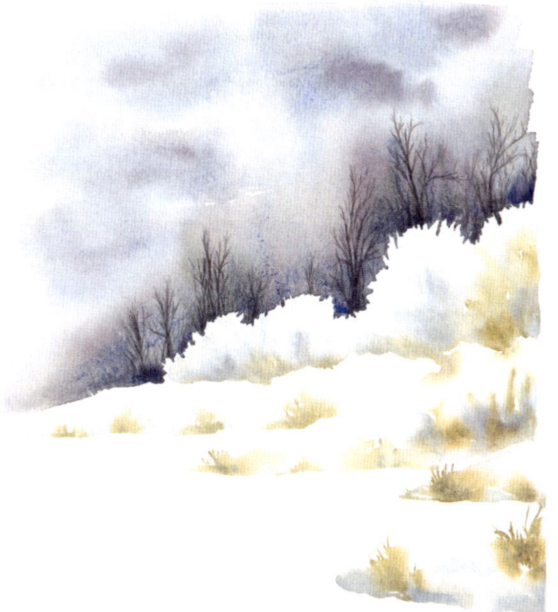

## Step 4

Using the tip of your brush or a detail brush with a dark brown mix, paint bare tree trunks and branches in the background (at the bottom of the sky).

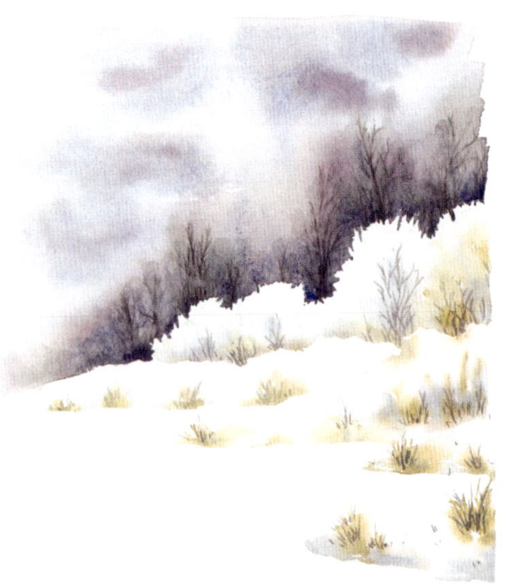

## Step 5

Use the same dark brown to add some loose branches to the bushes and additional definition to the tufts of yellow grass in front.

Take a medium round brush and load it up with a dark grey and a generous amount of water to dilute the sharpness of the tree branches in the background. Make small circular brushstrokes to create a washed-out effect. This is to soften the far perspective field and get rid of excessive detail.

## Step 6

Using a brush loaded with water, lay down a wash in between the bushy 'islands' that protrude from the water. While the layer is wet, pick up some dark grey and drop it beneath the edge where the ground meets the water. I also dropped in a little muted orange. This imitates reflections of the land on the surface of the lake.

Using a diluted grey, soften some of the branches of the bushes by applying a layer of the watery mix on top, similar to how you smoothed over the trees in the background.

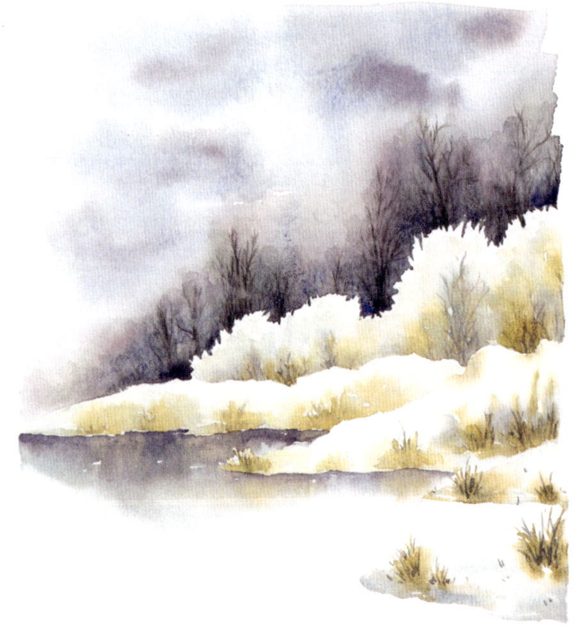

# Step 7

The last step is to extend the wash on the surface of the lake. With a lot of water and minimal amounts of grey and blue mixes, cover the rest of the empty space with a soft wash, leaving some spaces empty (you can introduce a bit of a dry brush technique). Using the tip of your brush, add an outline to the lake shore in the foreground, to enhance the contrast.

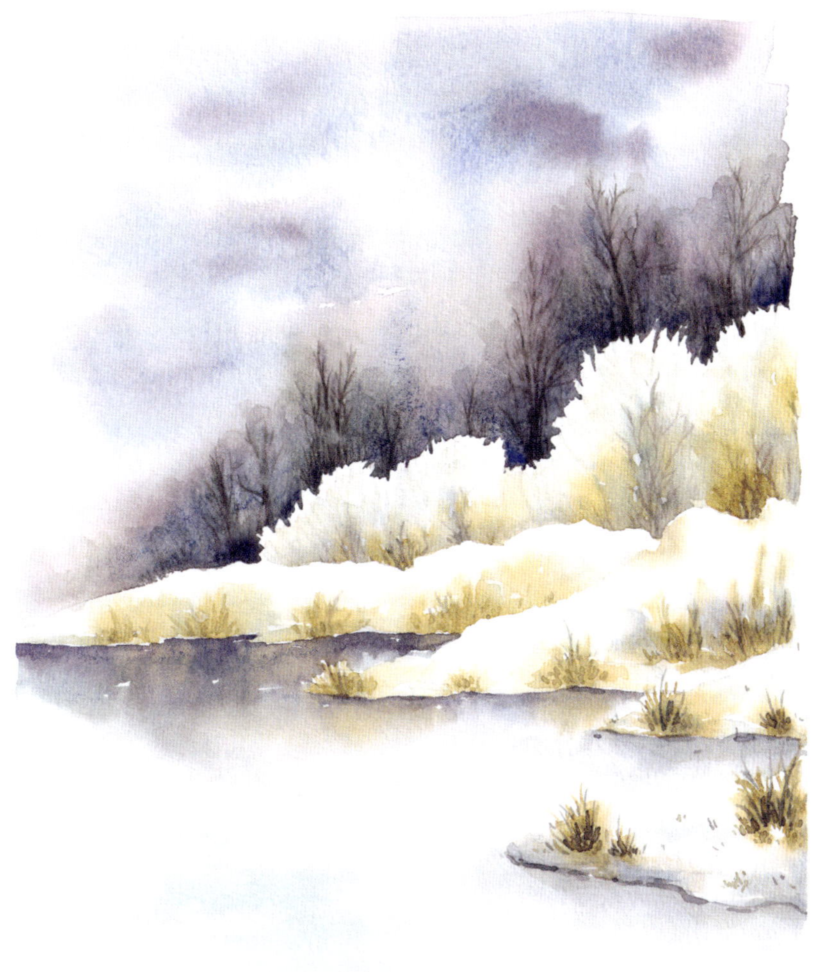

# 24/A Spring Walk

This landscape exercise will prompt you to practise many skills: perspective drawing, wet-on-wet application, painting shadows, creating vibrant colour palettes. It's the kind of illustration you could try to recreate in a sketchbook when *plein air* painting on a spring walk.

SUGGESTED ART SUPPLIES: COLD-PRESSED PAPER, IDEALLY 100% COTTON, PENCIL, MOP BRUSH, LARGE POINTY ROUND BRUSH

## PREP

Prepare a selection of bright, saturated colours: a few warm shades of green, a deep blue for the sky, deep brown, sunny yellow and rich pink for the flowers, and a muted purple for the tree's shadow.

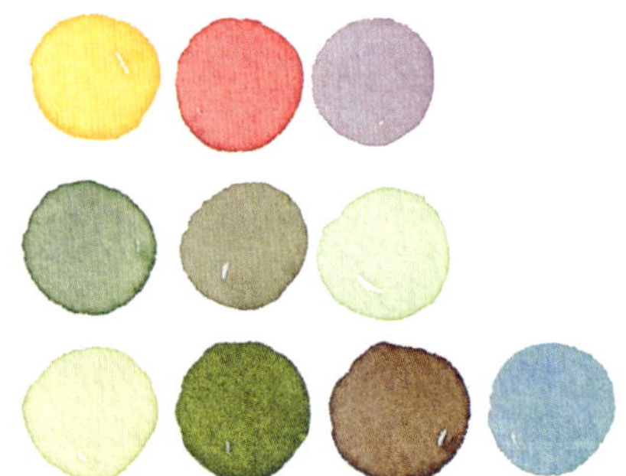

# Step 1

Make a delicate pencil sketch using sketch 3 on page 185 as a reference.

Pick up a large brush (round or flat) and load it generously with clean water to lay down a flat wash in the sky area, leaving the bottom a bit uneven and ragged.

Quickly load up the brush with your mix of blue and drop the pigment down at the top of the sky to create soft clouds using wet-on-wet application.

Before the sky dries, pick up a bit of soft green and touch the bottom edges so the green merges with the sky a little.

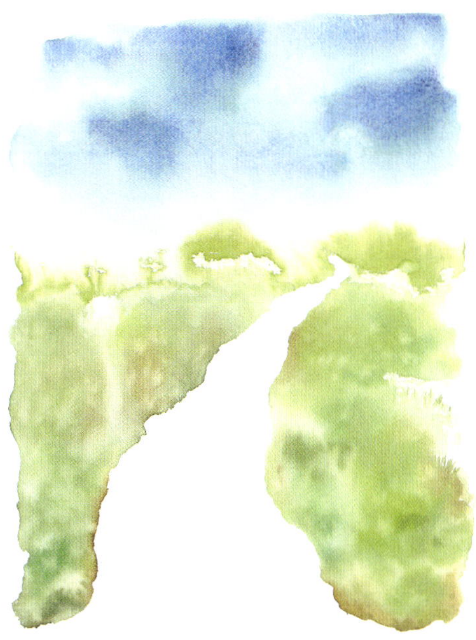

# Step 2

Continue using your greens to lay down a flat wash on both sides of the path. You can mix the various shades of green, which will create interesting dimensions. Try to leave a few empty gaps between your strokes for the same reason. At the bottom of the grass areas and by the path's edges, drop a little soft brown to indicate soil poking through.

When the grass area is still moist, clean off your brush and load it up with clean water. Lay down a few drops onto the green wash – the water will push the wet pigment sideways, creating little blooming effects across the grass.

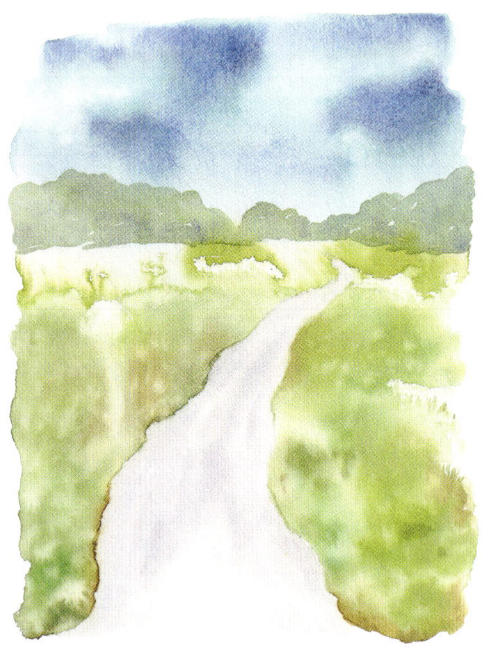

## Step 3

Let everything dry completely. Then, load up a round brush with a subdued bluish green and paint a layer of trees in the background. Make sure the strokes are soft and rounded and not detailed – the further away an object is in perspective painting, the less rigid its shapes and colours.

Clean off the brush and mix up a very pale muted yellow with hints of purple in it. Use it to fill in the path shape.

## Step 4

Let it dry completely. With the tip of your brush, add a few wonky, soft brown lines on the path to create a ragged texture.

Then load up with a darker green to paint some soft sprigs across the grass, concentrating them from the bottom to the middle of the entire grass area. Remember the further into the distance, the less detail we should see.

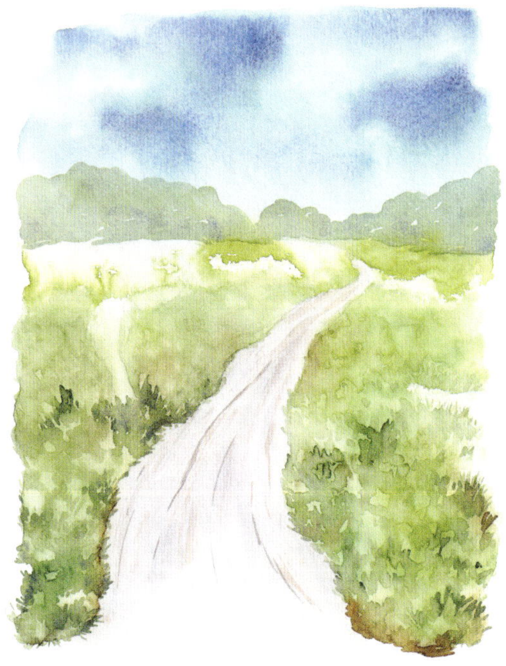

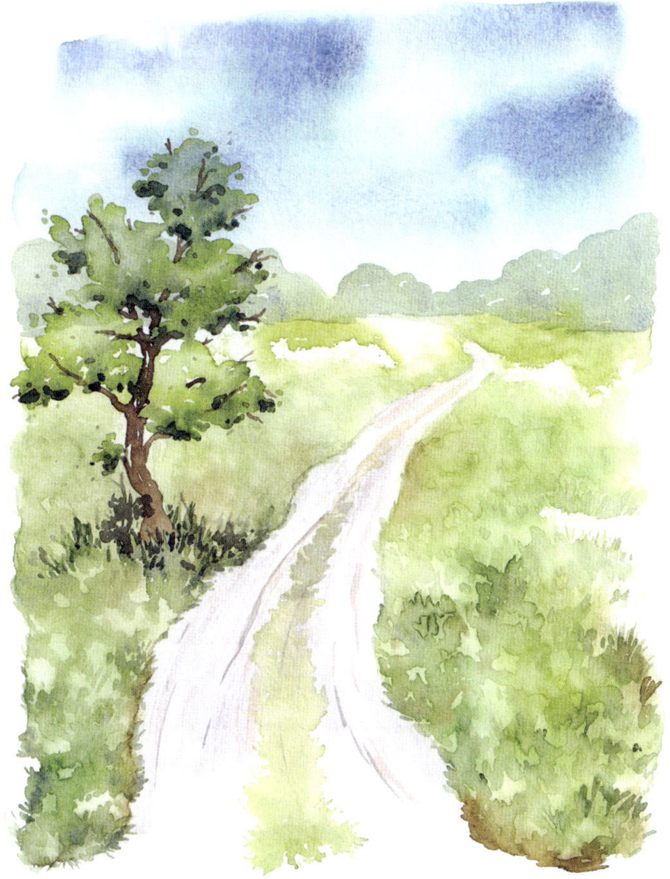

# Step 5

Keep your brush green but add more saturated colour to it to paint the tree foliage on the left. Make your strokes as loose as possible here, with some empty gaps to preserve highlights. The underside of the branches should be a darker green to indicate shadow areas.

Let the tree dry a little and pick up a dark soft brown to paint the trunk and branches. Some of them should be hidden behind the leaves – don't paint them as merely straight lines.

The brown you still have on the brush will serve well as the tree's shadow when mixed into some green. Lay down a few irregular strokes beneath the tree.

Then dilute the green and add a soft line of grass in the middle of the path. Next to the tree, the grass should be a little darker as it is shaded by the tree.

# Step 6

Pick up more green and add some individual blades of grass in the middle of the path. Then, using the same kind of scattered brushstrokes, go around the grass area and add more texture to it.

Now switch to the pale purple you have mixed at the start. Lay down a shadow beneath the tree that falls onto the path. There should be empty gaps between your strokes here too, to indicate that light is passing through the branches.

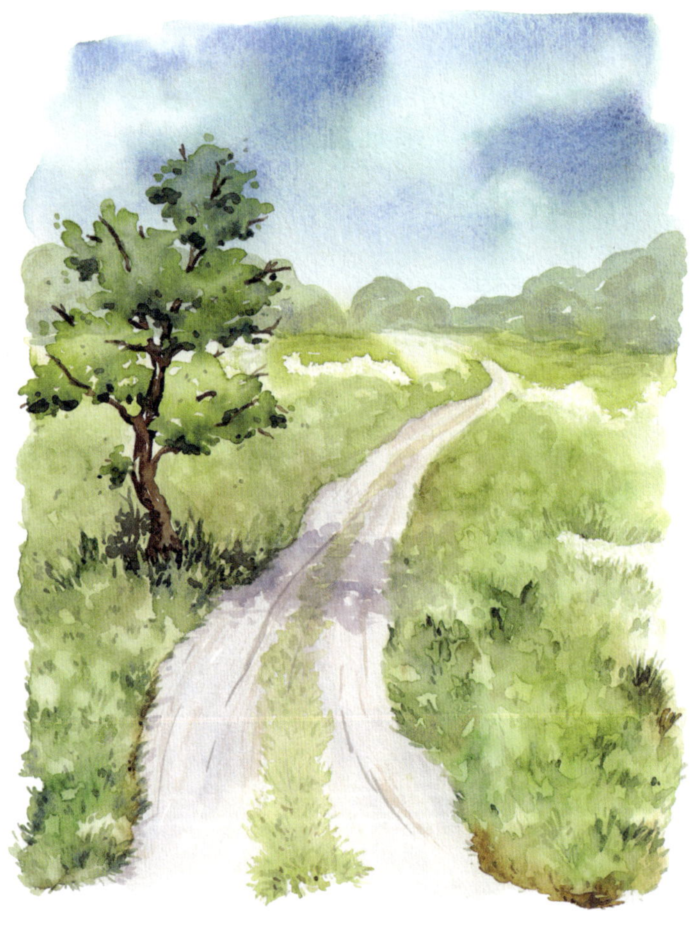

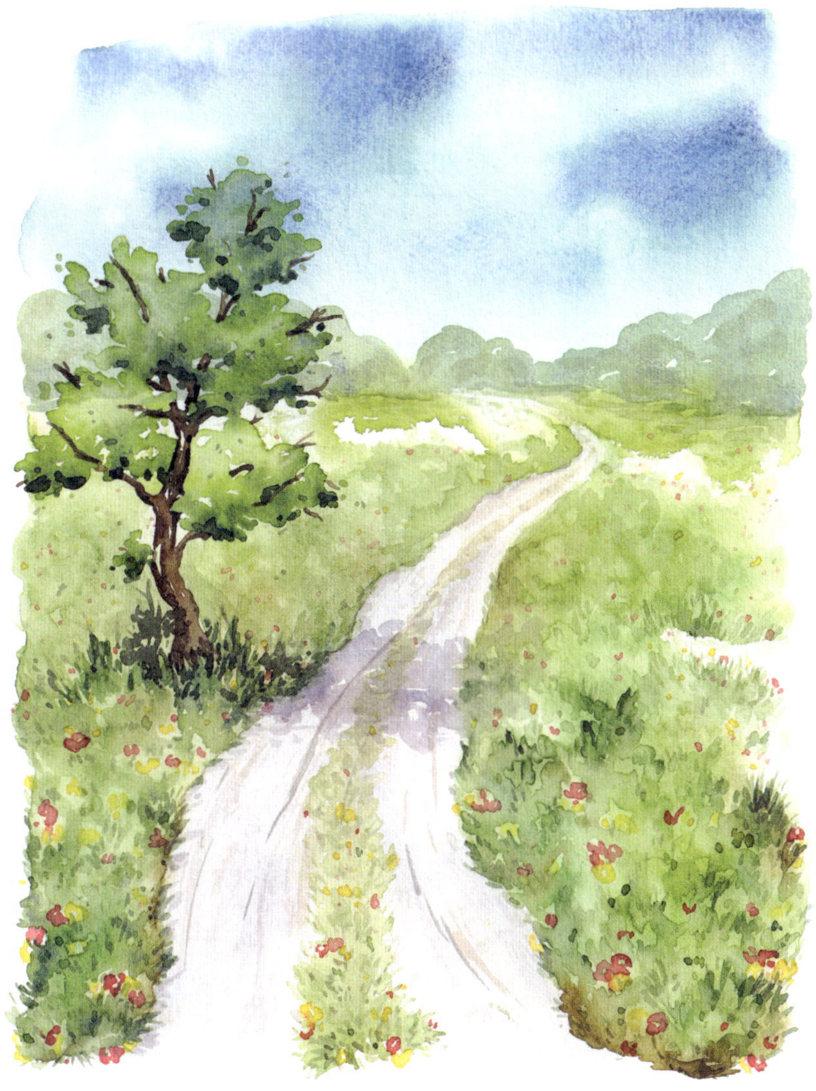

# Step 7

The last step, which feels like the cherry on top, is to paint some wildflowers.

Load your brush with vibrant warm yellow to paint a few dainty flowers and then switch to red to do the same. The petals should be bigger at the bottom of the composition and start getting smaller and more transparent as you move towards the farther distance. This will elevate the sense of perspective.

# 25/*Fig Lemon Vine*

The great thing about drawing and illustrating is that you can come up with abstract ideas and give them life on paper. This is how the marriage of lemons and figs on a vine came to be: I thought of some of my favourite fruits to paint and decided to join them in a watercolour union!

SUGGESTED ART SUPPLIES: COLD-PRESSED PAPER, PENCIL, MEDIUM POINTY ROUND BRUSH, DETAIL BRUSH

## PREP

Mix some vibrant, earthy colours in your palette. You will need a few shades of yellow ranging from bright to muted, at least one cool and one warm green, some warm browns, pale subdued orange, a red and a couple of purples for the figs.

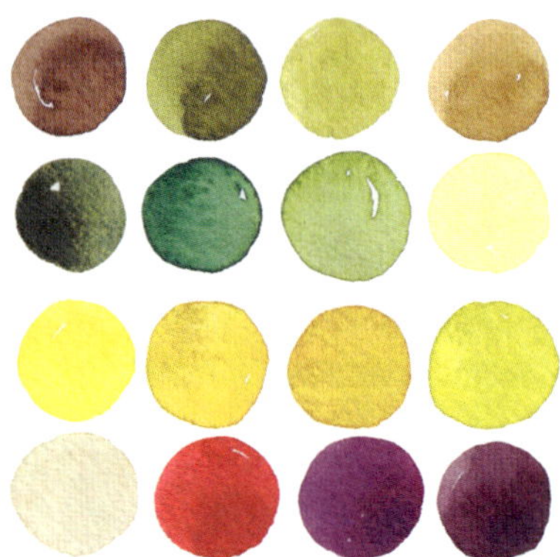

# Step 1

Before painting the final illustration, spend a little time practising the individual elements. Notice the lemon is painted as a gradient of yellow – starting from a brownish, dark shade and becoming a more transparent yellow as we add more water.

To paint a whole fig, start with the green stem and gradually change the colours as you move down its plump body. Leave a few empty gaps between the brushstrokes to preserve highlights.

The fig cut in half needs a base of a very pale yellow with an empty round shape left inside. When the shape is still wet, drop in a little reddish pink in the middle, and a bit of pale green to the stem. Once it all dries, use darker values of red to add ragged texture to the middle to create the fig's flesh.

Practise painting the lemon and fig leaves. The citrus pips are small so use a detail brush for those.

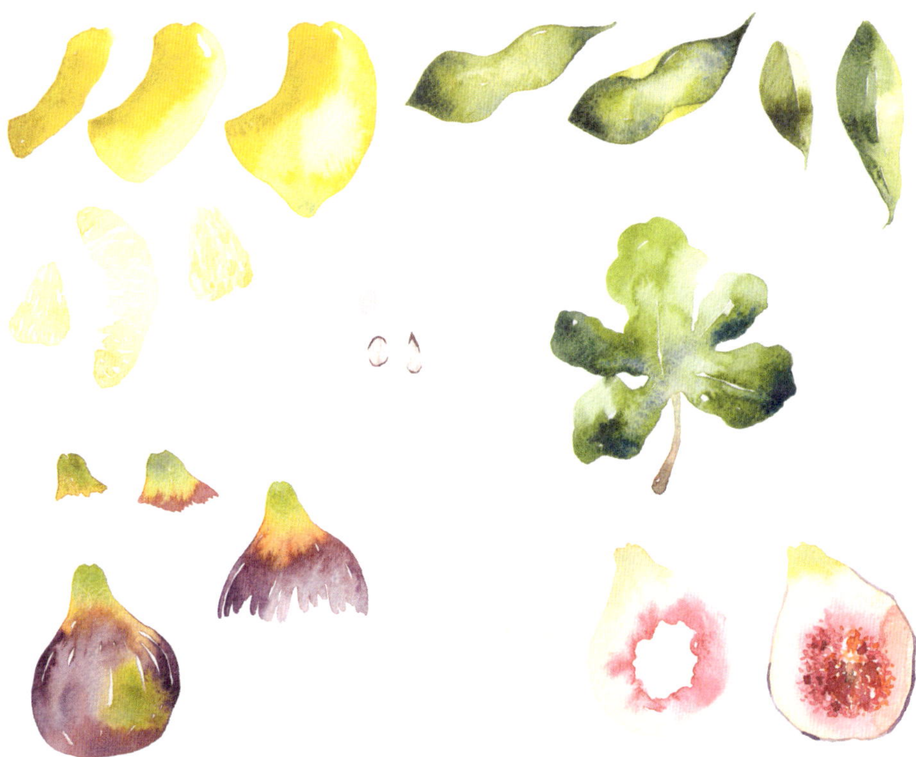

## Step 2

Make a pencil drawing using sketch 1 on page 186 as a reference. The two brown branches are the starting point, which works as an anchor for the composition. Load up a round or detail brush with light brown to paint some wonky twigs.

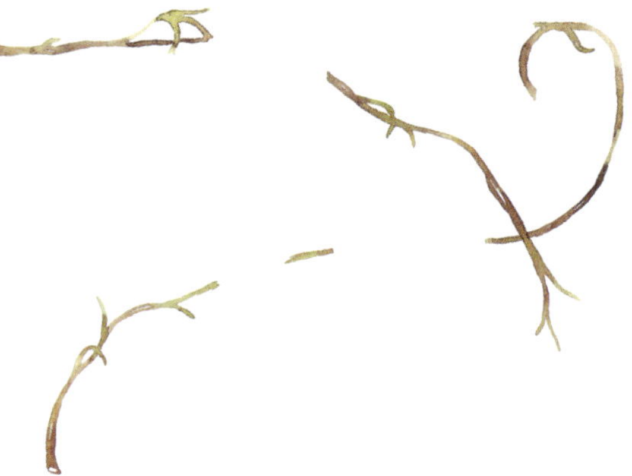

## Step 3

Load up a round brush with deep green and paint all the lemon and fig leaves. Notice that they point in different directions and vary in size, saturation and colour temperature. All of this adds up to make dense-looking foliage.

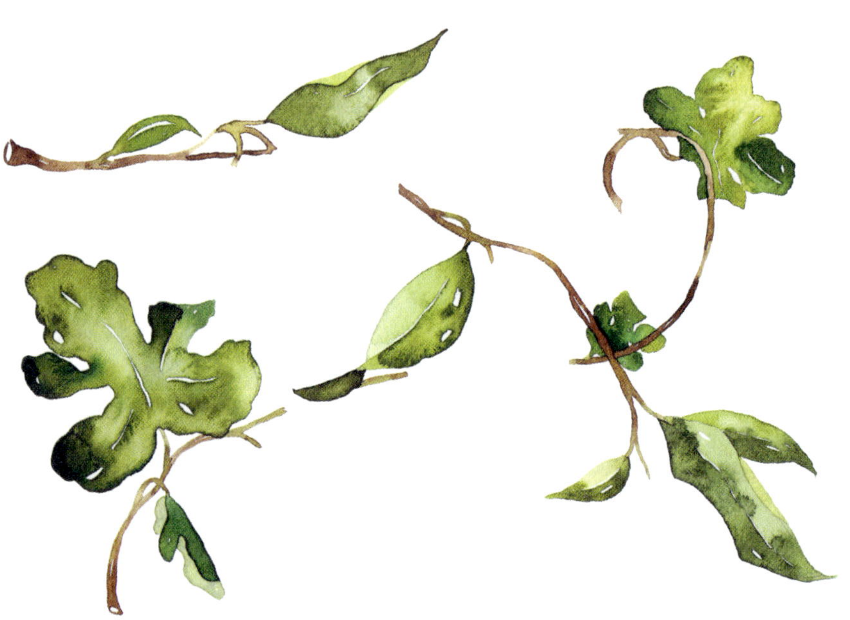

# Step 4

Let the leaves dry before loading up your brush with yellow to paint the lemons. The darker the yellow, the more you will indicate the fruit's shadows and textures. Dilute the colour to accentuate highlights. Drop in a little muted green at the tip of the middle lemon.

The lemon cut in half only requires an outline at this point – make sure you leave two crescent-shaped empty gaps inside it.

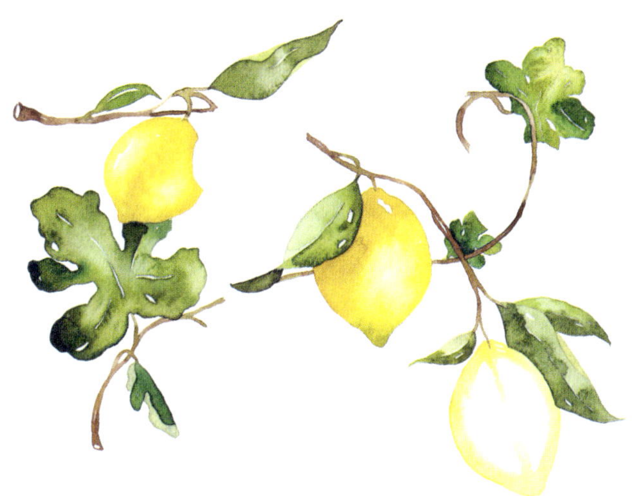

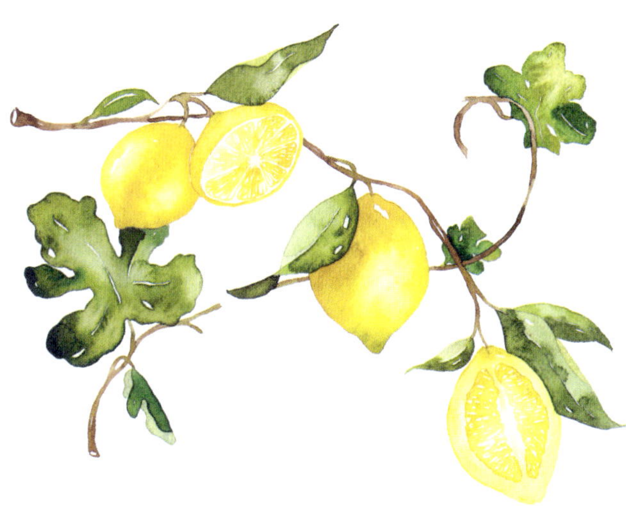

# Step 5

Let it dry. Add the remaining lemon, cut horizontally. Use a detail brush to add the lemon segments, as well as the segments of the cut lemon you painted in Step 4. Paint the segments with small irregular brushstrokes, leaving empty gaps between each one, to showcase light reflecting off the lemon flesh.

# Step 6

Move on to the figs. Paint the three whole figs first, using the technique shown in Step 1. Let them dry. Then, using a generous amount of water, apply a pale muted yellow base to the two figs cut in half. When they are still wet, drop in a little red in the middle, and some pale green at the stem, as practised in Step 1.

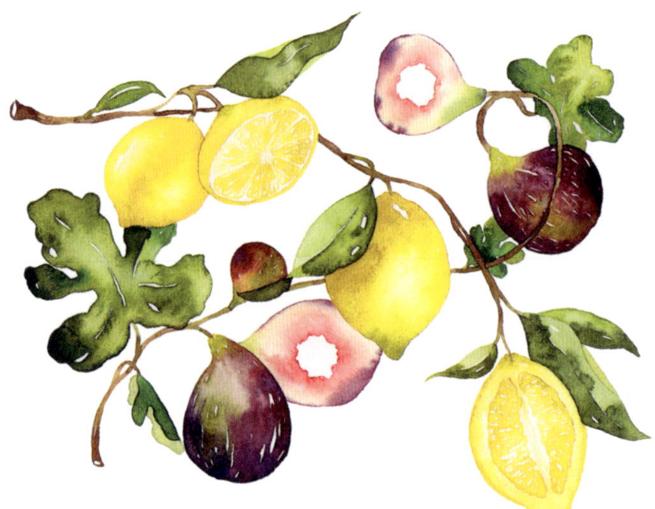

# Step 7

Using a detail brush, fill in the two cut figs with ragged irregular brushstrokes to illustrate the textured flesh. I used a combination of yellowish orange and red to achieve this effect.

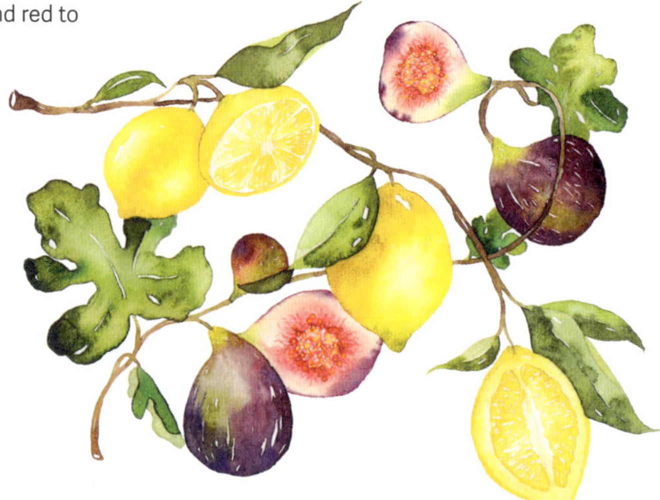

# Step 8

The last step is to add remaining details such as lemon pips, extra shading in the fig flesh, faint leaf veins across the foliage, some scattered dark dots around the leaves and extra textures along the brown branch.

Seemingly insignificant details can really elevate a painting – for example adding a sliver of dark green over the side of the bottom lemon to give that part extra depth.

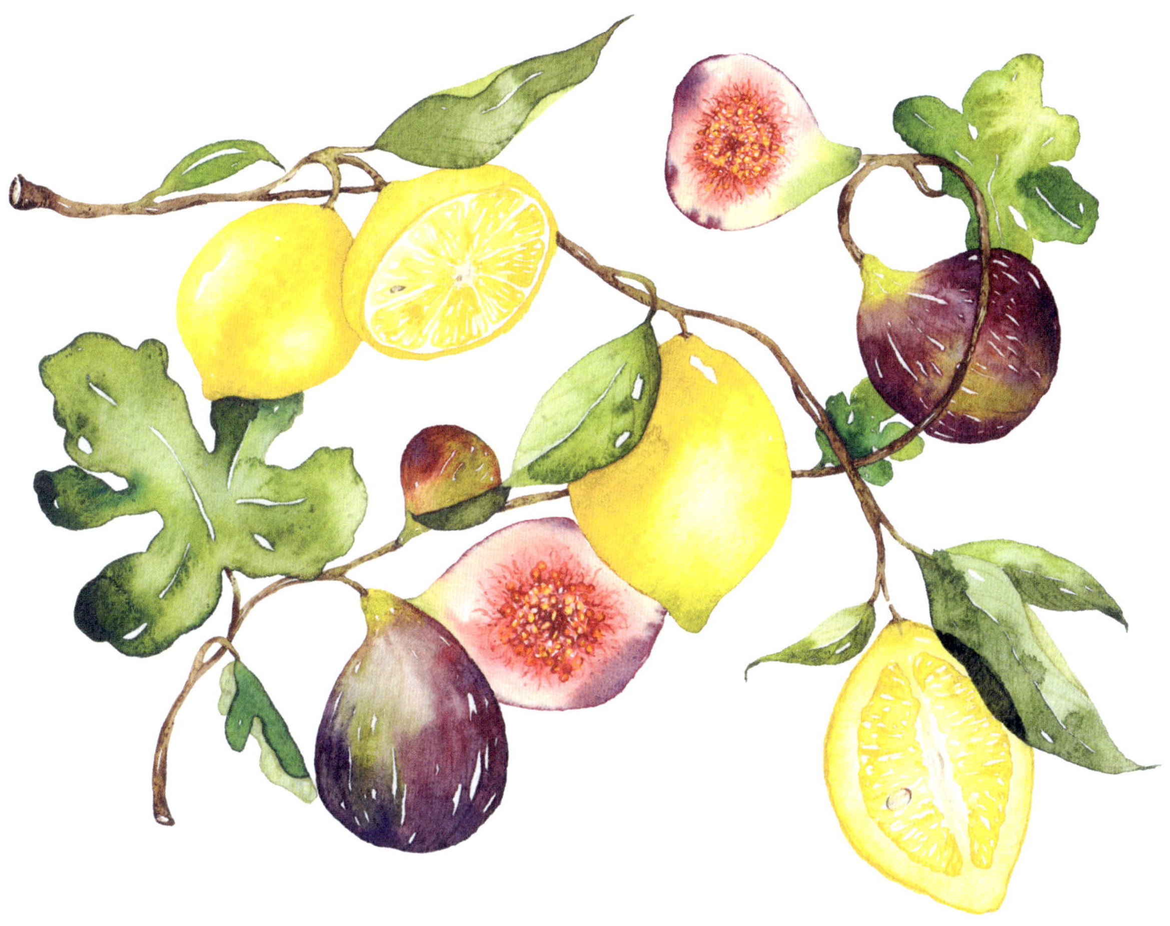

# 26/*Zebra*

The black and white stripes of a zebra are so striking in their contrast; it would be a shame not to tackle this stunning animal in watercolours.

SUGGESTED ART SUPPLIES: COLD-PRESSED OR ROUGH PAPER, PENCIL, MEDIUM ROUND OR MOP BRUSH, DETAIL BRUSH, FLAT BRUSH (OPTIONAL)

## PREP

It may seem odd to need so many colours to paint a black and white animal, but trust the subtle colour-mixing process, as the undertones will do most of the work for us here.

Prepare some black and dark brown, as well as warmer shades of brown and muted orange. Mix a pale subdued blue and a watered-down brownish yellow.

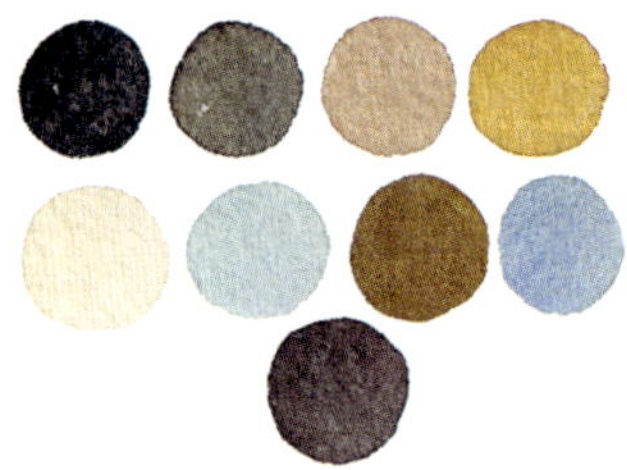

## Step 1

Sketch the zebra lightly with a pencil, using sketch 2 on page 186 as a reference.

With a medium-sized brush, pick up a generous amount of clean water and cover the entire area of the animal's body with a flat wash. While it is still wet, quickly pick up watered-down values of muted yellow and gently drop them onto the ears, nose, neck area, legs and back.

Clean off the brush and pick up a muted greyish blue, then drop it where the legs meet the body to create a base of shadows.

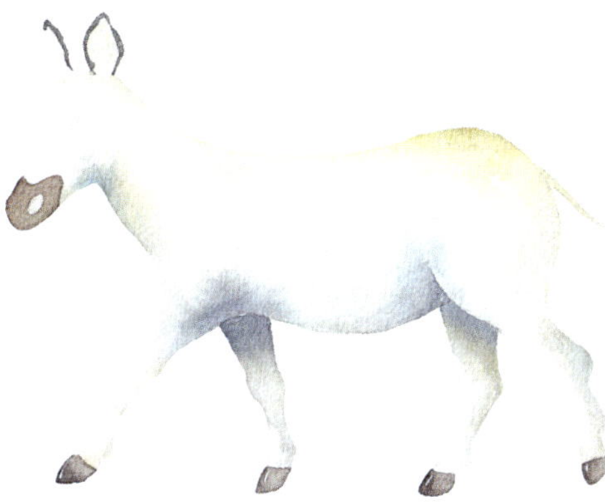

## Step 2

Wait for it to dry. Add a few more pale blue shadows to the same areas to accentuate the contrast.

Using a detail brush, pick up a pale brown to paint the outline of the ears, the nose and the four hooves.

Paint the tail a pale, muted yellow.

## Step 3

Pick up a warm, muted orange and, with short parallel brushstrokes, paint the hair on the head and neck, and add some hair to the tail. Add extra shading to the tail with some dark brown.

Use black to outline the eye shape and fill in the nostril.

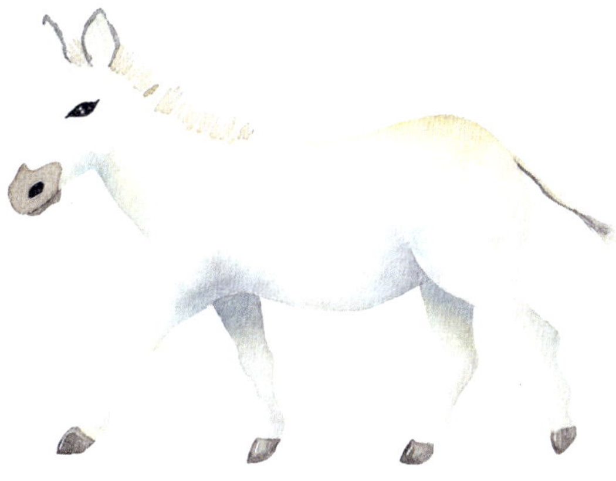

# Step 4

Now for the stripes! Using a brush with a fine point, paint dark grey curved lines across the body. Feel free to follow the stripe pattern of my zebra, as the lines can get confusing.

Notice that the insides of the legs have fewer stripes on them.

A fun little detail: add a small eyelash by the zebra's right eye.

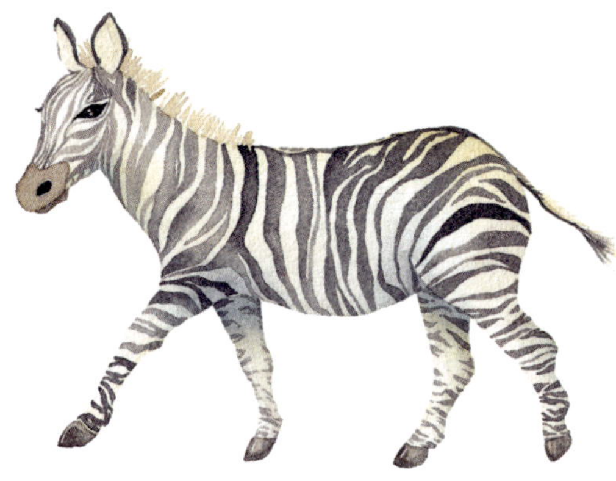

# Step 5

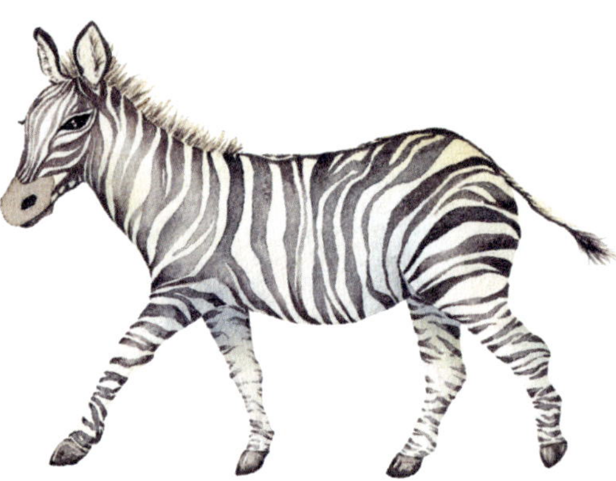

Now we will go over the body of the animal and enhance the contrast throughout. Pick up an earthy dark brown to add more definition to the hair, the inside of the ears and the outlines of the hooves.

Load up a dark brown (or black) and use it to add contrast to the tail hairs and the outlines of the ears.

Finally, go over the dark brown and black stripes again to add extra depth. I like to add extra layers of shading on the edges of the stripes, for example at the top of the back and the rear.

# Step 6

The last step is to give our zebra somewhere to stand. Pick up a large brush – I used a flat one – and pick up earthy tones of brownish orange and muted yellow.

Using a dry brush technique, make sweeping brushstrokes underneath the zebra's feet to create dry grassland, being careful not to paint over its legs.

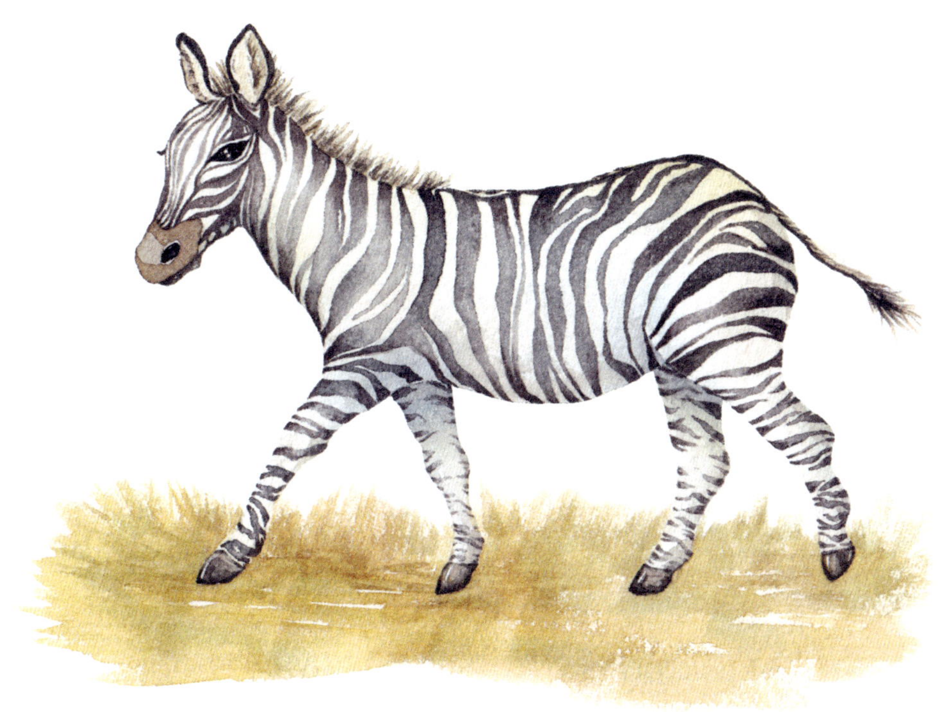

# 27/*View of an Abbey*

This charming view is of the Benedictine Abbey in Tyniec, Poland. The monastery is located close to Kraków; its age-old history and picturesque location attract many visitors. It is built on a rock cliff overlooking the majestic Vistula River, surrounded by lush greenery. It is a great subject for a landscape painting which incorporates a little architecture. The scene has depth and complexity, but at the same time is not overly difficult to illustrate.

SUGGESTED ART SUPPLIES: COLD-PRESSED PAPER, IDEALLY 100% COTTON, PENCIL, FINE-LINE DRAWING PEN, LARGE ROUND BRUSH OR MOP BRUSH, DETAIL BRUSH, TABLE SALT

## PREP

Prepare a selection of warm greens in different shades, some muted browns for the stone walls and rocks, a pale sky blue and a brick-red for the abbey's roof.

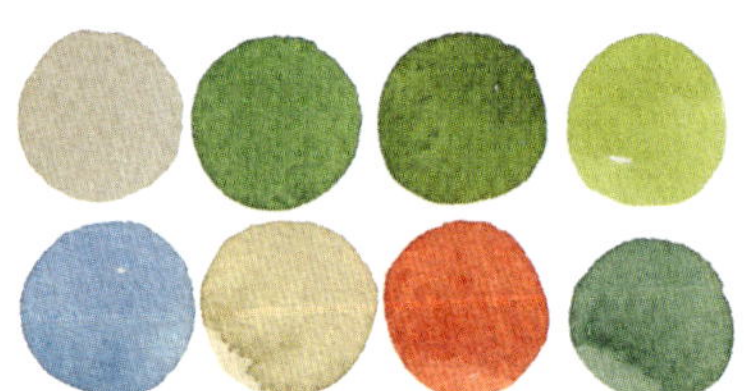

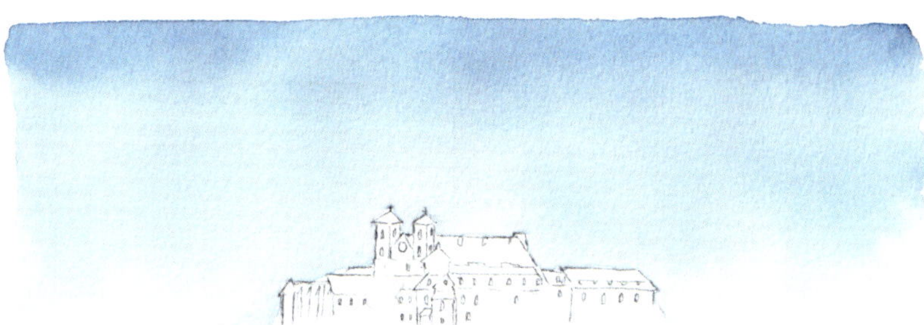

## Step 1

Sketch out the shape of the Tyniec Abbey using sketch 3 on page 187 as a reference. I drew it with a pencil first, and then went over the outlines of the walls, roof and windows with a fine line drawing pen to make the building pop against the background.

Pick up a mop or a large round brush and load it up with a lot of water. Lay down a flat wash of just clear water on the sky area, then quickly pick up your blue and drop it down from the top of the paper to create a soft gradient – you want the blue to become nearly transparent when it reaches the building.

## Step 2

Wait for the sky to dry. Then load up a smaller brush with the muted yellowish brown to fill in the walls of the abbey. Switch to the brick-red colour and fill in the roof area. Add a little cool bluish green to fill in the monastery's two tiny towers.

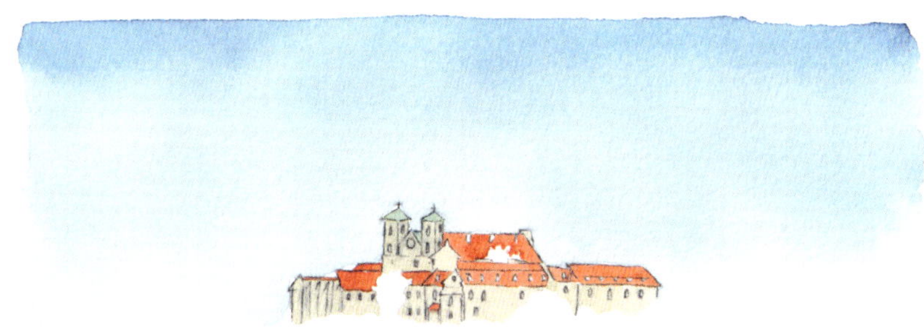

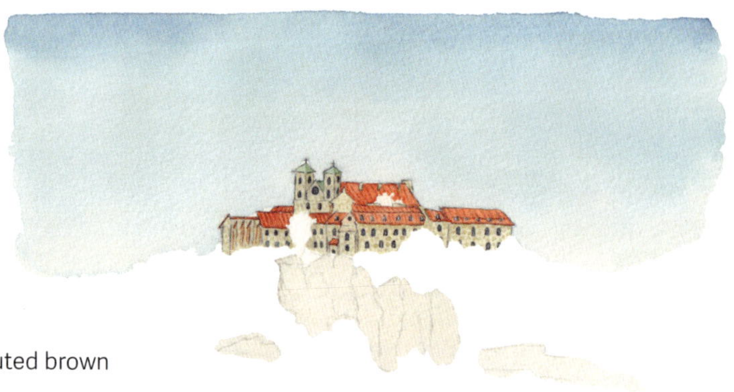

## Step 3

Switch the colour to the soft muted brown to fill in the rocks. Let it dry.

Then, using your fine-line pen, add some more defined lines to the windows.

## Step 4

Using a large round or a mop brush, load it up with plenty of water and a warm, saturated green. Fill in the greenery around the building and the rocks with a varied but evenly-laid wash. Apply a denser pigment in shadow areas such as by the riverbank and behind the abbey; use more water in your green mix in the sections more exposed to light.

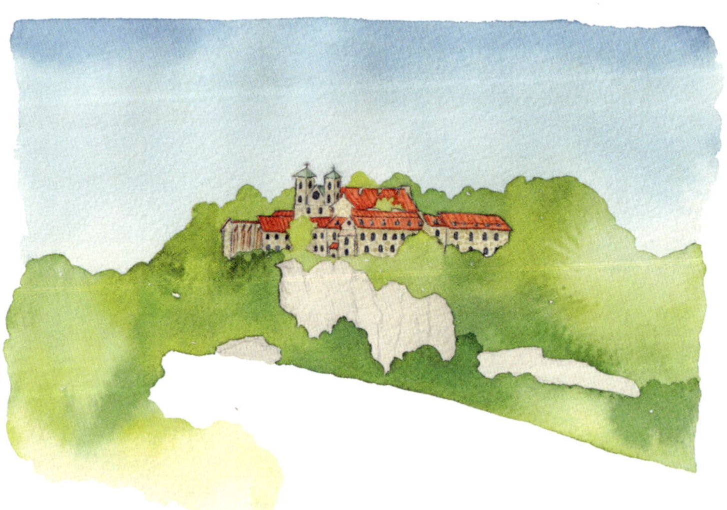

# Step 5

Let the greenery dry a little. Pick up a greyish blue and fill in the river area, dropping in a little muted yellow by the shoreline to indicate sand showing through and reflecting off the water.

When the river area is still wet, drop a little table salt across it. Wait for it to dry.

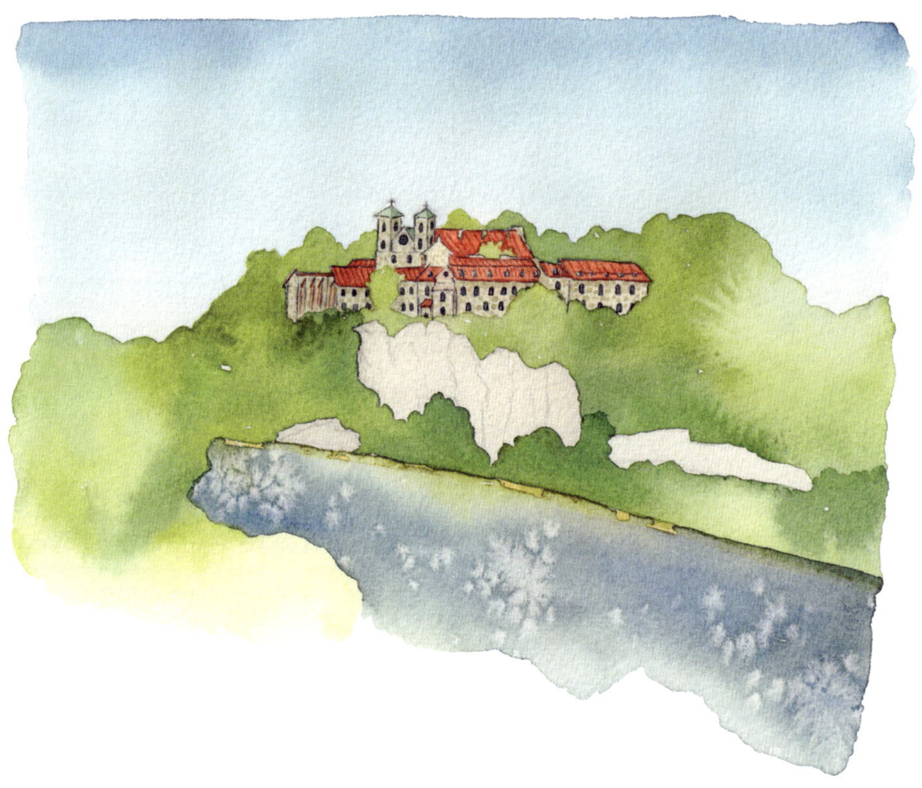

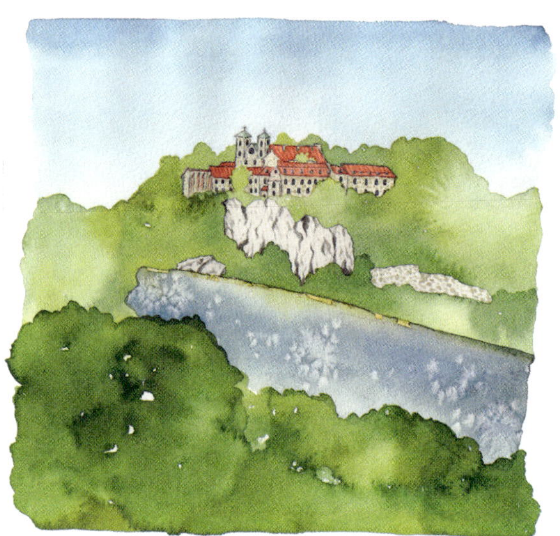

## Step 6

Get a detail brush and mix a mid-toned grey to mark the cracks in the rock and indicate small bricks on the ancient wall to the right.

Return to a larger round brush or a mop brush, and your green mixes – this time picking up a darker shade. Using a rich application, paint the bushy greens in the foreground, leaving some empty gaps between brushstrokes to enhance texture.

## Step 7

Dilute the dark green a little and return to the background trees. Give them some texture and layers by putting down soft round brushstrokes all around the foliage – don't make it too dark though, as the further away things are in a composition, the less detail they usually need.

Add some extra bits of greenery on the rock surfaces. Go back to the muted brown and add a little shading to the rocks, especially by its edges and along the bottom.

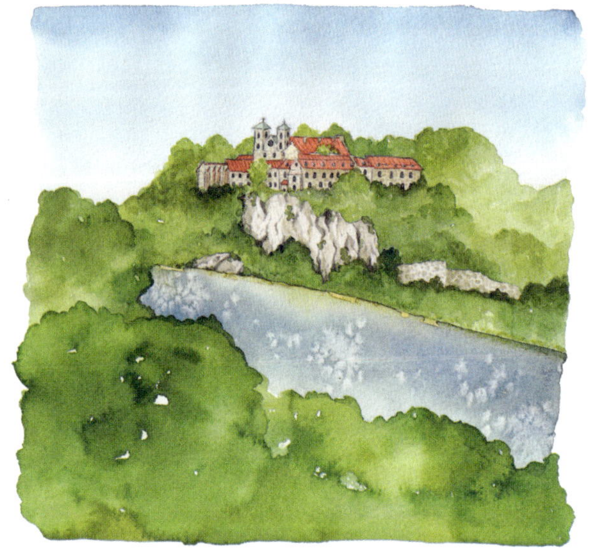

# Step 8

The last step is to add more texture to the greenery in front. Using a rich, deep green mix, go over the bushes by laying down soft, rounded brushstrokes. Make some of them darker than others.

At the end, pick up a detail brush or the tip of a round brush and add scattered, irregular dots all around the foreground foliage to elevate the uneven surface of the greenery, using the same deep green as Step 7.

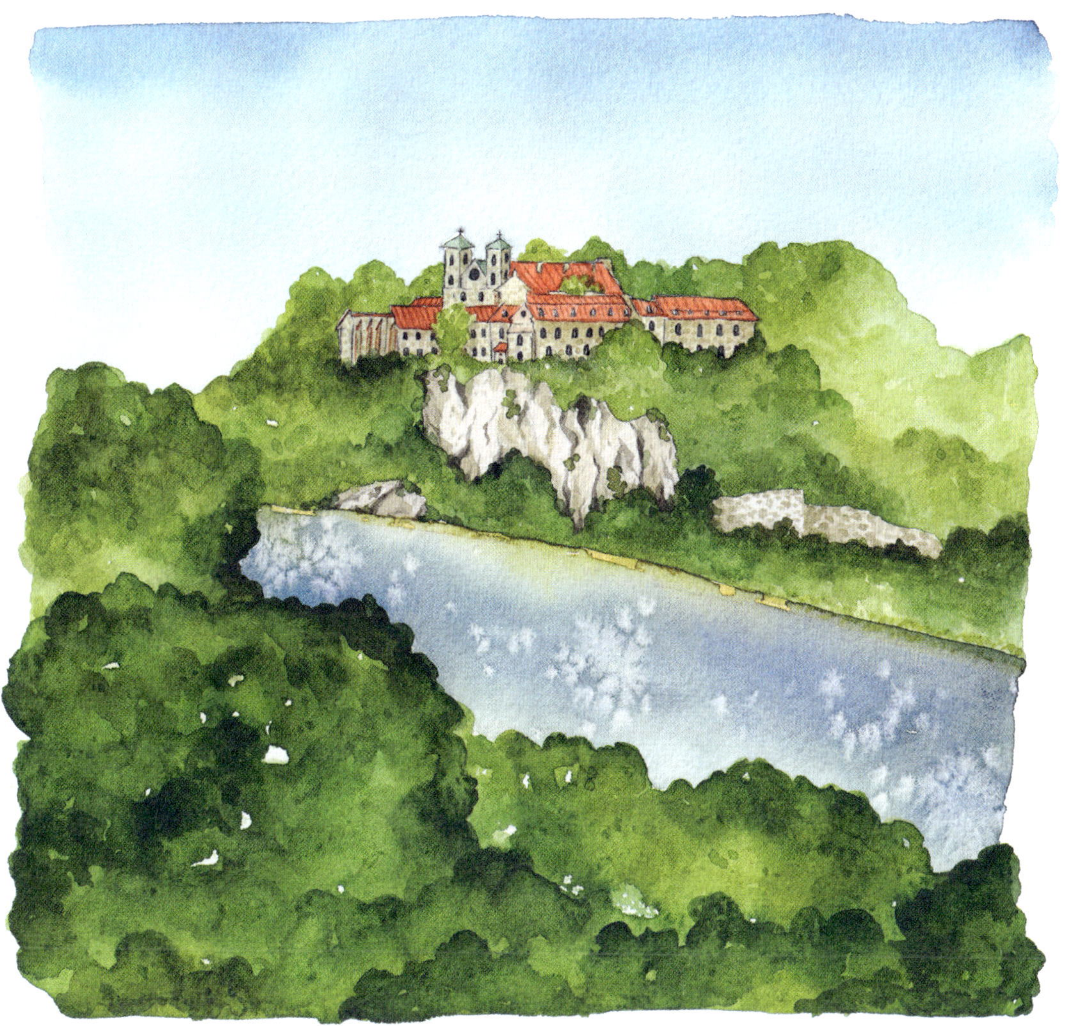

# 28/*White Wisteria Flowers*

If you are new to watercolour painting, you might think painting white objects means using white paint – like in acrylic or oil painting. In watercolours, however, it is best to work with the transparency of different pigments to achieve an illusion of the colour white, as that will give the most delicate and subtle effects.

SUGGESTED ART SUPPLIES: HOT- OR COLD-PRESSED PAPER, PENCIL, POINTED MEDIUM ROUND BRUSH, DETAIL BRUSH

## PREP

Prepare a range of colours: soft pinks and a purple, a few shades of warm and muted greens, subdued yellows and pale greys with little hints of blue.

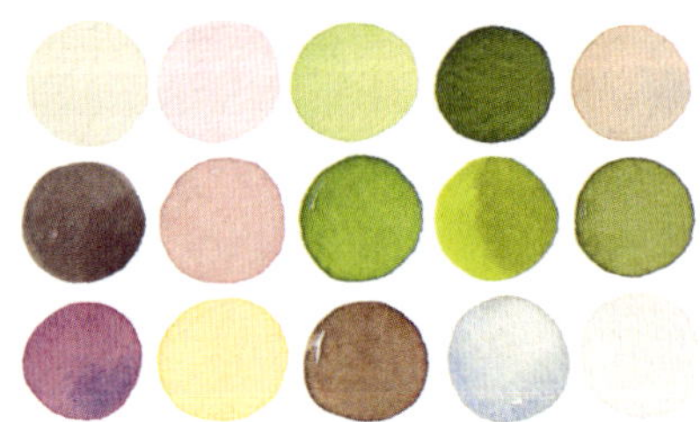

# Step 1

### TRIAL 1: WHITE PETALS

Before you tackle the cascading wisteria, I would like you to familiarise yourself with the individual shapes that make up these dainty flowers. Start small and sketch out some petals. Using a generous amount of water, paint some oval shapes and drop in tiny bits of grey, green, pink and yellow to give them subtle tints, but keep them transparent – and therefore 'white'.

### TRIAL 2: FLOWER SHAPES AND BRANCHES

Use the petal shapes above to make up compound flower shapes. It is good to practise painting the petals pointing in various directions to build up the variety of composition. Always drop a tiny bit of yellow in the middle of each flower. Sketch some flower buds too, and a curved brown branch.

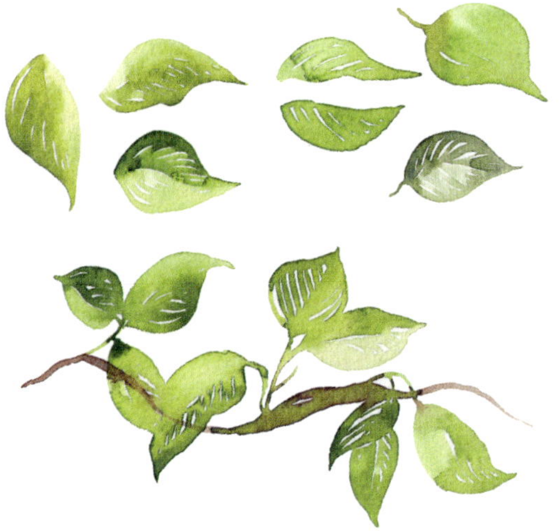

### TRIAL 3: LEAVES

Now practise painting rounded leaves. I like to leave empty gaps in between the brushstrokes that make up a leaf to preserve luminosity. Again, get familiar with 'twisting' the leaves in various directions and working with varying paint saturation to create contrast and depth.

# Step 2

Let's paint the cascading wisteria composition.

Now that you feel more comfortable with all the elements of the white flowers, I would like you to try and paint an entire branch of flowers loosely so that you can get immersed in the process. Move from top to bottom, using a generous amount of water and hints of other colours dropped around the petals.

Once the flowers are painted, pick up a detail brush, load it with a warm green and add the vertical stem – some of it should poke through, but most of it should be hidden behind the flowers.

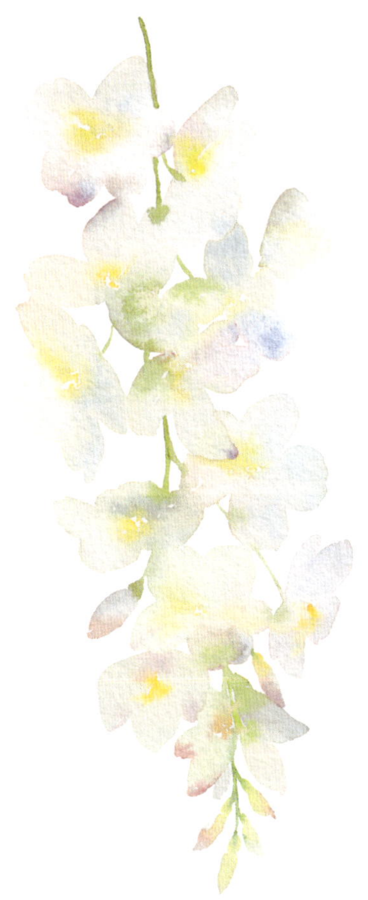

## Step 3

Pick up some warm dark brown and add a branch above the flowers. Leave gaps in the line of the branch so there is space for leaves to overlap it later.

## Step 4

Before we move on to the leaves, paint another cascading cluster of white flowers next to the first one. Use the same technique but begin a little lower down and finish lower as well – this is to create a dynamic composition.

Are you now able to notice how even though we are not using white paint, the transparency of watercolour is creating an elegant imitation of whiteness? It is important to remember that white, like other colours, comes in a variety of shades.

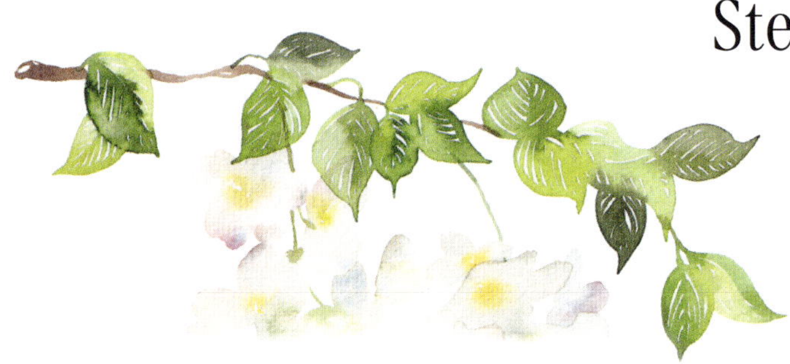

## Step 5

It is time to add the pop of colour – foliage. Go back to your vibrant greens and paint some leaves coming off the branch, as practised in Step 1, Trial 3.

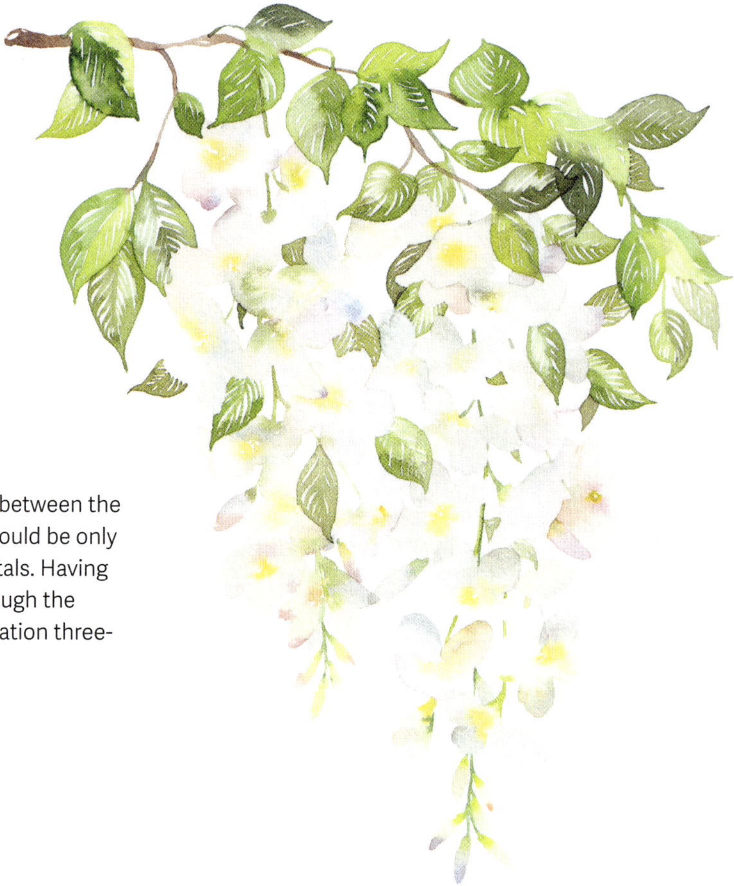

## Step 6

Add a few more leaves in between the flowers. Some of them should be only half visible behind the petals. Having parts of them poking through the cascade makes the illustration three-dimensional.

# Step 7

Lastly, working with a detail brush, go over the illustration to add some textures and irregularities. I added little dots of warm yellow in the middle of the flowers to indicate pollen. You can add faint grey lines to the petals to give them a little more texture. Add a tiny bit more contrast to the branch by layering some more brown on top.

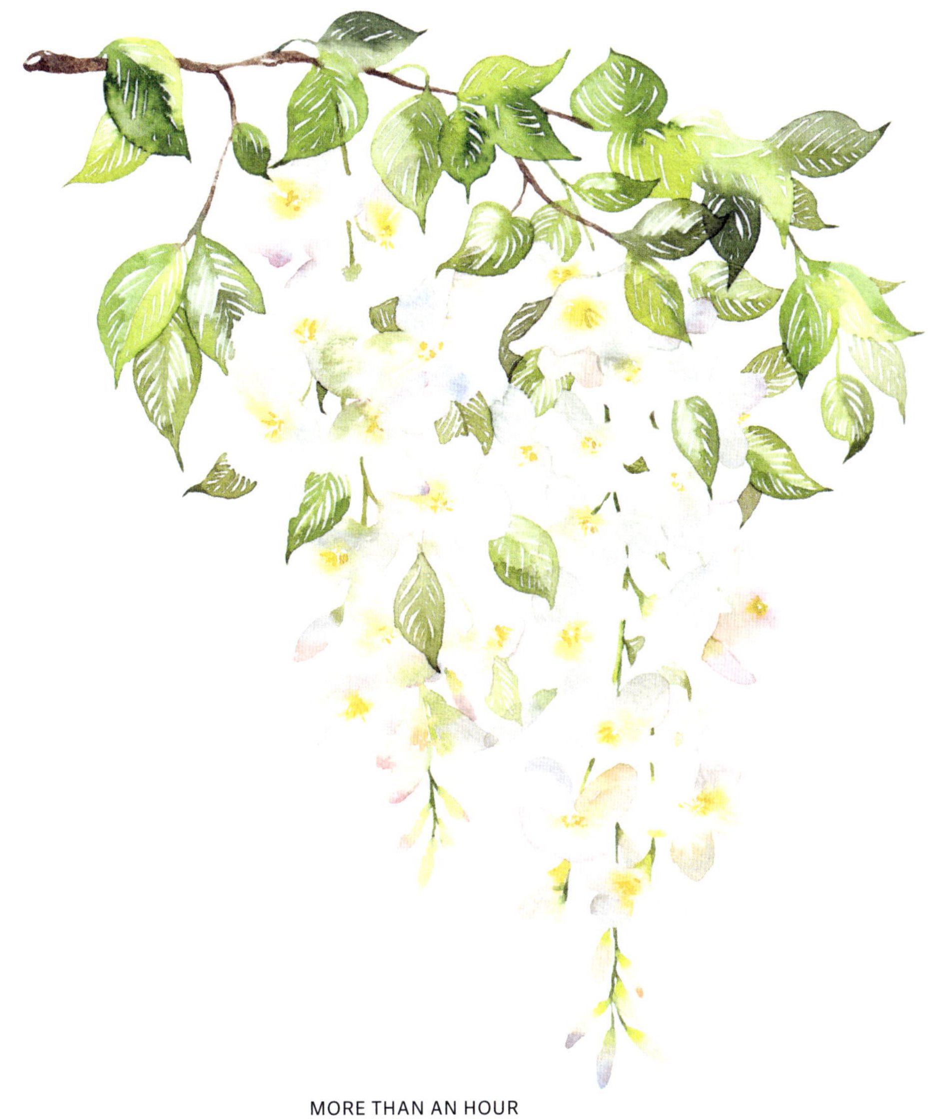

# 29/*Italian Oranges*

Drift away into a daydream where the scent of fresh leafy Sicilian oranges fills a room in a seashore house where you are staying. The blue window shutters create a magical contrast between the ledge and the lush seascape outside. A real room with a view.

SUGGESTED ART SUPPLIES: COLD-PRESSED PAPER, PENCIL, MEDIUM POINTY ROUND BRUSH, DETAIL BRUSH

## PREP

Prepare an array of colours so that you can lean into the painting and have all the shades ready to hand. I mixed a few dark blues in both cool and warm temperatures, a soft sky blue, an array of warm greens, a few shades of deep orange plus some browns in light and darker values.

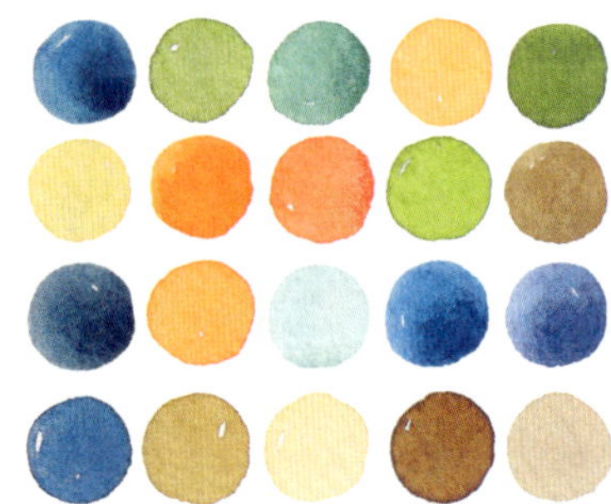

# Step 1

Sketch the window composition lightly with a pencil using sketch 1 on page 188 as a reference.

Start by laying down a very faint wash of pale blue across the sky and the sea. Leave empty spaces where the oranges will hang, as well as the protruding piece of land to the left.

# Step 2

Wait for the layer of blue to dry before picking up some muted yellow to indicate the sand. Then immediately pick up a warm mid-toned green to apply to the land; the sand and the greenery should blend into one another for a soft look.

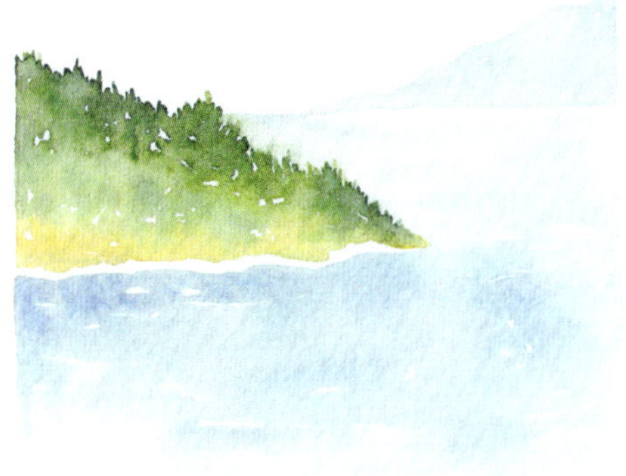

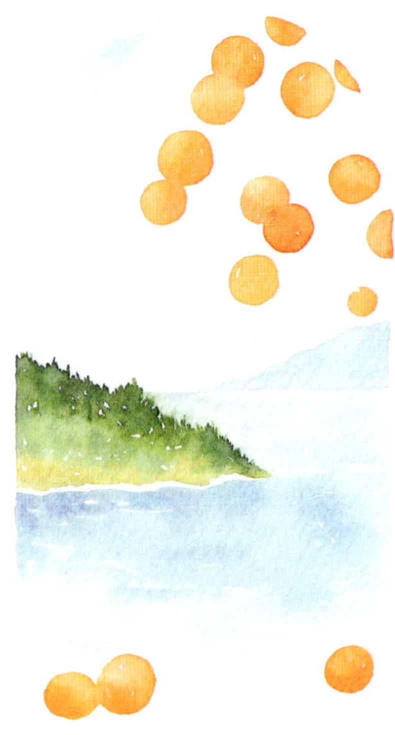

## Step 3

Load your brush with a rich, saturated orange. Varying the ratio of water to pigment constantly, fill in the circular gaps with orange shapes, making some of these paler than others.

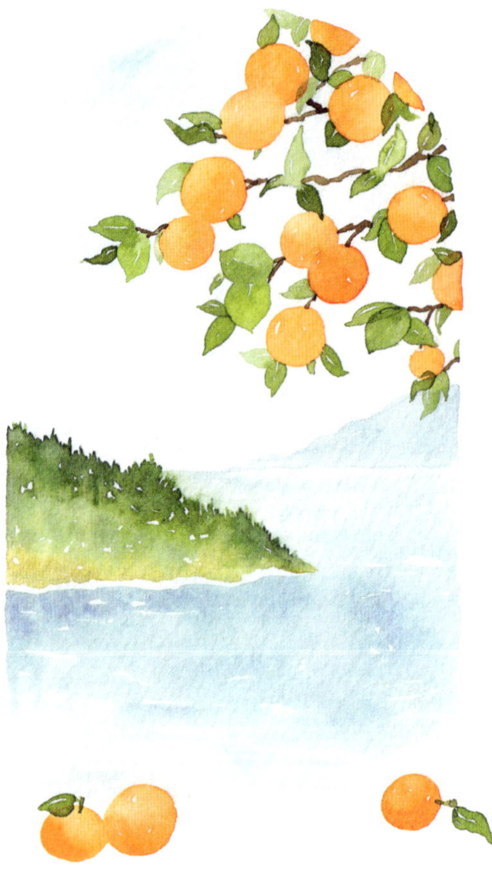

## Step 4

Let the oranges dry completely before going back to a green to add the leaves scattered over the tree and on the windowsill.

Pick up a warm brown and paint in some branches between the fruit and the foliage.

## Step 5

Keep the brown on your brush for now and fill in the outline of the window and the windowsill. Using small brushstrokes, go over the area of the wood but leave small empty gaps. Vary the amount of brown pigment you are applying, sometimes making the colour darker and then diluting it with some water. The more variety in the saturation, the more captivating the colour depth will be.

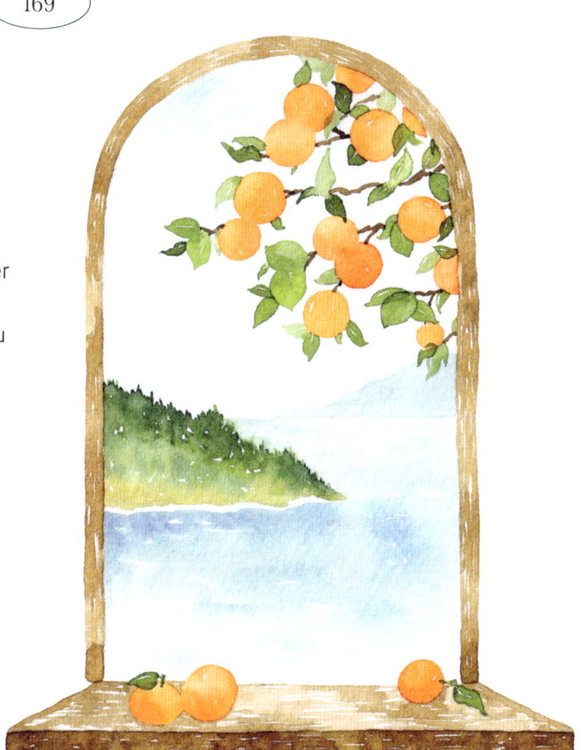

## Step 6

Load the brush with a deep ocean blue colour and paint the shutters in a similar way to the wooden window frame, but with slightly larger brushstrokes. As before, keep the empty gaps between your strokes.

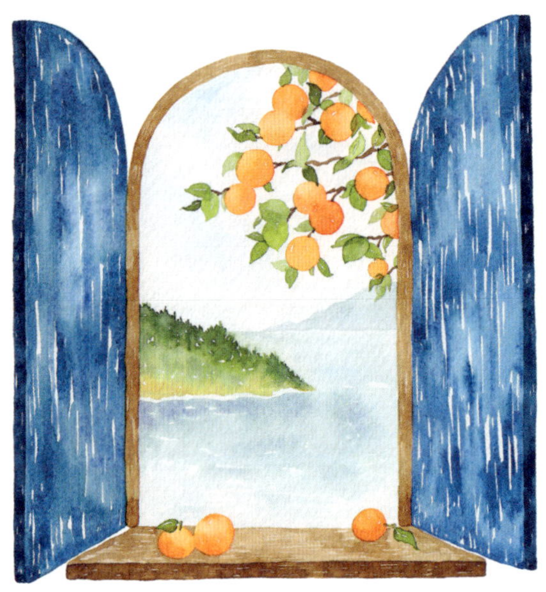

## Step 7

Mix a very dark blue and paint the free edges of the shutters on both sides to give them extra volume.

Then, go back to the brown used to paint the wooden frame and mix it with some extra water to achieve a semi-transparent value. Go over the wood with a flat wash of the colour to soften the wood grains.

## Step 8

Soften the shutters as you did for the window frame in Step 7 by picking up the blue you used to paint the shutters and mixing it with a little more water to create a wash on the surface of the wood grain and make it softer.

While this is drying, pick up a detail brush and load it up with a mid-toned orange. Add scattered dots across the orange fruits to give them a naturalistic texture.

Pick up a bit of muted soft brown to add faint shadows beneath the three oranges resting on the windowsill.

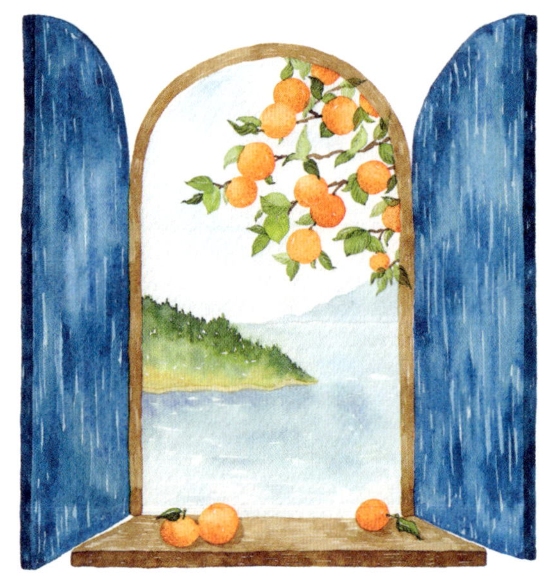

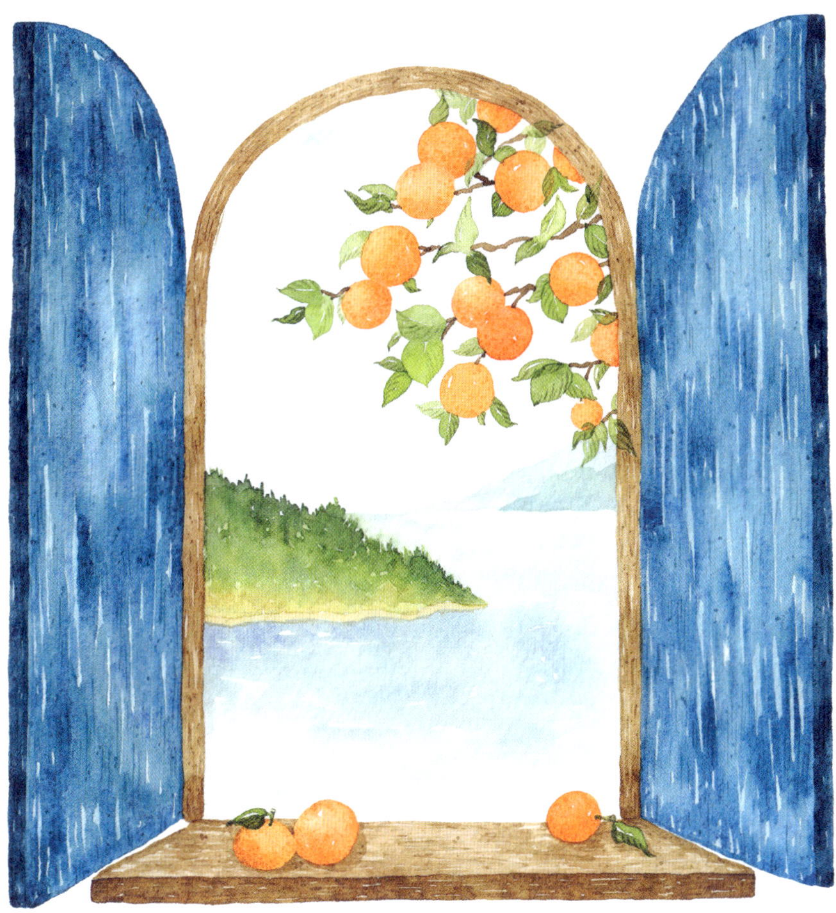

# Step 9

The last step is to tie everything together by adding any remaining details.

I added extra shading to some areas of the windowsill and frame. Then I picked up the dark blue again and added irregular scattered dots across the shutters. Switching to green, I added soft leaf veins to the orange leaves and laid down an additional wash of soft green to the landscape rising out of the water, to give it a little more saturation.

Finally, I went back to a muted, semi-transparent blue and placed an additional hill in the background of the seascape.

# 30/*Summer Breakfast*

Picture this: it is a slow summer morning, you are having a late breakfast soaking up the sun and birdsong, you don't need to rush to get anywhere, and you are sipping coffee in peace while reading a newspaper and eating a pastry. Doesn't it sound dreamy? Let's paint this into reality and carry this feeling forward!

SUGGESTED ART SUPPLIES: COLD-PRESSED PAPER, PENCIL, POINTY MEDIUM ROUND BRUSH, DETAIL BRUSH

## PREP

Mix a selection of summer-inspired colours: rich oranges, vibrant red, muted blues and soft greens, warm browns and pale greys.

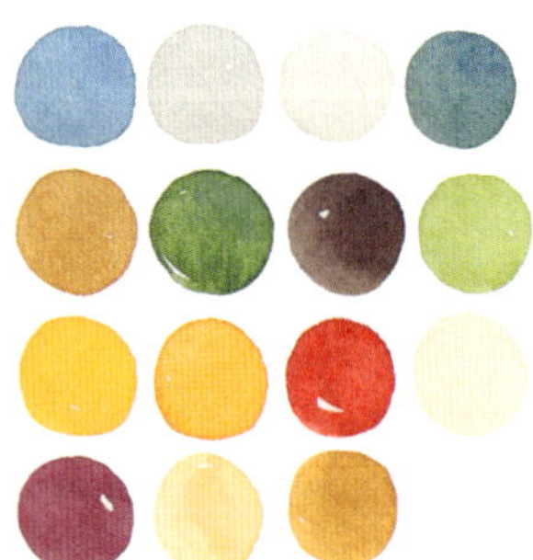

# Step 1

Sketch the breakfast table using sketch 1 on page 190 as a reference.

Using the muted soft blue, start off by painting the stripes of the tablecloth. Leave empty gaps for every other element that will come along in further steps.

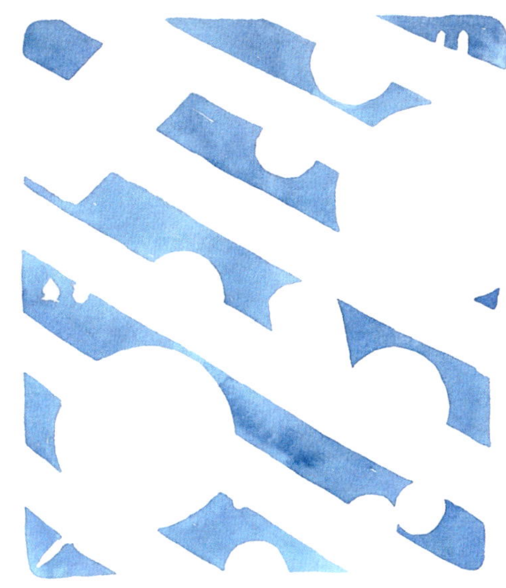

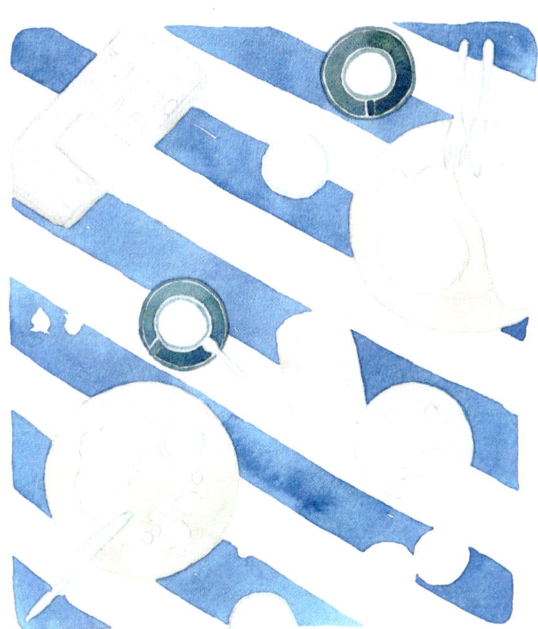

# Step 2

Mix a pale grey with a hint of yellow and lay down the initial layers of the two plates, a small butter dish and the little bowl next to it. Use the same colour for the newspaper in the upper left corner.

Pick up a cool green and fill in the outlines of the coffee cups.

# Step 3

Working on this illustration feels a bit like solving a puzzle game!

Fill in further shapes with the ready-mixed colours. Paint a subdued orange croissant, two bread slices, the vibrant orange egg yolk and two glasses full of bright orange juice.

Add in a few strawberries and blueberries. Paint the three oranges scattered across the table and fill in the cups with coffees – one black coffee painted in dark brown and one flat white painted with a muted orange to imitate the milky foam. Use a little reddish purple to paint the jam next to the croissant.

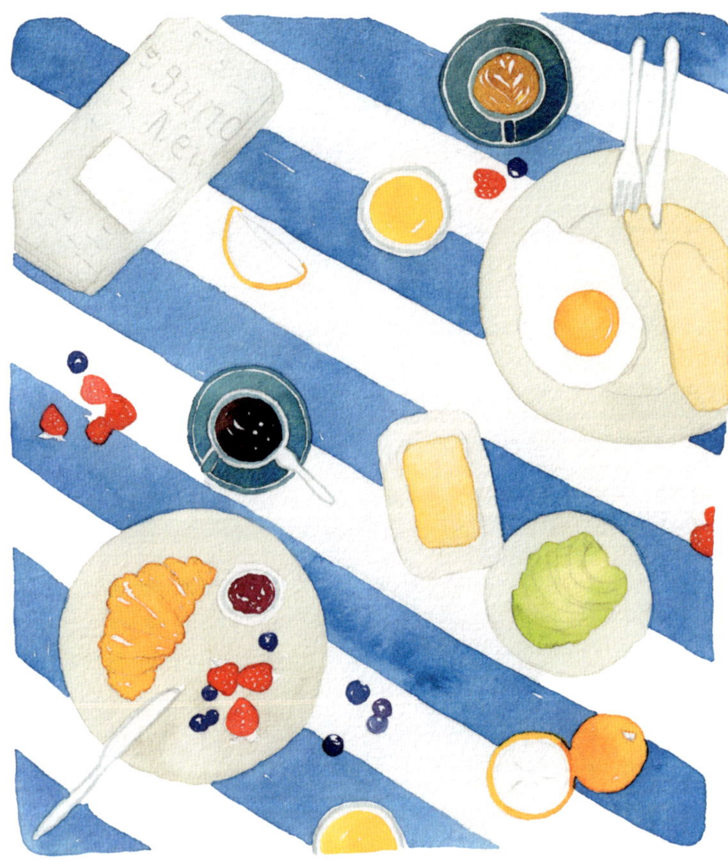

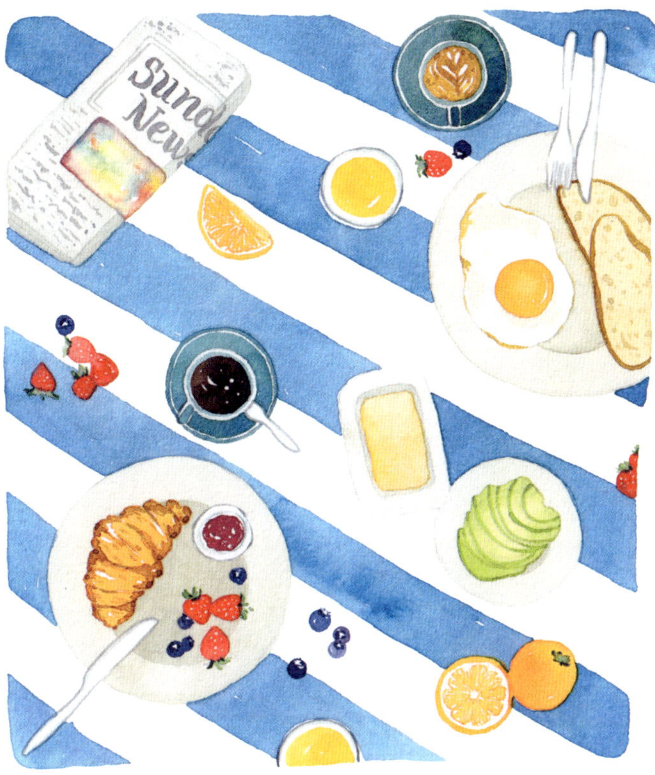


# Step 4

It's time to add some details and textures. Paint some printed text on the newspaper and add a colourful little image to the empty box under the paper's masthead.

Pick up a diluted grey to outline the cutlery and add some gentle shading to the egg white. Then switch to a warm, dark orange to paint its fried edge.

Fill in the middle of the plates with another layer of creamy grey to give them extra depth and add a shadow to the butter dish (around the butter) as well.

Outline the avocado slices with warm green brushstrokes and fill in the sliced oranges with citrus segments.

Use a dark blue to paint thin circular brushstrokes around the rim of the orange juice glasses and then the jam jar, to accentuate them.

Add irregular, pale little dots across the bread slices to give them texture and use warm dark brown to paint stronger edges around the croissant.

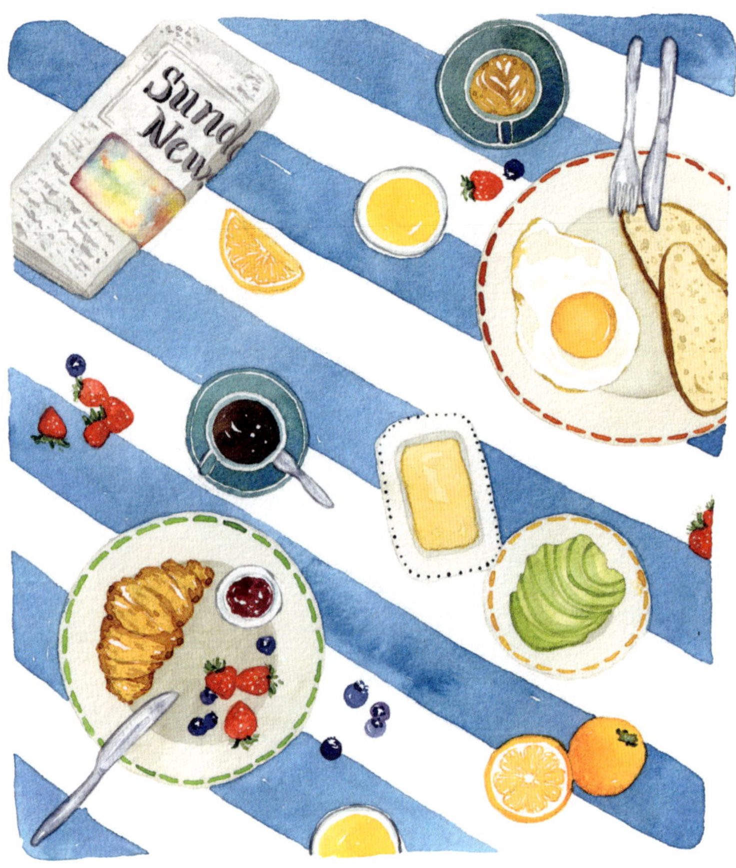

# Step 5

Choose a few colours to add decoration to the plates. I opted for a warm green, a deep red and an orange. Using even brushstrokes within the rim of the plates, I placed colourful little stripes to enhance the composition. The butter dish edge has been decorated with little dots, too.

I also accentuated the green strawberry leaves and added an extra layer of muted yellow to the butter.

# Step 6

The final step is to add shadows to everything sitting on this breakfast table. Mix a little pale grey to paint faint shadows beneath each object where it touches the white stripes of the tablecloth. To add shadows to the blue stripes, switch to a muted blue and add them in the same manner. Bon appetit!

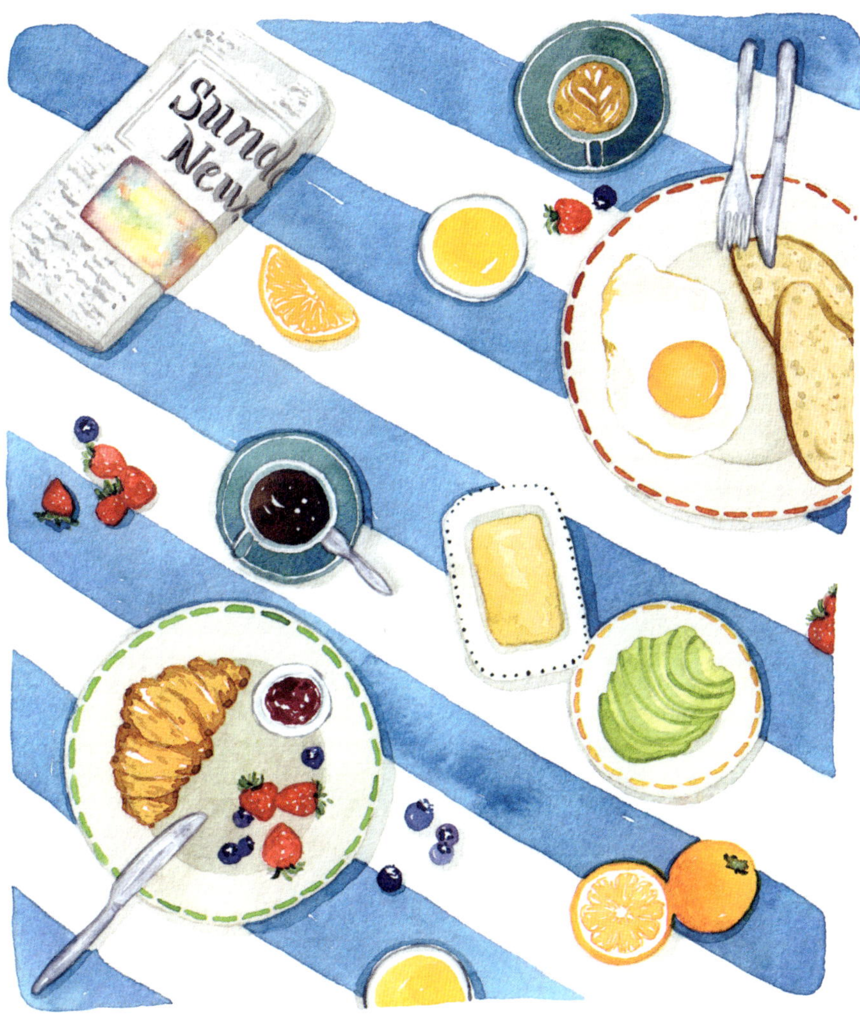

1. BEETROOT (P.48)
2. TROPICAL FRUIT (P.56)
3. CUCUMBERS (P.72)
4. FLOWERS AT DUSK (P.76)

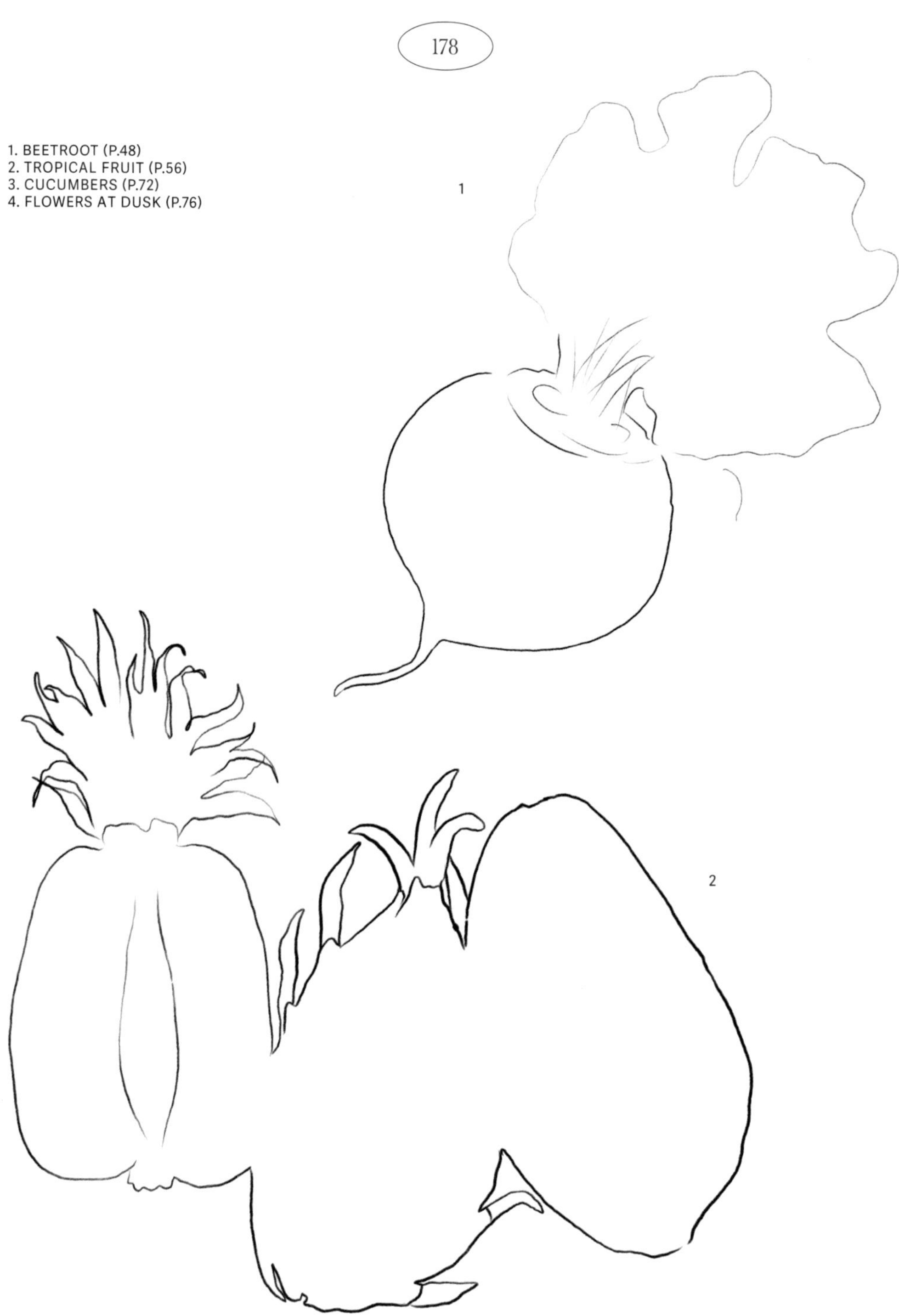

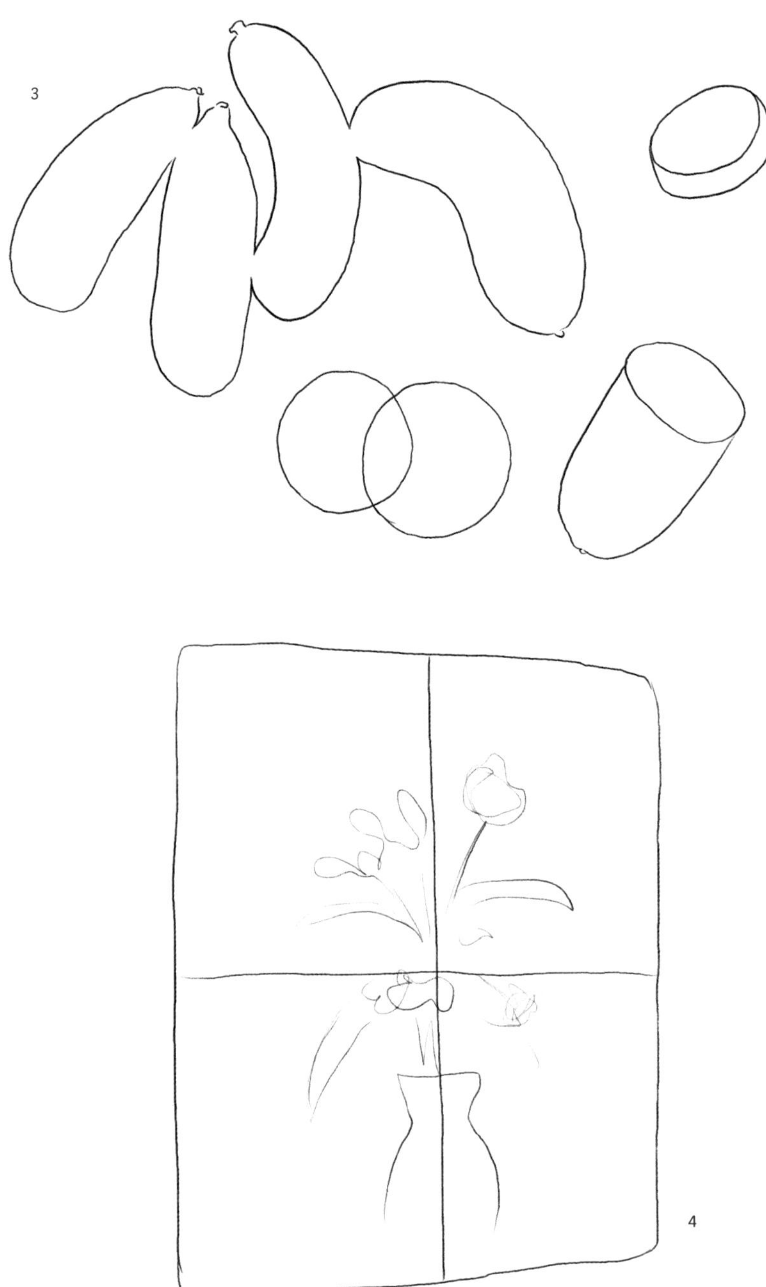
3
4

1. ARTICHOKE (P.114)
2. STORK (P.92)
3. APPLES AND PEARS (P.96)
4. AUTUMN LEAVES (P.81)

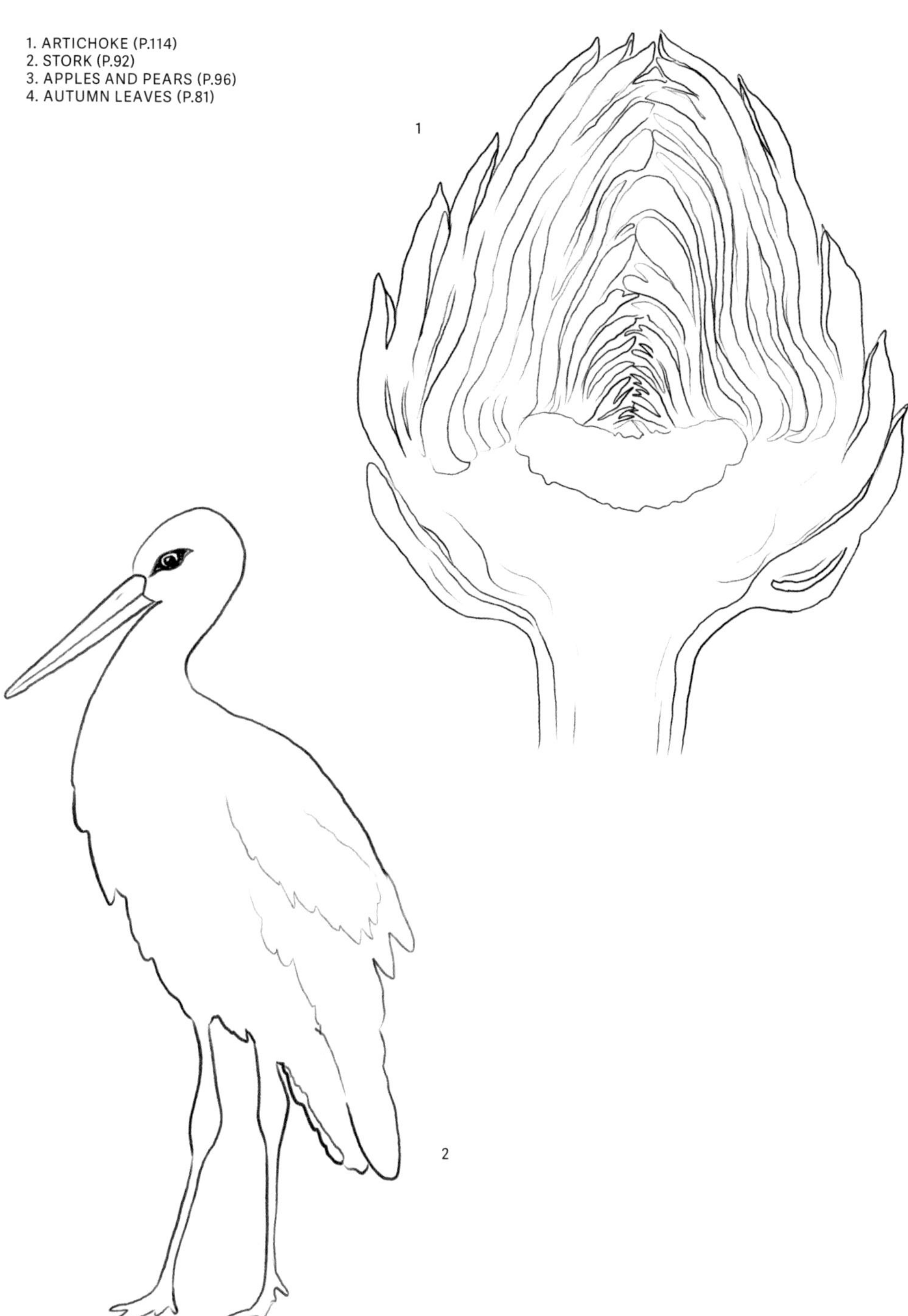

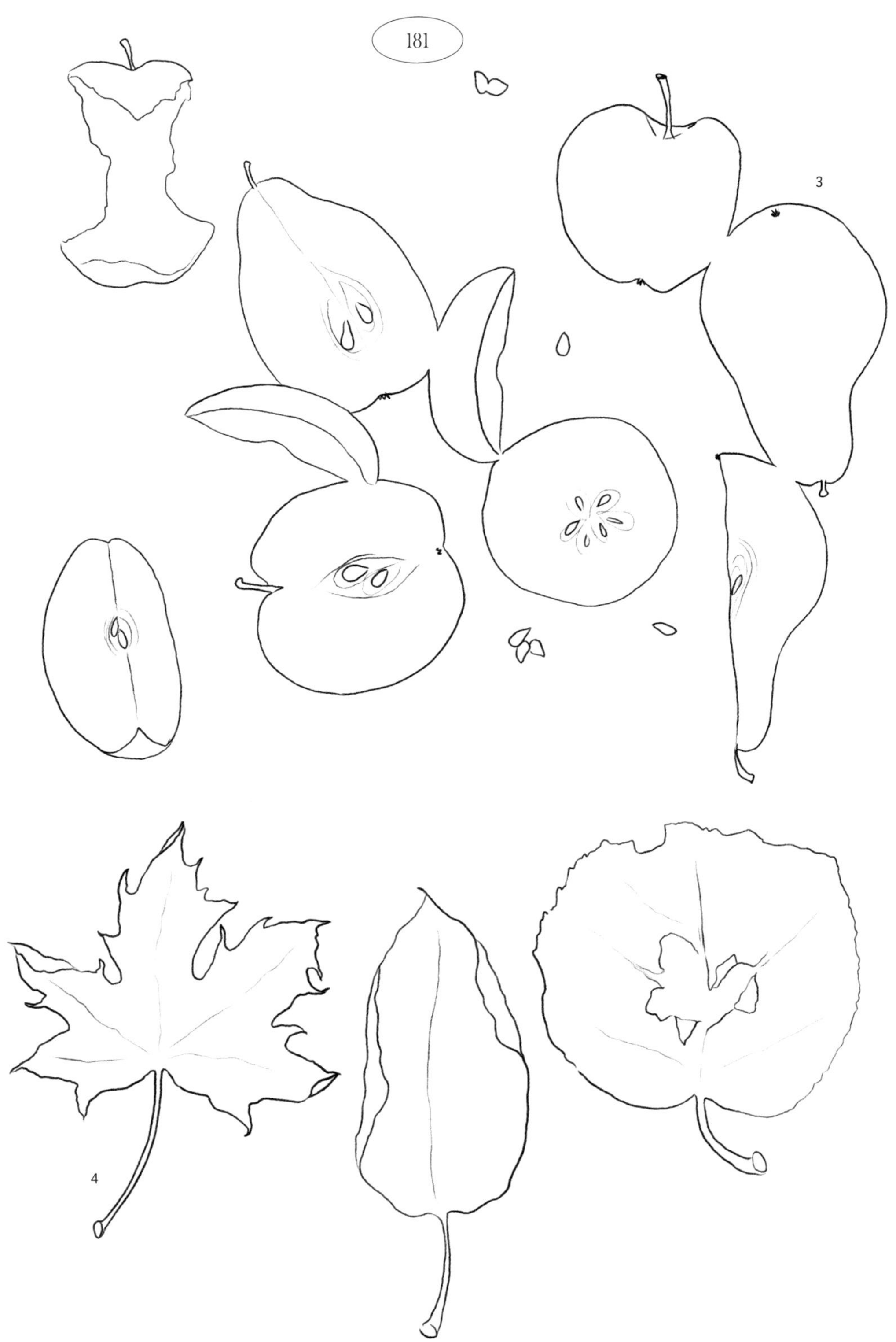
3
4

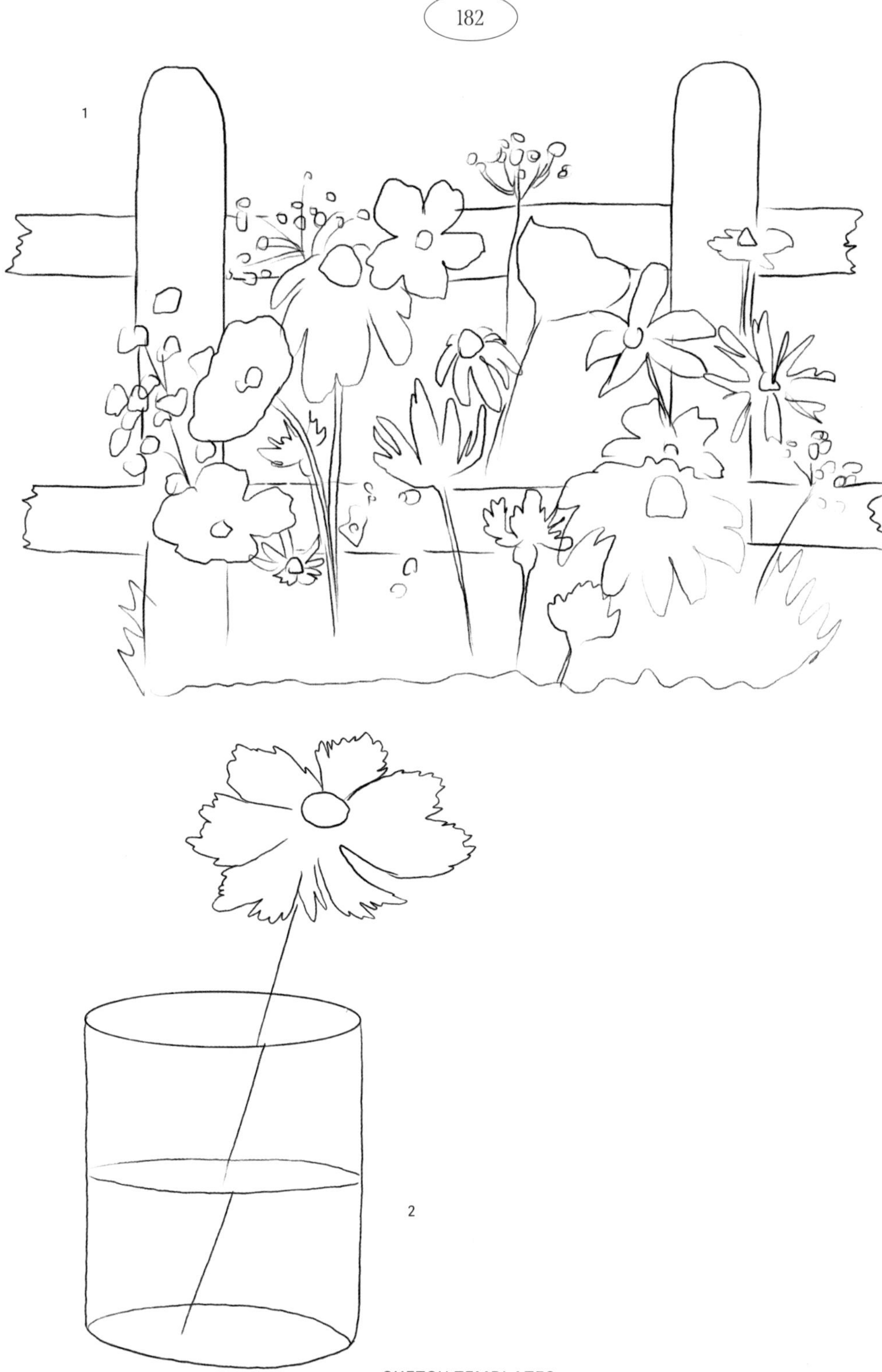
1
2

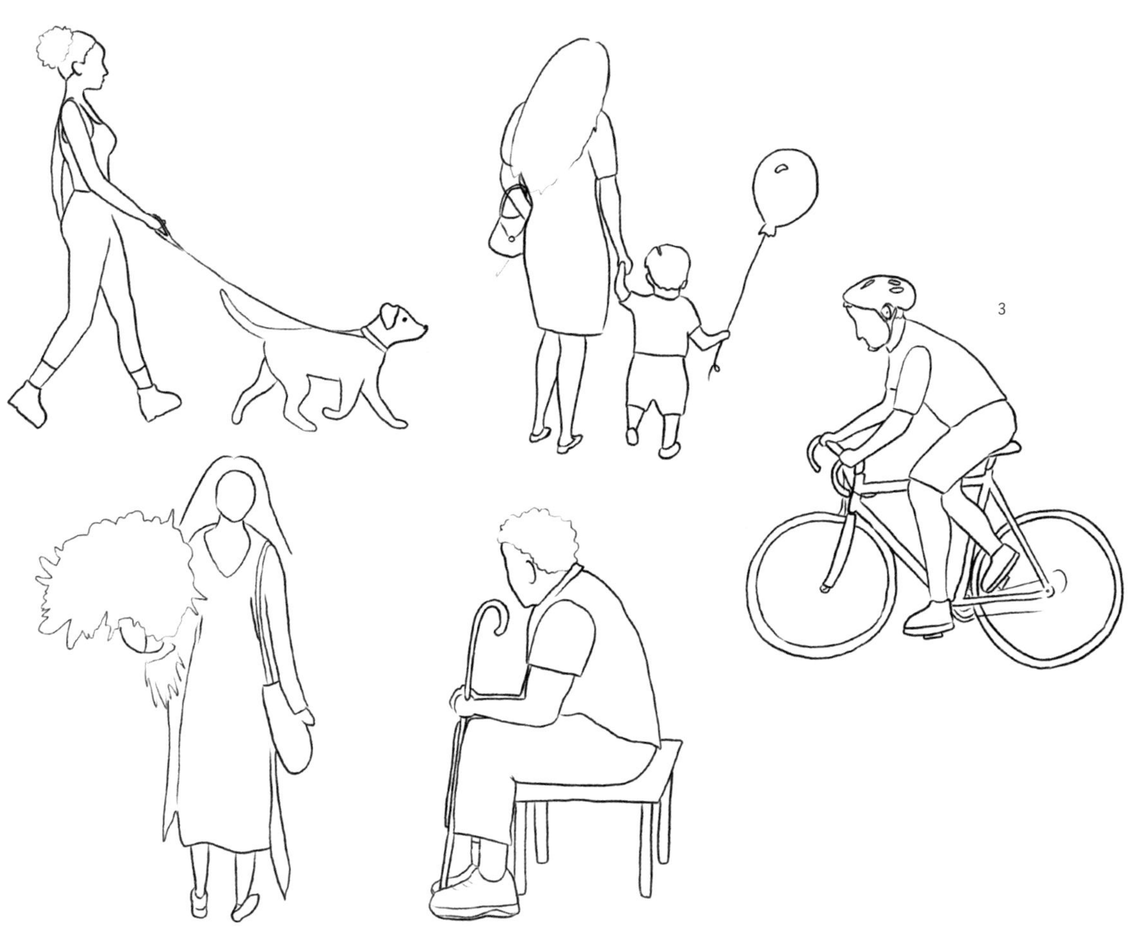


1. COUNTRYSIDE FLOWERS (P.100)
2. GLASS FLOWER VASE (P.109)
3. PEOPLE (P.128)

1. FOREST MUSHROOMS (P.123)
2. MOON (P.88)
3. A SPRING WALK (P.138)

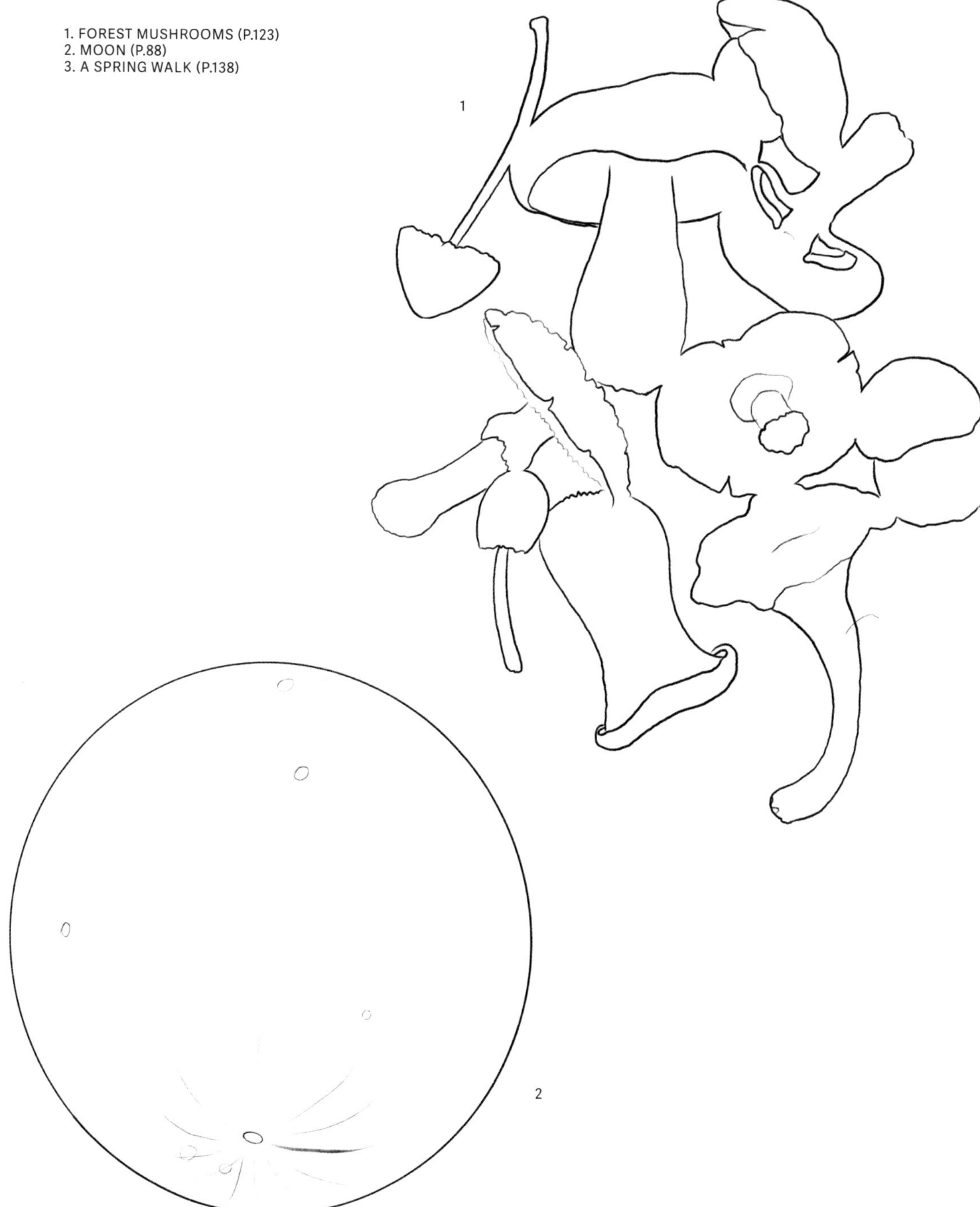

3

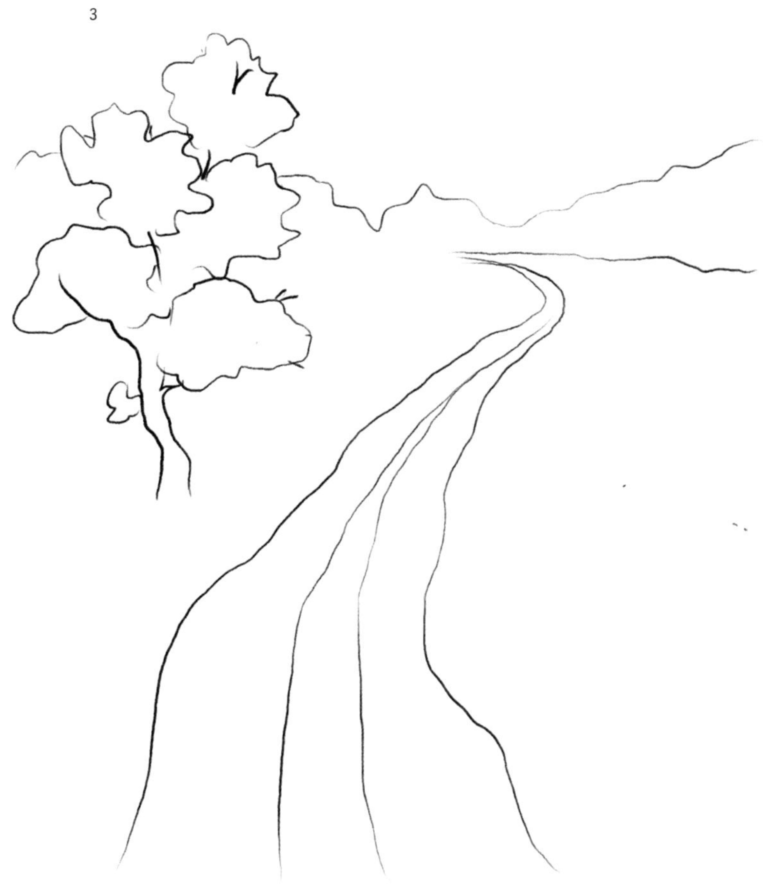

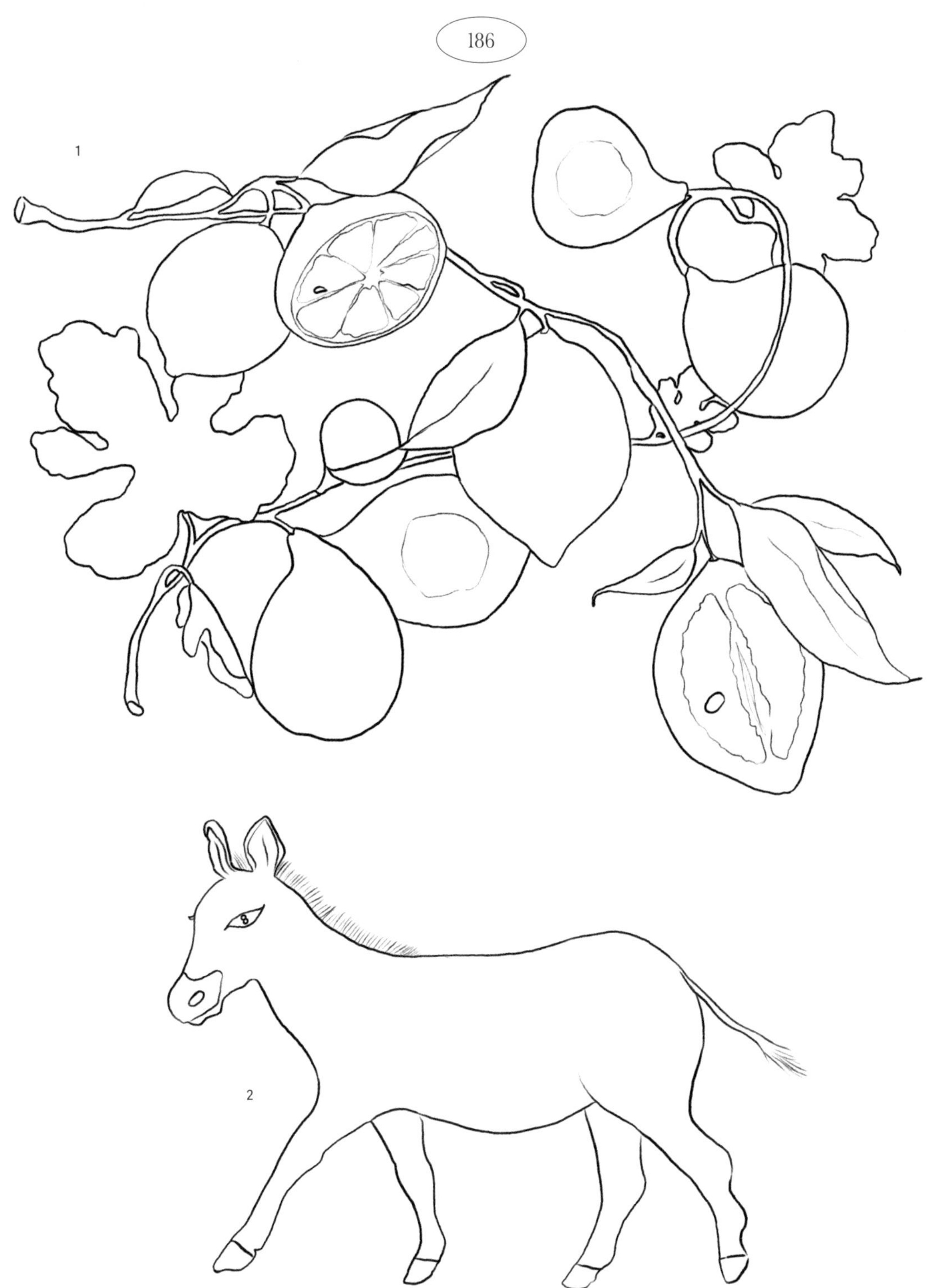
1
2

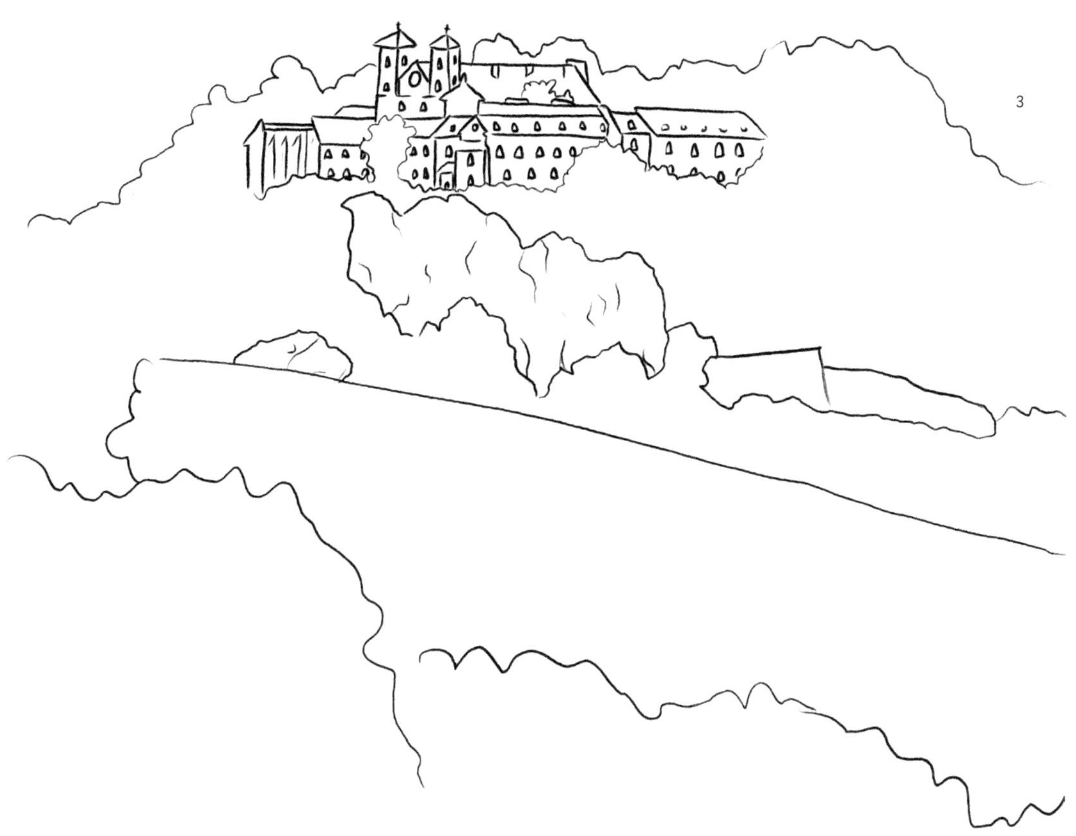


1. FIG LEMON VINE (P.144)
2. ZEBRA (P.150)
3. VIEW OF AN ABBEY (P.154)

1

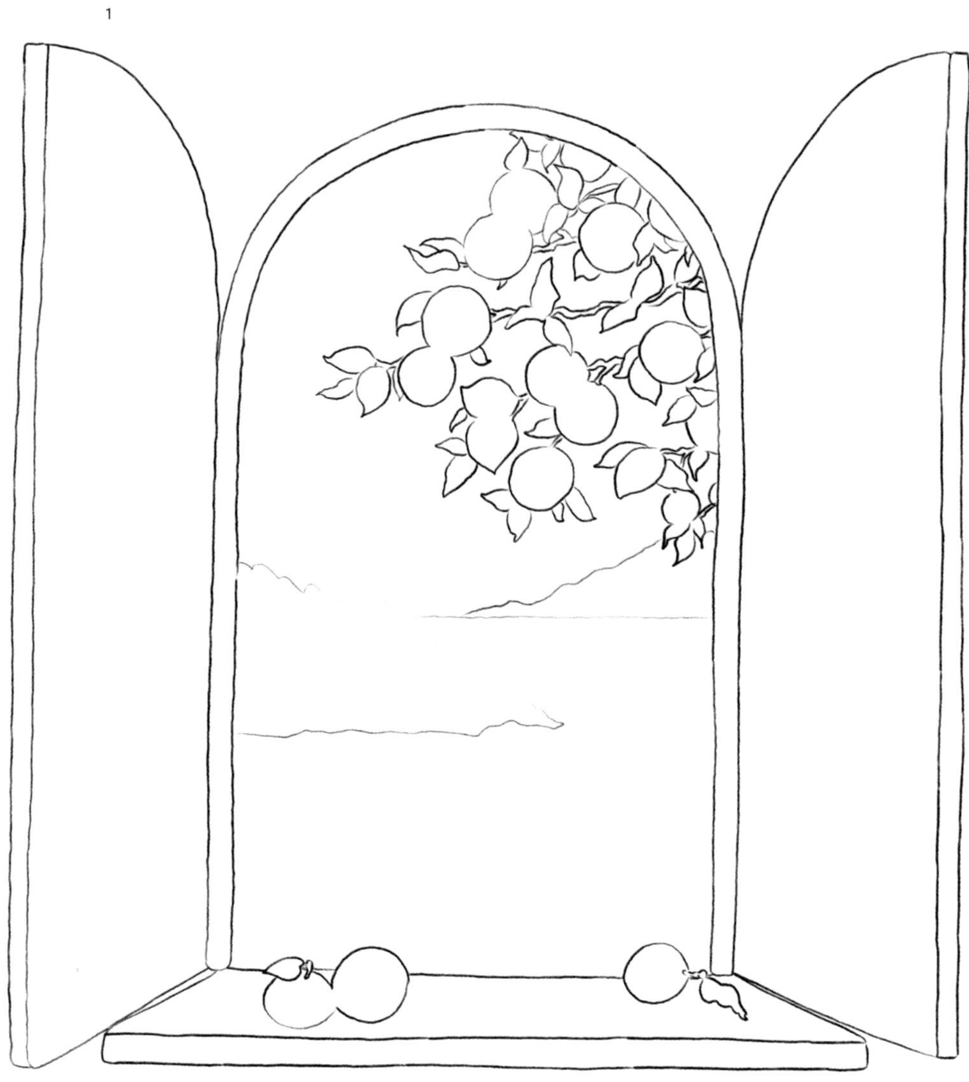

2

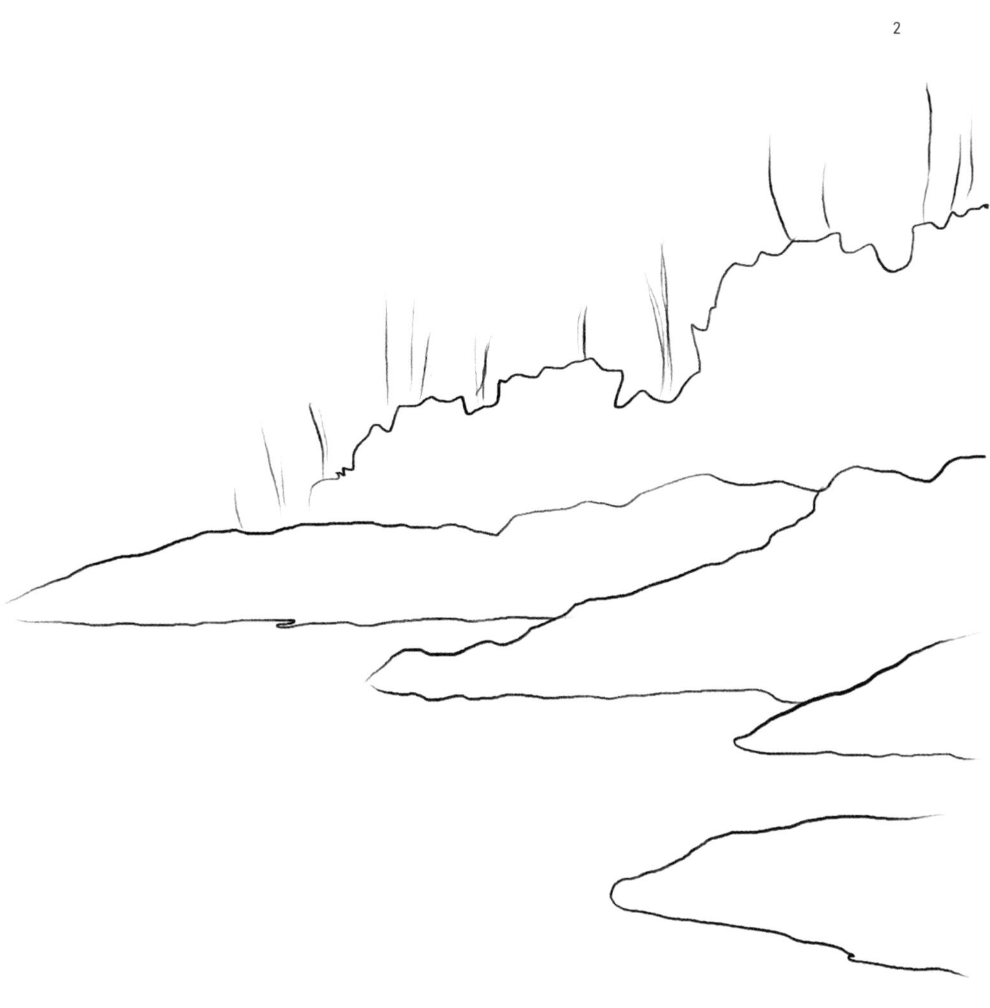

1. ITALIAN ORANGES (P.166)
2. WINTER LANDSCAPE (P.133)

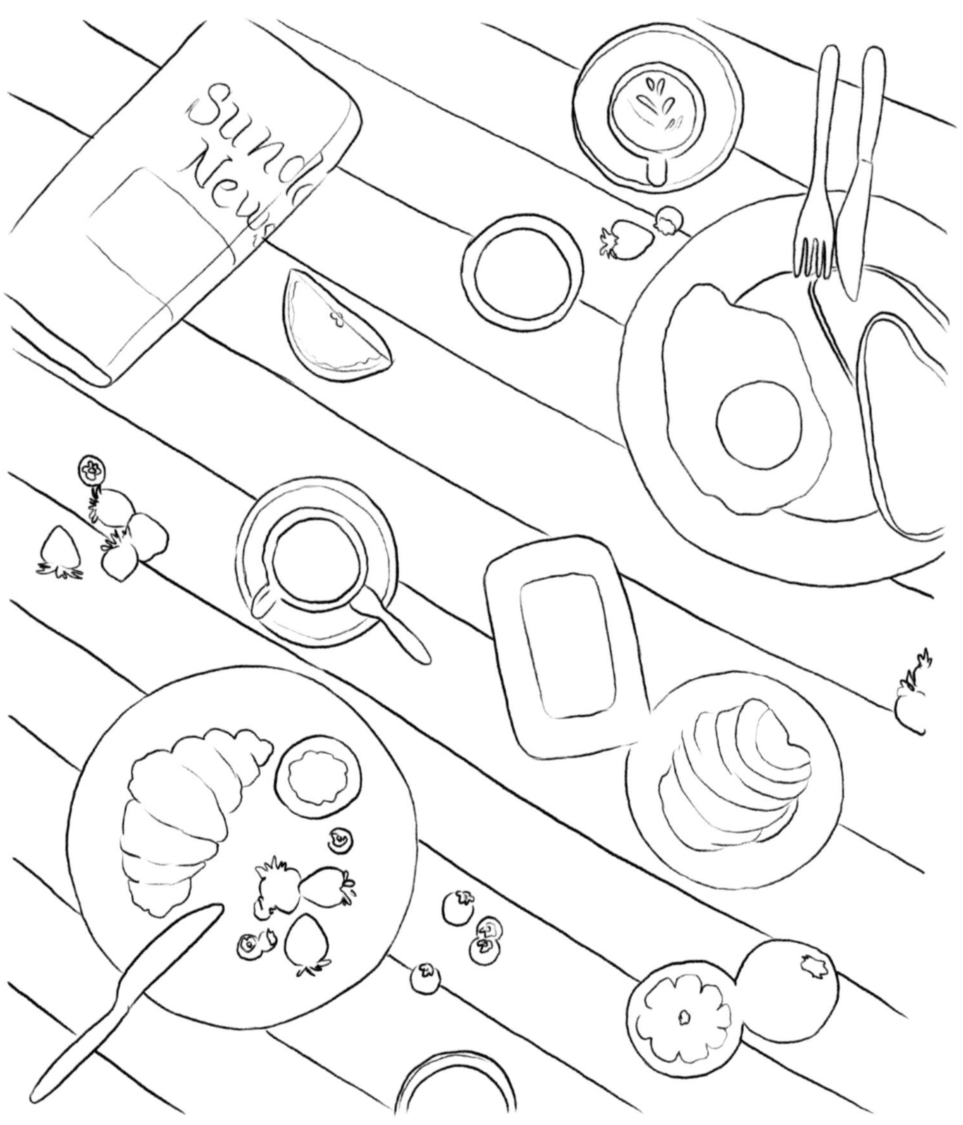

1. SUMMER BREAKFAST (P.172)

# About the Author

Jola Sopek is a self-taught watercolour artist from Poland. She works as an illustrator, art instructor and author. Her first book, *15 Minute Art: Watercolour* was released in 2024 by Hardie Grant Publishing and subsequently translated into Spanish (Editorial GG, 2025). She lives in the south of England with her husband and child.

# Acknowledgements

This book would not have come to fruition without the immense support of my family and friends, who enabled me to focus on writing and painting at a particularly chaotic time in our life, with a lovely albeit very energetic toddler in tow! Special thanks to my Mama, my patient husband and mother-in-law for their unprecedented assistance; my Dad for passing on his work ethic and to my child for existing and single-handedly giving me heaps of motivation and new waves of inspiration. Massive thanks to my wonderful editors Kate Burkett and Chelsea Edwards for having trust in my work, the autonomy and constructive advice they offer, as well as the proofreading, design and editorial teams at Quadrille. A huge thank you to anyone who has ever supported my illustration journey by commissioning an artwork, participated in a painting workshop, engaged with my content online or bought a copy of *15 Minute Art: Watercolour* – the book you are holding in your hands would not have appeared on shelves if not for your continued interest and priceless feedback. May the spirit of watercolour joy live on and on and continue to expand further. Dziękuję!

Quadrille, Penguin Random House UK, One Embassy Gardens, 8 Viaduct Gardens, London SW11 7BW

Quadrille Publishing Limited is part of the Penguin Random House group of companies whose addresses can be found at global.penguinrandomhouse.com

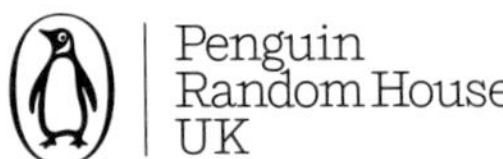




Published by Quadrille in 2026

www.penguin.co.uk

A CIP catalogue record for this book is available from the British Library

ISBN 9781837836406
10 9 8 7 6 5 4 3 2 1

**Managing Director, Publishing:** Sarah Lavelle
**Editorial Director:** Harriet Butt
**Managing Editor:** Chelsea Edwards
**Copy Editor:** Clare Double
**Proofreader:** Sara Goldsmith
**Designer:** Claire Rochford
**Production Manager:** Stephen Lang

Colour reproduction by F1

Printed in China by C&C Offset Printing Co., Ltd.

The authorised representative in the EEA is Penguin Random House Ireland, Morrison Chambers, 32 Nassau Street, Dublin D02 YH68.

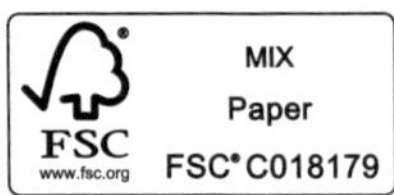


Penguin Random House is committed to a sustainable future for our business, our readers and our planet. This book is made from Forest Stewardship Council® certified paper.